STREETWISE®

SALES LETTERS

2,500 Professionally
Written Sales and
Marketing Letters

**by Sue Reynard
and David Weiss**

Adams Media Corporation
Avon, Massachusetts

Copyright ©2001, F+W Publications, Inc. All rights reserved.
This book, or parts thereof, may not be reproduced in any form without permission from the publisher; exceptions are made for brief excerpts used in published reviews.

A Streetwise® Publication.
Streetwise® is a registered trademark of F+W Publications, Inc.

Published by Adams Media, an F+W Publications Company
57 Littlefield Street, Avon, MA 02322. U.S.A.
www.adamsmedia.com

ISBN: 1-58062-440-5

Printed in the United States of America.

J   I   H   G   F   E   D   C

Library of Congress Cataloging-in-Publication Data
available upon request from the publisher.

This book was developed and produced for Adams Media Corporation by CWL Publishing Enterprises, John Woods, President, 3010 Irvington Way, Madison, WI 53713, www.cwlpub.com.

This publication is designed to provide accurate and authoritative information with regard to the subject matter covered. It is sold with the understanding that the publisher is not engaged in rendering legal, accounting, or other professional advice. If legal advice or other expert assistance is required, the services of a competent professional person should be sought.

— From a *Declaration of Principles* jointly adopted by a Committee of the American Bar Associationand a Committee of Publishers and Associations

Cover illustration by Eric Mueller.

This book is available at quantity discounts for bulk purchases.
For information, call 1-800-872-5627.

Table of Contents*

* Titles correspond to the file names on the CD-ROM

Chapter 2: Current and Former Customers.103

Contents

Chapter 3: Prospecting 171

Prospecting Specific People

Contents

Introduction

You now hold in your hands the most comprehensive guide to sales letters available. No other book, disc, or CD-ROM has as many examples, covers as many situations, and saves you as much time as *Streetwise Sales Letters*.

As a professional, you probably have chosen this book to accomplish two major goals. First is to save time. Why struggle to put your thoughts into words when your time is better spent on dealing directly with customers, making improvements, and staying ahead of your competition.

Second is to communicate effectively and professionally. Let's face it, there's no point in saving time by using prewritten business letters if they're not top-notch.

Streetwise Sales Letters will save you time and money and present your business in the most professional manner possible. For starters, you can't find as many example letters anywhere else. The book portion of this package provides more than 360 samples from some of the most common, everyday sales and marketing situations you'll face. If the version presented in the book doesn't fit your needs, there's more than 2100 more letters on the CD-ROM, providing you with alternatives. You simply can't beat that.

What's Here

To be effective, sales and marketing staff need to have a variety of tools at their disposal. They have to contact potential customers, maintain current customers, exchange information with others, and perhaps even deal with distributors. The letters here cover all these situations and more.

You'll find everything from cover letters to send with a brochure mailed to a purchased list, to notes you could send to a customer you know personally, to letters dealing with RFPs and even inviting customers to join a focus group. There are sample letters for companies who will be developing their own sales communication, as well as examples for companies who will be hiring an advertising agency—and even examples for ad agency staff.

The variety of letters doesn't stop with just subject matter. You'll find letters in a variety of formats (faxes, e-mails, memos) and style (from standard, formal business style to humorous and emotional). In short, no matter what your need or interest, no matter how experienced you are in writing, you'll find something in *Streetwise Sales Letters* to help you out.

Getting Started

All the letters in this book are on the enclosed CD-ROM, along with the other 2100 examples. Locating a letter in the book is easy: We've included the computer "address" of each letter at the bottom of each page. All you need to do is insert the CD-ROM and click through the various folders and subfolders to find the letter you want. To find other variations on the letter you're interested in, simply browse through the other letters that are in the same folder.

Using these letters will help you accomplish both your goals. Using just *one* letter from this book will likely save you an hour right off the bat—an hour that is worth in dollars more than you spent on the purchase price! And if you continue to use this resource throughout the life of your business, you'll save countless hours and dollars! In choosing this book, you've also made a commitment to achieving your second goal: communicating in an effective and professional manner. Each letter was written by an experienced, professional business writer.

So whether you want to send out mass correspondence to a purchased mailing list, write a simple thank-you note to a customer who gave you a referral, or inform your colleagues of important sales information, *Streetwise Sales Letters* has the right letter ready for you.

General Promotion

Chapter 1

Despite many advances in technology that make it easier for businesses to know specific information about their customers, there are still many times when you won't know much about the audience who receives your communication. Examples include mass mailings done to purchased mailing lists, "open" letters posted on a Web site, announcements sent to mailing addresses based on zip codes, mailings sent to tradeshow participants, and so on.

The letters in this chapter are designed for such situations, where you may know only the most general information about potential readers—such as where they live or that they've purchased a particular product or service in the past.

The first subset of letters here (and the corresponding sections of the CD-ROM) represent a new breed of mass mailings. Some are written in a standard, straightforward business style. But most are either targeted at a specific *type* of potential customer (that you'd see labeled with terms such as "achievers" or "actualizers" in the marketing literature), or are written with a strong style (such as "humorous" or "emotional").

You can increase the chances of success by knowing *something* about the targeted group and tailoring the style and approach to those characteristics. To select and customize a letter in this chapter that comes closest to your needs, you should know:

1. How the letter fits in with your overall marketing scheme. Is this a prelude to another mailing, perhaps of a brochure or postcard? Will it follow up a brochure or ad?
2. How you will define "success." What do you want this particular letter to accomplish? What action, if any, should the reader take? (Call your company to order the product? Visit your Web site to get more information? Return an

enclosed card? Come to a tradeshow booth?) Make sure the content of the letter makes this desired action clear.

3. What message(s) you want to send. Be careful with this issue—one of the most common mistakes in business communication is trying to crowd too much into one letter. You want the reader to come away with a clear mental picture of one thing—be that your product, service, values, key selling point, company, etc.

The more you know about your audience and your marketing strategy, the more easily you can answer such questions, and the more effective you can be in writing a letter that will generate "success" by your own definition. Yet it would be an absolute waste of your time—and your company's money—to send out any old letter to any group, and never understand why you got (or did not get) the response you wanted. If you don't know much about the audience except in the most general terms—which happens often when purchasing a mailing list from a professional group, journal, etc.—design the communication strategy as an experiment. Send several different types of letters to well-identified subgroups, and include ways to track the response rates from each subgroup. Or change the type of letter posted on your Web site and track responses when each style is posted. Make every attempt to learn what style and approach is most effective for your audiences.

Announcing a new product

[Name]
[Company]
[Address]
[City, State ZIP]

Dear [   ]:

It's not often [company/organization] sticks our neck out for someone else. But [product company] has developed such a terrific [product type] that we couldn't remain silent!

[Product company's] [product name/type] is great. [Easy to use. Convenient. Durable. Reliable.] Everything you want in a [product type].

And we should know. We've used [product name/type] for [# months] now. And here's what some of our employees say:

- [Employee quote #1]
- [Employee quote #2]
- [Employee quote #3]

We think you should give [product name] a try. And [product company] is willing to make it worth your while! Act now and receive a [XX% discount] if you mention [company's] name when you order. That's a savings of [$xx].

It's easy! Just call [800-555-5555] or visit [product company's] Web site at [www.productcompany.com].

And if you're just half as satisfied as we've been, you'll be glad you called!

Sincerely,

[Name]
[Title]

P.S. Take our advice! We've tested [product name] for [weeks/months] and love every aspect of it.

- **Having a third-party endorse a product is unusual enough that an opening like this will raise the reader's curiosity.**

- **Describe the product, then provide additional endorsements.**

- **Close with the call to action.**

- **Use the postscript to either reiterate the endorsement or describe a particularly appealing feature of the product.**

Path on CD-ROM: General Promotion→ Mass Marketing→Announcing a new product→Retailer~1

Announcing a new product

Wondering when the parts you want will arrive?
Can't schedule [groundbreaking] until the [permits are secured]?
Turn to [Virtual Switchboard]!

[Name]
[Company]
[Address]
[City, State ZIP]

Dear [   ]:

In today's fast paced world, instant and effective communication is critical to getting projects done on time and under budget. That's where [Virtual Switchboard] comes in.

[Virtual Switchboard] is the latest [scheduling software] from [software developer]. With [Virtual Switchboard], you can coordinate the efforts of dozens...even hundreds...of employees and vendors.

Using [Virtual Switchboard] is simple! [Employees and vendors] simply log onto your Web site and enter a password specific to the project they're working on. They then enter a central project-tracking screen that lets them...

- Enter updates on their parts of the project
- Check progress on other parts of the project
- Find alerts to important changes or delays
- Leave message for any other member of the team

You've never seen anything like it before! No more delays and work order changes because of miscommunication!

To see for yourself, log on to [www.softwaredeveloper.com] and click on "Try Me." Or to speak with one of our representatives, call [800-555-5555].

Sincerely,

[Name]
[Title]

- **Emphasize what's new or different about the product.**

- **Sound enthusiastic.**

Path on CD-ROM: General Promotion→ Mass Marketing→Announcing a new product→Software-2

Announcing a new product

[Name]
[Company]
[Address]
[City, State ZIP]

Dear [   ]:

Last month, [Jim Reeves] almost lost his business to fire. Old wiring finally wore out and caught fire.

Luckily, [Jim] had recently installed new [SensAlarm System] from [HomeSafe, Inc.] They detected the smoke while the fire was just an ember, sounded an alarm, turned on the sprinklers, and dialed the local fire department...all in the space of seconds.

["SensAlarm saved my business, and more importantly, the lives of 53 employees," says Jim.]

If you're concerned about the safety of your employees, you owe it to them to install [SensAlarm] in your buildings. Call 555-5555 today for a free estimate.

Don't wait until AFTER disaster strikes! Call now.

Sincerely,

[Name]
[Title]

- **Business is supposed to be cold and unemotional, but many employers feel strong loyalty towards their employees (and vice versa).**

- **Close with a strong emotional statement that everyone will feel compelled to answer with an affirmative—"Yes, I'm concerned about the safety..."**

Path on CD-ROM: General Promotion→ Mass Marketing→Announcing a new product→Alarm-1

Announcing a new product

[Name]
[Company]
[Address]
[City, State ZIP]

Dear [   ]:

We hate to say it, but there are a lot of companies out there who say they support [name of charity or cause] when really they don't. If you look at their bottom line, you'd see the profits go to corporate officers and shareholders, not to the people who really need the help.

[Nonprofit company] has been around for [##] years. We've employed [hundreds] of [disadvantaged] workers while establishing a strong presence in the marketplace. That's why we're so excited about introducing our new [product].

[Product] is made entirely by [type of disadvantage] workers, yet we maintain the highest standards in the industry. It is guaranteed to perform to your satisfaction, or we'll refund your money.

Best of all, [product] is priced below the competition, so you can save your business money, get the performance you need, AND support [disadvantaged] workers all at the same time.

Won't you call today to place an order?

Sincerely,

[Name]
[Title]

P.S. Visit our Web site, [www.nonprofit,org] to see the full range of our products.

- **This same type of letter could be used by a for-profit company that championed a worthy social or environmental cause.**

Path on CD-ROM: General Promotion→ Mass Marketing→Announcing a new product→Nonprofit-1

Announcing a new product

[Name]
[Address]
[City, State ZIP]

Dear [   ]:

When was the last time you sat back in your easy chair and really enjoyed [reading a magazine]? Most of them are so full of ads that you have a hard time finding the meat!

Here's a new [magazine] just for you. [*Handy About the House*] is brought to you by [Harry Reeves, best-selling author of *Harry's Handy, Helpful Hardware Book*]. This [bimonthly magazine] is filled with practical tips and how-to advice on home maintenance and repair.

You'll find step-by-step instructions for everything from repairing cracks in the plaster to installing ceiling fans, from fixing leaks to removing stains. [Harry] also compares brand-name tools and shows you how they measure up in every-day use!

Return the enclosed card and receive the special introductory price of just ($24.95 per year)—that's [40%] off the newsstand price!

Then sit back in your easy chair and relax with something worthwhile for a change.

Sincerely,

[Name]
[Title]

P.S. Don't delay! Act now and receive a FREE copy of [*Harry's Top 100 Home Repair Tips*].

- **Build credibility by describing the credentials of the author (but keep it short).**

- **The postscript provides an additional incentive for prospective subscribers.**

Path on CD-ROM: General Promotion→ Mass Marketing→Announcing a new product→Magazine-2

MASS MARKETING

Announcing a new product

[Name]
[Address]
[City, State ZIP]

Dear [   ]:

I've got some good news and some bad news.

The bad news is you probably paid too much for your last [product category].

The good news is that it never has to happen again.

In a recent survey of [# of local retailers], [company] found that our [product] is consistently priced lower than our competition.

So why are you paying too much for the features you want most, like [features].

The next time you need a [product category], do your wallet a favor and look for [product] on the shelves.

Sincerely,

[Name]
[Title]

- **This letter is written with one-line paragraphs, much like a comedian would tell one-line jokes.**

- **Match the humor to the benefit you want to highlight; here it's price.**

Path on CD-ROM: General Promotion→ Mass Marketing→Announcing a new product→Generic-10

Announcing a new service

[Name]
[Company]
[Address]
[City, State ZIP]

Dear [   ]:

JoAnn is intelligent, resourceful, and loyal. Thomas is good with his hands. Carlita is a dynamic whirlwind who loves people. An employer would be lucky to have any one of these people. But most don't even know they exist.

Why? Because all three of these people have a physical or mental disability that makes it challenging to find good jobs. Yes, it's illegal to discriminate against people with disabilities. But because many employers simply don't know how to go about finding qualified employees who happen to be physically or mentally challenged, many of these extraordinary people are not placed in jobs that take full advantage of their skills and abilities.

That's where [New World Job Service] comes in. We're a new employment agency that specializes in matching employers with qualified employees who face extra barriers in the workplace. These are people who are strongly motivated to work and willing to learn.

But [New World Job Service] goes beyond just placing employees. We provide extra support to any of our candidates who need it even after they are placed— all at no cost to you, the employer. That includes on-the-job training, nursing care, and other forms of support.

The next time you are hiring, have your HR director give [New World] a call. We'll select several prescreened candidates who meet your hiring criteria to send for interviews. You've got nothing to lose and everything to gain by giving deserving people a chance at a rewarding job.

Enrich your work force by hiring from [New World Job Service]. We're an employment agency for the next century.

Sincerely,
[Name]
[Title]

- **Emotional/ guilt letters often start with stories of real people to elicit an instantaneous response in the reader.**

- **Make the readers feel that they will feel good if they act in the way you recommend.**

Path on CD-ROM: General Promotion→ Mass Marketing→Announcing a new service→Employment-1

Announcing a new service

[Name]
[Company]
[Address]
[City, State ZIP]

Dear [   ]:

With medical miracles happening every day, it's getting more and more likely that you'll live to a ripe old age. But will you be able to support yourself? What if you live well into your 80s or 90s, but your money runs out at 75? You say you want to save but have mortgage payments and kids headed to college? How can you meet today's financial needs, let alone worry about tomorrow?

[Penzee Associates] is here to help. We now offer [retirement planning services] for families and individuals. We'll help you look out ten, twenty, or even thirty years and plan out where you want to be. Then we'll help you get there.

[Penzee Associates] is not associated with any single retirement plan provider. So you'll get a solid, independent assessment of your current investment strategies, retirement plans offered through your work, and personal assets. And you don't have to worry if you don't know a stock from a bond—our experts are knowledgeable about all the oldest and latest investment options.

Call [555-5555] today and start planning for your future.

Sincerely,

[Name]
[Title]

P.S. Even if you don't have much to invest, there are simple, painless investment tricks that can help you achieve your goals.

- **Fear is another emotion you can build on in this type of letter.**

- **Try to identify the key fears that would prevent people from using your service and address those in the letter. Here, the P.S. addresses a key customer concern—they don't possibly see how they could carve anything out of their current expenditures to save.**

Path on CD-ROM: General Promotion→ Mass Marketing→Announcing a new service→Retirement-1

MASS MARKETING

Announcing a new service

[Name]
[Company]
[Address]
[City, State ZIP]

Dear [   ]:

Do you know the legal difference between raw jokes and sexual harassment?
Do you know if you're compliant with federal regulations regarding nondis-
criminatory hiring practices? Do you know for sure that your employees aren't
violating any copyright laws—and putting your business at risk?

The legal issues surrounding any business can seem overwhelmingly complex.
And small business owners are especially at risk since they often lack the time
and expertise to learn all they need to know.

That's why [Barnett, Trask, & Ritter] is introducing new comprehensive legal
services for small business owners called [Clarity]. [Barnett, Trask, and Ritter]
has been providing legal services to business owners for three generations. But
[Clarity] represents the first time we've brought together all the services that
small business owners need. With [Clarity], your legal team is always on the
lookout for you. They know the answers before you have the question.

[Clarity] covers all the legal needs of most businesses, including hiring,
employment, firing, health and safety standards set by OSHA, taxes, and insurance. You name it, and we've got lawyers who specialize in it.

Don't trust your small business to just anyone. Come to [Barnett, Trask, and
Ritter]. We're big on small business.

Sincerely,

[Name]
[Title]

- The opening
  questions are
  designed to elicit
  a "no" answer
  from the reader,
  thereby exposing
  a need they may
  not have known
  they had.

- The text should
  describe what is
  of particular
  benefit to your
  specific audience
  (here, small
  business owners).

Path on CD-ROM: General Promotion→ Mass Marketing→Announcing a new service→Legal-1

Announcing a new service

[Name]
[Company]
[Address]
[City, State ZIP]

Dear [   ]:

The strong economy has meant that it's a buyer's market when it comes to filling jobs. Potential employees can afford to be picky, to look around for which company offers the best deal in terms of salary and especially benefits.

Let [Fitz Associates] help make your company more competitive in the job market. We don't just prescribe the same benefits for each client—we study your culture and strategic goals and custom design a benefits package just for you. And it won't cost your company an arm and leg either!

A solid benefits package has innumerable benefits. Not only will it attract highly qualified job applicants, you'll also be able to retain more of your current employees. And that means less turnover, which translates to less time spent on recruiting, hiring, and training.

If you're having trouble attracting and keeping qualified job applicants, let [Fitz Associates] help you today.

Call [800-555-5555] now to speak with one of our representatives. You'll be glad you did.

Sincerely,

[Name]
[Title]

- **This letter uses a hot topic in the market place to build strong selling points.**

- **In soft sell letters, stick to the facts and benefits as best you can. Avoid anything that sounds like hyperbole or undue pressure.**

Path on CD-ROM: General Promotion→ Mass Marketing→Announcing a new service→Benefit-1

Announcing a new service

Dear [   ]:

If you're like most managers, you probably struggle with [problem]. I'd like to introduce you to a new service from [Company] that will help you.

[New Service] is an innovative approach to [describe need]. We take care of all the [describe activities involved in the service].

Because we spend so much of our time on [activity], our staff are experts in the field. They're up on the latest trends and technologies—experience that's bolstered by extensive training. That means we can do everything more efficiently and effectively than most companies can do themselves.

With [New Service], you don't ever have to worry again about [activity] getting done right and on time ever again.

Call [800-555-5555] now to speak with one of our representatives and see how [New Service] can improve your bottom line.

Sincerely,

[Name]
[Title]

- **Nearly every issue in business boils down to being cost-effective, so make a link between what your services offer a company and what they will save.**

- **Use anything you do to invest in your staff's credentials as a selling point. People aren't going to hire someone else to do something they think they can do better themselves.**

Path on CD-ROM: General Promotion→ Mass Marketing→Announcing a new service→Generic-4

Announcing a new service

[Name]
[Company]
[Address]
[City, State ZIP]

Dear [   ]:

It used to be that computers were tools only for scientists and geeks. But now it's become an essential business tool. As a business leader, your job is especially challenging because you're going to be managing young kids who grew up with computers. How can you keep your own computer skills fresh?

Sign up for [WorkNet's] new [Comp Exec] workshops. These workshops are designed especially for busy executives. We can come to your home or office for half-hour, one-on-one tutorials, or you can join small classes of no more than five other executives at [WorkNet's] training center on [Deming Road].

[Comp Exec] workshops cover everything from basic computing skills to word processing, creating and using spreadsheets, efficient Web surfing, and developing CD-ROMs. You can learn about hardware components if you like, or concentrate on the latest business software for both PCs and mainframe computers. You name it, we teach it.

Don't get left behind in the twentieth century. Keep on top by updating your computing skills regularly.

Call [555-5555] for more details or stop by our Web site at [www.worknet.com].

Sincerely,

[Name]
[Title]

- **This letter frankly preys on the insecurity of executives who rose through the ranks before computing skills were considered essential. Make it clear they need to learn these skills to keep out in front of their employees and colleagues.**

Path on CD-ROM: General Promotion→ Mass Marketing→Announcing a new service→Training-1

Selling an existing product

[Name]
[Company]
[Address]
[City, State ZIP]

Dear [   ]:

The REVOLUTION has begun! And [product] is right in the middle of it!

[Product] is the cost-effective way to SAVE your company's [describe type of business].

Your customers are demanding higher and higher levels of quality. Well, [Product] can help. We offer a patented [name of feature] that is [##] more efficient that anything else on the market. And that will help YOU save time and MONEY.

[Product] also helps you avoid costly delays and shutdowns on your manufacturing lines. It has all the durability and reliability that [Company's] products have been known for.

Enclosed you'll find detailed literature describing [Product's] engineering specifications. If you're worried about keeping ahead of your competition, you owe it to yourself to read this brochure.

Stay competitive. CALL OUR TOLL-FREE number today and learn more about what [Product] can do to position your company for the next century.

Sincerely,

[Name]
[Title]

P.S. DON'T WAIT. Think how good your bottom line will look when a small investment in [Product] saves thousands—if not millions—of dollars down the road!

- Link your product to helping the reader serve their customers.

- Link your product to their competitiveness.

- This type of short letter is suitable for a product that has a single strong selling point.

Path on CD-ROM: General Promotion→ Mass Marketing→Selling existing product→Generic-4

Selling an existing product

[Name]
[Address]
[City, State ZIP]

Dear [   ]:

Are you tired of having to pay top dollar to get shoes that fit? Tired of having shoes that don't last more than one season?

[SpringStep Shoes] has the solution for you! We carry the widest selection of shoe sizes and styles in the city. All our shoes are made of the finest materials, guaranteed to last and look great for years to come. And each has the special [Comfort Step] feature that provides great support even when you have to be on your feet all day!

Best yet, we carry a full range of widths, from AAAA to EEE and everything in between.

Come in today and try [SpringStep Shoes] for yourself. Get the perfect fit, and the right style for every occasion, at a price you can afford!

[SpringStep Shoes]. See how fashionable comfort can be!

Sincerely,

[Name]
[Title]

- **Open with the frustration that you're trying to solve.**

- **Close with your company's slogan.**

Path on CD-ROM: General Promotion→ Mass Marketing→Selling existing product→Shoes-2

Selling an existing product

[Name]
[Address]
[City, State ZIP]

Dear [   ]:

We have seen the future of golf. And its name is [TitanPro golf clubs].

[TitanPro] clubs are made of [Titanium Plus], a new material that gives them [strength, flexibility, and unbelievable accuracy] whether you're driving off the tee, chipping for the green, or trying to sink that 45-foot putt! And they've got a revolutionary design, including [SureGrip] pads to help keep your hands steady during every part of your swing. You'll drive longer, straighter, and smoother with [TitanPro]. Guaranteed.

But don't take our word for it. As a member of the [GolfView Country Club], you can try the [TitanPro clubs] for a full round of 18 holes. Just call the club-house manager at least 24 hours in advance to reserve a test set. There's no obligation to buy, but once you see what they can do for you, you'll be hooked (only on the clubs, not on your drives!).

[TitanPro. The future of golf has arrived.]

Sincerely,

[Name]
[Title]

- **Focus on what's new or revolutionary or ahead of the market to get a "flash" effect.**

- **If the product is really different from existing products, you may want to offer customers the ability to test the product before purchasing.**

Path on CD-ROM: General Promotion→ Mass Marketing→Selling existing product→Golf Clubs-1

Header and body:

Selling an existing product

[Name]
[Company]
[Address]
[City, State ZIP]

Dear [   ]:

What would make [Bill Gates] walk around his office…barefoot?

[SWANK]. Executive carpet from [Wall-to-Wall, Inc.]

[Swank] is so plush, you'll think you're walking on clouds. It comes in a rainbow of colors to match any décor—and textures to complement any design.

[Swank] is made of [FibR-Con], a new fiber that's softer and tougher than anything you've ever felt before. It's a subtle message that says power and prestige with every step.

Come into [Wall-to-Wall] to see this new carpet for yourself.

And come barefoot!

Sincerely,

[Name]
[Title]

P.S. If [Swank] is good enough for [Bill Gates's] feet, isn't it good enough for yours?

- To achieve a "flash" effect, place your product in the presence of someone famous.

- Highlight the new, innovative features.

MASS MARKETING

Selling an existing product

[Name]
[Address]
[City, State ZIP]

Dear [   ]:

You're expecting an important phone call from work but headed out to the theater. Your spouse is waiting on one from the doctor's office. The kids are always on the phone chatting with friends—and heaven forbid they would miss a phone call!

What do you do?

Let [Home Answer] voice-mail do the answering for you! [Home Answer] is better than an answering machine. It works just like your voice-mail at work. You can have different extensions, each with its own recorded message. So callers can choose to leave a message just for you, your spouse, one of the kids, or the family as a whole.

[Home Answer] kicks in any time your phone is busy, or you can set it to answer all incoming calls any time you don't want to be interrupted with calls (like in the middle of dinner!).

Just call [800-555-5555] to order [Home Answer] for your telephone. Don't let phone calls run your life! Get control of your calls with [Home Answer].

Sincerely,

[Name]
[Title]

- The "you" voice helps put the reader in the situation you're describing.

- Sell the "control of your life" benefit.

Path on CD-ROM: General Promotion→ Mass Marketing→Selling existing product→Voice mail-1

Selling an existing product

[Name]
[Company]
[Address]
[City, State ZIP]

Dear [   ]:

Have you noticed that most shopping malls looks exactly the same? That when you're in a McDonald's you could just as easily be in New York as El Paso? And nowadays, most office buildings seem to be following that trend. You've seen one, you've seen them all.

And what about your office environment? What does it say about your personal tastes and interests? Anything?

Probably not. That's why we invented [Art for Work], a program that places original art in office buildings. We know from personal experience with hundreds of companies that the work environment has a direct impact on people's creativity and productivity. Sterile work environments breed sterile imaginations.

So liven up your office space. [Art for Work] has or will commission art for any taste in any style. We have recreations of oil paintings in everything from Gothic to Impressionist masters. We carry original African-American folk art and modern multimedia sculptures. You can preview our collection at [www.workforart.com] or stop by our showroom at [address].

Don't settle for a boring workspace. Create your environment—don't just react to it.

Sincerely,

[Name]
[Title]

- **Since this product is unusual in that it doesn't have a direct use or bottom-line impact, it takes a longer lead-in to make the case that the product is needed in the workplace. So the product isn't named until the third paragraph. This approach works as long as you keep the introduction interesting.**

Path on CD-ROM: General Promotion→ Mass Marketing→Selling existing product→Art-1

Selling an existing service

[Name]
[Title]
[Organization]
[Address]
[City, State ZIP]

Dear [   ]:

It's 9:00 P.M. The kids are in bed, and the dog is asleep at your feet. You've put a lot into making your home safe and secure.

But just how safe are you? Do your kids know what to do if there's a fire? Are your valuables protected from burglary? Do you know what's in those old cans out in the garage?

Let us here at [HomeSafe, Inc.] help you make sure your family and home are fully protected. [We don't just offer alarm systems—our new Home Protector Security Program will help you identify and remedy all the major risks in your house and garage. Our professionals will work closely with your family to:]

[• Analyze security risks and install a patented HomeWatch electronic alarm system customized for your needs]

[• Identify and safely store or remove all dangerous/outdated chemicals in your home, basement, and garage]

[• Develop emergency and disaster preparedness plans, including dry runs with your entire family]

Don't leave your family's safety to chance. Call [555-5555] now or return the enclosed postcard and let [HomeSafe] help you protect your family.

Sincerely,

[Name]
[Title]

- **Achievers are closely tied to family, stability.**

- **Service is becoming a stronger selling point than hardware or product features; emphasize value-added services that your competitors don't offer.**

Path on CD-ROM: General Promotion→ Mass Marketing→Selling existing service→Security-1

Selling an existing service

[Name]
[Company]
[Address]
[City, State ZIP]

Dear [   ]:

Remember what it was like to report on a daily deadline for the first time? Or to interview a city official for the first time? Or even to begin to maneuver a desktop publishing program?

We know that the journalism program at [college or university] was a source of many of these firsts for you. We're still providing these important first experiences to budding young writers and editors. And we're hoping you'll be willing to help these students make it through.

As you know, the costs of providing top-notch education just keep going up. We've done everything we can to contain costs without compromising quality. One of those things is to set up a special scholarship fund for students with special financial needs.

Would you contribute generously to our fund? Simply complete the enclosed form and send it along with your check. Of course, your donation is tax deductible. And, you'll get a great feeling knowing you're helping support the formation of future leaders in the profession.

Thanks for your help.

Sincerely,

[Name]
[Title]

- **Remind the prospect of college days.**

- **Appeal to the prospect's sense of "giving back" to those following in their footsteps.**

Path on CD-ROM: General Promotion→ Mass Marketing→Selling existing service→Donation-1

MASS MARKETING

Selling an existing service

[Name]
[Company]
[Address]
[City, State ZIP]

Dear [   ]:

You kept putting it off, thinking there will always be time to find that perfect someone. Trouble is, it's getting harder and harder to meet new people.

Don't let life slip by while you wait for it to happen to you! Take charge of your future. Let [Perfect Partners] help you meet that special someone! We can introduce you to intelligent, successful singles who share your special interests, goals, and values. These are people looking for someone like you!

[Perfect Partners] is one of the most successful dating services in the country! We have a full staff of professional counselors who will take the time to get to know you—your goals, ambitions, relationship history, interests, work—all the things that make you one of a kind. We then introduce you to people who are likely to be compatible...similar enough to share your values, but different enough to introduce a little spice into your life!

If you or a friend would like to control your own future, take a step in our direction. Just fill out and return the enclosed Confidential Profile, or call your nearest [Perfect Partner] center at [800-555-5555]. There's no obligation—and you pay nothing up front!

Best regards,

[Name]
[Title]

P.S. You've got nothing to lose—and everything to gain in finding someone to share your life with.

- **The opening creates an image the target reader will identify with.**

- **Make the letter action oriented.**

- **Emphasize how easy it is for them to solve their problem.**

Path on CD-ROM: General Promotion→ Mass Marketing→Selling existing service→Dating-1

Selling an existing service

Nothing is more important than your good name!

[Name]
[Address]
[City, State ZIP]

Dear [   ]:

Thankfully, there's still some people to whom a good name is something of value. We know you're one of those people. And we want to help you protect yours.

That's why [Riverland Credit Union] is extending this special offer. We're inviting you to sign up for our [Protector™ overdraft protection service]. We all go through times when we forget to write down a check or an ATM withdrawal—and the next thing we know, our checking account is overdrawn. That may not sound like a big deal, but to people who track your credit rating, it sure is!

With [Protector], you never have to worry about getting overdrawn. If your checking or savings accounts ever dip below $0, [Protector] automatically extends you a temporary loan to cover any overdraft balance. And you'll have up to [60] days to pay it off.

Get a little peace of mind. Sign up for [Protector] today! Just drop by any of our branch offices or call [555-5555]. You can also get quick approval over the Internet at [www.riverland.org].

Don't put your good name—and credit rating—at risk! Get [Protector] today!

Sincerely,

[Name]
[Title]

- The opening addresses the core belief or value you think will be important to a believer.

- Use of "we" voice makes it sound like you're in the same boat as the reader and therefore understand his/her concerns.

- Describe the benefits of the service.

- Re-emphasize the core value several times in the letter.

- End with a call to action.

Path on CD-ROM: General Promotion→ Mass Marketing→Selling existing service→Financial-1

Selling an existing service

Question: How much did your company spend on training last year?

Next question: What have you gotten in return?

[Name]
[Company]
[Address]
[City, State ZIP]

Dear [   ]:

Having a trained, educated workforce is a MUST in today's business world. Companies—and employees—who aren't constantly developing their skills are falling behind! That's why so many companies invest so heavily in training and education.

The trouble is, much of that money is going down the drain. You probably know from your own experience that there often isn't much noticeable change after staff have completed a training program.

[Gasey Training] can change all that. We have an excellent staff of instructional designers and training specialists who can help make sure that you get your money's worth out of each and every dollar you invest in employee development. We'll analyze your training design, implementation, and staff and suggest changes to improve their effectiveness.

We will help you get the most out of training packages, or develop customized training specifically designed for your organization.

The money you spend on employee development is one of the most critical investments you can make as a business. Make sure you're getting your money's worth. Call [Gasey Training] at [800-555-5555] or visit our Web site at [www.gasey.com].

Sincerely,

[Name]
[Title]

- **Start by describing the area of business expense that your service targets.**

- **Make the link between your services and the customer's bottom line.**

Path on CD-ROM: General Promotion→ Mass Marketing→Selling existing service→Design-1

Selling an existing service

[Name]
[Company]
[Address]
[City, State Zip]

Dear [   ]:

Isn't it time you put your business on the Web?

Having a World Wide Web site isn't just for small businesses. And it isn't a luxury. It's becoming as basic as a phone listing or a business card. A site on the World Wide Web helps put your business on the map and shows that you're serious about business.

[Turnerton Associates] can build an impressive Web site for your firm complete with custom graphics and descriptions of your principle products or services and host it for [less than $1 per day]. That's right—for [less than $1 per day] for your total cost and virtually none of your time, you can have a Web site that you can be proud of.

To learn more about [Turnerton Associates] give us a call at [800-475-9000]—or better yet—visit our Web site at [www.turnerton.com]. You'll find hot links to other Web sites we've built for businesses just like yours.

And what's your Web site address? Call [Turnerton Associates] today and you won't have to apologize for not being on the World Wide Web any longer!

Sincerely,

[Greg Turnerton,]
[Partner]

Path on CD-ROM: General Promotion→ Mass Marketing→Selling existing service→Web-1

Selling company's image or feature

[Name]
[Address]
[City, State ZIP]

Dear [   ]:

The most important thing about a [bank] isn't the size of the building or how many glitzy services it offers. The most important thing is whether you trust the people inside.

Hello, my name is [famous name], and I'm the [President and CEO] of [First Personal Bank]. My family has been involved in [banking] for years. In fact, [we started the first bank in [city] back in [18xx]. We have always been strongly committed to supporting [city] and its [citizens].

And isn't that what you want in a bank? A partner who is interested in you personally? A champion who will be on your side when you need it? That's what you'll find at [First Personal Bank]. We really want to get to know you personally and determine the right set of banking services just for you.

If you're tired of being just a number to an international conglomerate, if you're tired of having your mortgage or loan sold to out-of-state banks, come to [First Personal Bank].

We're committed to this community and to you.

Sincerely,

[Name]
[Title]

- Open by stating the point you're selling as a matter of fact.

- Introduce the letter signer and describe his/her credentials.

- Describe what makes the company trustworthy.

Path on CD-ROM: General Promotion→ Mass Marketing→Selling company's image or feature→Banking-1

Selling your company

[Name]
[Company]
[Address]
[City, State ZIP]

Dear [   ]:

If you have heart trouble, you want to be treated by an experienced heart specialist, right? That's the same philosophy that [DB Consulting] brings to the table. All of our Senior Consultants are experienced professionals—not young kids fresh out of business school! They have the knowledge—and scars—that comes from being on the frontline and in the board room, making the tough calls and living with the consequences.

[DB Consulting] provides consulting and coaching in areas such as [name areas]. When we work with a client, we assign a Senior Consultant to lead the team, someone who has the specific knowledge, training, and experience that relates to your particular needs. That's why we get results—results that improve your bottom line, increase ROI, and make your organization more effective and efficient.

If your company could do a better job of [describe relative areas], I encourage you to look at the enclosed brochure. You'll find a complete list of the types of services that [DB Consulting] offers, testimonials from many of our clients, and resumes for all our senior consulting staff.

If you want experienced professionals working to help you solve your problems and meet your challenges, call on [DB Consulting].

Sincerely,

[Name]
[Title]

- **This style of letter indirectly slams your competition by setting up a false comparison (you hire experience professionals, others hire kids out of business school).**

- **Enclose case studies, resumes, or other material to support the "experienced" claim.**

Path on CD-ROM: General Promotion→ Mass Marketing→Selling company's image or feature→Consultant-1

Selling company's image or feature

[Name]
[Title]
[Company]
[Address]
[City, State ZIP]

Dear [   ]:

Are you tired of having to pay top dollar to get a [copier] that has more features than you'll ever use? Sick of dealing with behemoth corporations that only sell you [copiers] that do what THEY want them to do? Wouldn't you like to get the [copier] you need with only the features you want—and work with a [copier] company that cares about your needs more than their own?

We're the [copier] company you've been looking for!

We're [CustomCopiers, Inc.], and customized [copiers] are the ONLY kind we make. We can custom build a [copier] with all the features you want—and none that you don't want. So you'll only pay for the features you really use.

Take a look through the enclosed catalog, which shows our basic models and how they can be customized to meet your needs. Then give us a call at [800-555-5555] and let one of our service representatives help you meet your needs.

Don't pay for features you're not using! Call the customized-ONLY [copier] company— [CustomCopiers]—today!

Sincerely,

[Name]
[Title]

P.S. Our [copiers] can also be [hooked up to your file server so you can print multiple copies direct from your computer]. Call [800-555-5555] to find out how!

- Identify with the reader's frustrations regarding the types of companies he/she's used to dealing with.

- Let the reader see how both your company and its products are superior to what has been available.

- A postscript can be used to re-emphasize a key point in the letter or provide a tickler that provides additional incentive to call.

Path on CD-ROM: General Promotion→ Mass Marketing→Selling company's image or feature→Copiers-1

Selling company's image or feature

TO: [Name@company.com]
FROM: [Name]
SUBJECT: Come out of the Dark Ages!

Dear [   ]:

Before the dawn of civilization, humankind sent runners ahead of the tribe to scout for new game and track enemies. These scouts were vigilant, tireless, and reliable.

You may not be hunting mammoths, but scouts are still vital to your success. And [CyberScout Inc.] offers a line of products that harness Internet search technologies to help you scope out the landscape and track the competition.

Our [Market Scout] product scans the Internet for business news and trends and synthesizes the information into simple reports you can print from your own computer. All you have to do is tell [Market Scout] what types of business and consumers you want to track, the software does the rest.

[TechScout] brings you up-to-date on the latest Internet and new high-tech product developments. While [NewsScout] delivers urgent news bulletins in the categories of your choice, right to your e-mailbox.

New products from [CyberScout Inc.] Don't go hunting without them.

Click here to visit our Web site. You can download a trial version of the Scout product of your choice—Market Scout, TechScout, or NewsScout— ABSOLUTELY FREE.

- **Analogies are useful only if the comparisons make sense.**

- **If possible extend your unique technologies across a range of specialized applications.**

- **Offer sample versions to induce interest and trial; with brand new, untested companies, the opportunity to place the product in a prospect's hands is crucial.**

Path on CD-ROM: General Promotion→ Mass Marketing→Selling company's image or feature→Software-1

Selling company's image or feature

[Packaging innovations] come and go. But one name has provided more packaging solutions to more businesses than any other: [XPedient].

Now [XPedient] brings the latest innovations in packaging technology to every one of our packages. Our new [EverGreen] packing material is [stronger than plastic] and [made of 100% recycled products]. It offers more features than any other packaging material:

- Easily moldable to fit any product shape

- Strong but flexible to provide the ultimate protection for your products

- Lightweight construction saves on shipping costs

All that AND you're protecting the environment no matter which [XPedient] package you choose!

What's more, now you can let the name you've relied on for years meet your newest challenges, because now [XPedient] can custom design a packaging system just for your products.

Click here to see samples of [EverGreen] packaging. Or go to Customer Service to contact one of our sales representatives or call [800-555-5555]. See how [XPedient], more than ever, is the packaging company of tomorrow—and today.

- **An innovative feature that's deployed across a company's entire line is a great hook for selling the company.**

- **Even in a letter posted on the Web, intended to sell the company as a whole, provide information that lets people contact you by various means (mail, phone, fax).**

Path on CD-ROM: General Promotion→ Mass Marketing→Selling company's image or feature→Packaging-1

Brochure and catalog cover letters

[Name]
[Company]
[Address]
[City, State ZIP]

Dear [   ]:

Peace. You look for it at home, at work and at church. So why not look for it in your friends? You can find it by joining the premier service club in America today, the [Rotary Lions].

Maybe it sounds corny to call [Rotary Lions] "good people." But that's what we are. Our mission is to help others in need. Come to our next meeting on [date] to see for yourself. You'll find people just like you who care about this community and its citizens—and, more importantly, are doing something about it.

The enclosed brochure describes just some of the programs that [Rotary Lions] have participated in over the past year. We provided [## meals for the homeless, donated ## books to the Literacy Program, and help tutor ## grade school children in reading]. And that's just the tip of the iceberg.

So if you'd like to join an organization that's making a difference in our community, check out the [Rotary Lions].

Our next meeting is [date] at [time] at [location]. Won't you join us? There's no obligation—just a chance to meet great people.

[Rotary Lions]. Be part of the solution.

Sincerely,

[Name]
[Title]

- **Emphasize a belief in community values.**

- **Recap a few highlights of your organization's achievement, but leave the details for the brochure.**

- **The purpose is to get people to one meeting, not necessarily make them join right away.**

Path on CD-ROM: General Promotion→ Mass Marketing→Brochure and catalog cover letters→Nonprofit-1

MASS MARKETING

Brochure and catalog cover letters

"If it's so great, why don't you patent it?"

[Name]
[Address]
[City, State ZIP]

Dear [   ]:

That's what our customers kept asking us. And here's the answer: we did.

Our [Chef Magic pots and pans] are made with an incredible new material that provides the [cooking] performance everybody wants.

- They heat evenly

- They are fully nonstick

- You can put them in the dishwasher

- You can use metal utensils—nothing can scratch the surface!

The patented [Never-Scratch coating] is so revolutionary, you'll never have to buy another pot or pan! Guaranteed.

Take a look at the enclosed full-color brochure, then send in your order form, or just call [800-555-5555] now to order your own set for just [$299.99]. And if you respond by [date], we'll even cover the cost of shipping!

Sincerely,

[Name]
[Title]

P.S. Act now and get your [Chef Magic set] for just [$299.99]. Shipping is free!

- **Use this approach if your product has a special material or component that is new to the market.**

- **Flash approaches focus on what's new or different, which can be underscored by the inclusion of a well-produced brochure or catalog highlighting unusual visual elements of the product.**

Path on CD-ROM: General Promotion→ Mass Marketing→Brochure and catalog cover letters→Cookware-1

Brochure and catalog cover letters

[Name]
[Company]
[Address]
[City, State ZIP]

Dear [   ]:

We hate to say it, but there are a lot of companies out there who say they support [name of charity or cause] when really they don't. If you look at their bottom line, you'd see the profits go to corporate officers and shareholders, not to the people who really need the help.

[Nonprofit company] has been around for [##] years. We've employed [hundreds] of [disadvantaged] workers while establishing a strong presence in the marketplace. That's why we're so excited about introducing our new [Product line].

The [product] line is made entirely by [type of disadvantage] workers. Yet we maintain the highest standards in the industry. One look through the enclosed catalogue will convince you of that. And all of our [product line] products are guaranteed to perform to your satisfaction or we'll refund your money.

Best of all, [product line] products are priced below the competition, so you can save your business money, get the performance you need, AND support [disadvantaged] workers all at the same time.

Won't you go through our catalog and then call to place an order?

Sincerely,

[Name]
[Title]

P.S. Visit our Web site, [www.nonprofit.org], to see the full range of our products. And please call or order online today. To delay may mean to forget.

- **This same type of letter could be used by a for-profit company that championed a worthy social or environmental cause.**

- **Include photos of the workplace and workers in the catalog to help make the message/cause real.**

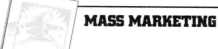

Brochure and catalog cover letters

[Name]
[Company]
[Address]
[City, State ZIP]

Dear [   ]:

It used to be that the computer was a tool only for scientists and geeks. But now it's become an essential business tool. As a business leader, your job is especially challenging because you're going to be managing young kids who grew up with computers.

How can you keep your own computer skills fresh? Sign up for [Office-Staff's] new [Comp Exec] workshops.

These workshops are designed especially for busy executives. We can come to your home or office for half-hour, one-on-one tutorials, or you can join small classes of no more than five other executives at [Office-Staff's] training center on [1627 W. Main].

Look through our brochure outlining our classes, on-site schedules, and prices for workshops covering everything from basic computing skills to word processing, from developing CD-ROMs to hardware components.

Don't get left behind in the twentieth century. Keep on top by updating your computing skills regularly. Register today. Just fill out the registration form in the back of the brochure or go to the Registration page on our Web site, [www.Office-Staff.com].

Sincerely,

[Name]
[Title]

- **This letter preys on the insecurity of executives who rose through the ranks before computing skills were considered essential. Make it clear they need to learn these skills to keep out in front of their employees and colleagues.**

- **Use the brochure to give the reader a complete breakdown of class options, schedules, and prices—and the opportunity to register immediately.**

Path on CD-ROM: General Promotion→ Mass Marketing→Brochure and catalog cover letters→Training-1

Brochure and catalog cover letters

[Name]
[Company]
[Address]
[City, State ZIP]

> **Answer: Alaska in the spring; New Mexico in the winter; southern Spain almost any time of the year.**
>
> **Question: Where do you like to vacation?**

Dear [   ]:

Most travelers worry about what items to pack and how to fit everything they want to take into the number of bags they can take. Not you. When you order all of your travel clothes and necessities from [Balboa Originals], your only concern is where to go next.

Just point your finger to a spot on the globe. Wherever you choose to go, [Balboa Originals] can outfit your trip—from cap to sandals, from desert hat to desert boots, or polar hood to snow boots. You get the idea.

Get the complete picture by reviewing the enclosed catalog. From gadgets to gizmos, [Balboa Originals] supplies all types of luggage and travel gear, as well as easy-care, great-looking clothing.

All orders are guaranteed. And ordering is easy. Just select your items from the catalog, complete the form, and mail in the postage-paid envelope provided. Or order online at [www.balboaorginals.com].

See you in Spain.

Sincerely,

[Name]
[Title]

- **Introductory teaser is in a question-and-answer format.**

- **Direct-mail copy is often very descriptive. It does not just list product benefits but explains specific selling points in focused copy.**

Path on CD-ROM: General Promotion→ Mass Marketing→Brochure and catalog cover letters→Travel-1

Brochure and catalog cover letters

[Name]
[Company]
[Address]
[City, State ZIP]

Dear [   ]:

Maybe you know where you are headed but don't know precisely what gear and clothing you will need. We have all been there.

Our customer service representatives are all experienced travelers who can advise you on the outfits you will need—whether you're off to the Andes in Peru or the Appalachians in Pennsylvania.

Our representatives can provide advice on the types of shoes and boots you will need to hike the canyons of Utah or the wilderness around Lake Superior. They can offer suggestions on bug spray and poison ivy salve and other products we don't even sell. They will take the time to answer all of your questions and point you to the right source for the items you need if we don't offer them.

What do you want to know? When does the rainy season begin? When do the flies disappear?

Pick up the phone and ask one of our representatives. While you're conversing, don't forget to place your order for several of our travel products. They will keep you and your gear dry, comfortable, and on track, whatever your destination.

Sincerely,

[Name]
[Title]

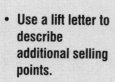

- **Use a lift letter to describe additional selling points.**

- **Invite the readers to order.**

Path on CD-ROM: General Promotion→ Mass Marketing→Brochure and catalog cover letters→Apparel-1

Brochure and catalog cover letters

A special note from the Editor...

Dear [   ]:

No one knows the challenges of leading today's colleges and universities better than you do. You know only too well the constraints of austere budgets, the pain of financial cutbacks, the low morale of faculty, the worries of students, and the anger of their parents at the high cost of tuition.

Yet you persevere, looking for the answers you know are there, seeking for the seeds of solutions in the heart of the problems.

You have a vision for the success and effectiveness of your institution well into the 21st century.

I want to help you get there.

[*Fundraising Alert*] is designed to extend your network of helpful colleagues at campuses across the globe—without the expense in time or money of traveling to another conference or hiring an outside consultant.

This new publication offers help from those already inside academia who understand its culture and environment. [*Fundraising Alert*] extends your dialogue on your financial issues with colleagues on other campuses. It extends your range of options when confronting tough situations and offers campus contacts to get more details on what worked elsewhere.

I invite you to take me up on the charter offer described elsewhere in this package. Experience for yourself the benefits of an expanded collegial network. Use [*Fundraising Alert*] as your personal advisory committee, beginning this fall.

Best wishes,

[Name]
[Editor and Publisher]

- **A lift letter sometimes accompanies a direct mail package and provides an additional teaser to the reader. Often it begins, "Open this only if you have decided not to order."**

- **This lift letter provides a more personal reason to purchase the product.**

Path on CD-ROM: General Promotion→ Mass Marketing→Brochure and catalog cover letters→Magazine-4

Brochure and catalog cover letters

[Date]

[Name]
[Company]
[Address]
[City, State ZIP]

Dear [   ]:

Did I mention that our new software guarantees your meeting planning success? If you try the latest release of [program] and your conference does not attract more participants and generate more excitement, we will refund your purchase price.

Of course, we don't think that will happen. We think you will want to use it for years.

As one customer explained, ["Your software saved me many days of work. In fact, I used to have to hire a limited term employee to help with our annual convention, but now I just use your program. It is worth its weight in gold."]

Test her words by trying our new software for yourself. See if your next meeting doesn't attract more praise from more participants. You have nothing to lose and a lot of compliments to gain.

Sincerely,

[Name]
[Title]

- **Use a strong guarantee to gain a response from the uncommitted reader.**

- **Consider offering a challenge to try the product.**

Path on CD-ROM: General Promotion→ Mass Marketing→Brochure and catalog cover letters→Software-1

Coupon promotions

Dear [   ]:

What with everybody shouting at you these days, sometimes it's hard to know which [type of store] has the best deals. WE know that [Company] is the best, but don't take our word for it.

Use the enclosed coupon and receive [XX]% off your next purchase. Then you can judge for yourself.

But don't delay—the coupon expires [date]. You wouldn't want to pass this deal by!

Regards,

[Name]

- **Though a soft sell, this memo still emphasizes the deadline.**

- **This approach sells your store by telling customers it will sell itself if only they come in.**

Coupon promotions

Never has traveling looked this good!

Dear [   ]:

Now you can travel the world in style with the new [Traveler] luggage from [Morby's]. And for a limited time, you can save [10%] off any purchase of [Traveler] luggage with the enclosed coupon.

[Traveler] luggage is perfect for any occasion. Take it to 5-star hotels or cabins in the wilderness, on business trips or family vacations. It will look great anywhere!

Better still, [Traveler] is light, durable, and scratch resistant. And it comes in a variety of sizes, finishes, and styles to fit any taste, any need. Larger pieces have built-in pull-handles with sturdy wheels. Smaller pieces have comfortable shoulder straps. Now you can travel through airports, hotels, and rugged backwaters with ease!

Hurry in today! Your [10%] discount expires on [date].

Sincerely,

[Name]
[Title]

P.S. Get a leg up on your summer traveling! Stop by [Morby's] today.

- Use an eye-catching headline to grab the reader's attention.

- Turn the reader's thoughts to what can be accomplished with the product (traveling).

Path on CD-ROM: General Promotion→ Mass Marketing→Promotions—Coupons→Discount-3

Introductory offers

"If it's so great, why don't you patent it?"

[Name]
[Address]
[City, State ZIP]

Dear [   ]:

That's what our customers kept asking us. And here's the answer: We did.

Our [CookRight pots and pans] are made with an incredible new material that provides the [cooking] performance everybody wants.

[• Even heating
• Fully nonstick
• Dishwasher safe
• Use metal utensils—nothing can scratch the surface!]

The patented [UnStick surface] is so revolutionary, you'll never have to buy another pot or pan! Guaranteed].

ACT NOW and get two [CookRight Cookie Sheets] ABSOLUTELY FREE! You'll never have to grease a cookie sheet again! And the special patented surface means your cookies will bake evenly!

Visit our Web site at [www.unstick.com] for more information, or call [800-555-5555] now to order your own set for just [$299.99]. Shipping is free!

Sincerely,

[Name]
[Title]

P.S. Act now and get your [CookRight set] for just [$299.99]. Shipping is free!

- **Use this approach if your product has a special material or component that is new to the market.**

- **Flash approaches focus on what's new or different.**

- **Provide enough description of the bonus to make it sound enticing and reinforce the special flash feature.**

MASS MARKETING

Introductory offers

[Name]
[Address]
[City, State ZIP]

Dear [   ]:

You're expecting an important phone call from work but headed out to the the-ater. Your spouse is waiting on one from the doctor's office. The kids are always on the phone chatting with friends, and heaven forbid they miss a phone call!

What do you do?

Let [Home Answer] voice-mail do the answering for you! [Home Answer] is better than an answering machine. It works just like your voice-mail at work. You can have different extensions, each with its own recorded message, so callers can choose to leave a message just for you, your spouse, one of the kids, or the family as a whole. [Home Answer] kicks in any time your phone is busy, or you can set it to answer all incoming calls any time you don't want to be interrupted with calls (like in the middle of dinner!).

Just call [800-555-5555] to order [Home Answer] for your telephone. And if you sign up for a 6-month service contract by [date], the first month is free!

Don't let phone calls run your life! Get control of your calls with [Home Answer].

Sincerely,

[Name]
[Title]

- **The "you" voice helps put the reader in the situation you're describing.**

- **Sell the "control of your life" benefit.**

- **With a service that's billed on a monthly basis, offering a free month to motivate commitment to a multimonth contract can be quite tempting.**

Path on CD-ROM: General Promotion→ Mass Marketing→Promotions—intro offers→Voice mail-1

Introductory offers

[Name]
[Address]
[City, State ZIP]

Dear [   ]:

You've probably seen the ads for the new [Rocky Mountain Bike] on TV. How would you like to try one out for 30 days, free!

[For 30 days, you can plunge down mountainsides, streak through forested paths, or bounce across rugged city streets! The Rocky Mountain Bike is classy and durable, lightweight but incredibly strong].

People tell us we're crazy for making this offer. Whoever heard of letting people try out a [mountain bike] free for 30 days? But that's what we're doing. For a limited time only you can purchase a [Rocky Mountain Bike] from [World Cycle] with no money down. Try it out for 30 days, and if you don't like it, we'll refund the entire purchase price.

Come into [World Cycle] today, and head for the hills tomorrow!

Sincerely,

[Name]
[Title]

- **Draw on a media image to make the product more attractive.**

- **Make the language action-oriented like the product you're selling.**

Path on CD-ROM: General Promotion→ Mass Marketing→Promotions—intro offers→Bikes-1

Introductory offers

[Name]
[Company]
[Address]
[City, State ZIP]

Dear [   ]:

When you're [name an outdoor activity], you want to have the best equipment possible, don't you?

The same holds true every time one of your employees gets into one of your fleet cars. That's why you should rely on [brand name] tires.

[Brand name] tires give you precise control under all road conditions, from a straight stretch of parched desert highway to ice-covered mountain hairpins. And they have [design feature] that makes them [puncture resistant], even when the tread begins to wear down, which won't be for a long time!

[Brand name] tires are built of the finest materials and pass rigorous quality standards, and [they're proven to last longer than other tires]. And they come in a full range of sizes, so they're perfect for everything from passenger cars to SUVs to light trucks.

Don't risk an accident with your current tires. Give your drivers the control they need on the road.

Check out our Web site at [www.tires.com] for a list of authorized dealers in your area, and note which dealers are featuring our factory-authorized introductory offer: 25% off your first fleet order if you buy by [date]. You're going to have to re-equip your fleet soon enough anyway, so why not do it at a time that makes financial sense and places your drivers more safely on the road than ever before.

Sincerely,

[Name]
[Title]

- **Create appeal for your product by equating it with a sensation the readers might have had.**

- **Emphasize action, control, and experience, even in the introductory offer.**

Path on CD-ROM: General Promotion→ Mass Marketing→Promotions—intro offers→Tires-1

Introductory offers

[Name]
[Address]
[City, State ZIP]

Dear [   ]:

We know the past wasn't as rosy as it's sometimes cracked up to be. But with all the scandal in sports these days, it's hard not to think that there really was something good about the old days. That's why [Golden Era] is proud to bring you memorabilia from the greatest sports heroes of the twentieth century.

We cover the early days of all the major sports—baseball, basketball, golf, tennis—and even Olympic champions from the early games. How would you like to have a baseball that Babe Ruth autographed? Or a golf club from Babe Didrickson? How about an original Arthur Ashe tennis racquet? We have all that, and much more!

And if you're a real classic sports fan, you'll appreciate our "get-acquainted" special offer: when you buy any item worth [$50] or more before [date], you'll get 50% off any other item of equal or lesser value.

So come into [Golden Era] today at [address] and browse as long as you like through aisle after aisle of original, authentic gear, clothing, and other memorabilia used by the great sports heroes of the century.

Sincerely,

[Name]
[Title]

- **This letter aims at balancing pure nostalgia with an acknowledgment that the past wasn't perfect.**

- **Briefly list or describe a range of products or memorabilia you carry, hitting the highlights.**

- **Acknowledge the value of your merchandise by tying the introductory offer to a significant first purchase.**

Path on CD-ROM: General Promotion→ Mass Marketing→Promotions—intro offers→Memorabilia-1

Introductory offers

[Name]
[Address]
[City, State ZIP]

Dear [   ]:

Your kids are home from school for the summer and you can hear them out in the yard screaming. And what are they screaming for? ICE CREAM, naturally!

Don't disappoint them! Come into [SugarCone Ice Cream Parlor]. Our famous HOMEMADE ice cream can't be beat! You'll never taste anything this creamy and delicious. And it's all made right in our store so you're guaranteed the freshest ice cream you've ever had.

Visit us before [June 25] and you can join our [Frequent Screamers Club— buy nine cones or cups and get the tenth free]. With summer already heating up, it's an opportunity you won't want to pass up.

So if you're tired of all the screaming, stop by [SugarCone Ice Cream Parlor] today. We're located just off [Main] on [W. 7th] across from [the bowling alley].

Sincerely,

[Name]
[Title]

- **The opening is a parody of an old saying that should resonate with readers.**

- **When selling food, you have to tempt the taste buds.**

- **Make the introductory offer tied to frequency and the season if possible.**

Path on CD-ROM: General Promotion→ Mass Marketing→Promotions—intro offers→Ice cream-1

Bonus offers

[Name]
[Title]
[Company]
[Address]
[City, State ZIP]

Dear [   ]:

Did you know that you don't have to put up with copies that are faded, streaked, or covered in black dots?

Did you know you don't have to wait [10] minutes just to copy a [20-page] report [back-to-back]?

Did you know that you can track the number of copies made by each department in your company?

AND DID YOU KNOW YOU CAN GET FREE TONER CARTRIDGES BY PURCHASING A NEW COPIER FROM [O.E. SYSTEMS]?

Stop by our showroom today or call [555-5555] and one of our representatives will come to your office to show you the wide range of copiers we carry. You'll find models from all the best brand names—[Canon, Royal, Minolta, Mita]. We can find a model to fit your exact needs. So whether you're looking for high volume copying, crisp resolution, or special digital effects, come to [O.E. Systems].

And we'll even give you three FREE toner cartridges to get you started.

Sincerely,

[Name]
[Title]

P.S. Did you know you can LEASE a copier from [O.E.Systems]?

- **Start out with typical problems that would cause someone to be in the market for a copier (even if they haven't realized it).**

- **Here, the bonus is set up relatively early in the letter to continue the pattern of "do you know" questions.**

- **The postscript carries on the theme set up in the opening and introduces another reason for the reader to use this company. Alternatively, you could put a reminder of the bonus in the postscript.**

Streetwise Sales Letters

[Name]
[Address]
[City, State ZIP]

Dear [   ]:

Just feel the exhilaration of riding just in front of the crest. Feel the thrill of speed, the excitement of being out in the world.

Yes, I'm talking about surfing, but not on Oahu! I'm describing the experience of Web surfing with [Pax Cable's SonicWeb™ Service].

AND FOR A LIMITED TIME...EXPERIENCE IT FOR FREE! That's right, get your first month of [Pax SonicWeb] free!

A lot of of people still think that 56K modems provide fast Internet access. But that's like driving a Model T compared to the super speeds you'll get through [Pax Cable's SonicWeb]! No more long waits for images to load, no more gaps in streaming audio or video. Just the total thrill of surfing at high speed.

Sign up for [Pax Cable's SonicWeb™ Service] and get the fastest access to the Internet and Web available! And it all comes through the cables you already have to your home.

For just a [$XX.XX] installation fee and [$XX.XX] a month, you can save HOURS each month by getting faster Internet service. Imagine being able to move from screen to screen in just seconds rather than minutes! E-mail large files to your friends or coworkers in just a fraction of the time it would take over the phone lines!

And remember, now you can try it for FREE the first month! Call your local [Pax Cable] company today at [555-5555] and sign up for [SonicWeb] service. Surf the New Wave of Internet access.

Sincerely,

[Name]
[Title]

P.S. This offer won't last for long! Call today.

- **Bonuses associated with services that are delivered regularly are often of the "get a month free" variety. That kind of offer can induce someone to sign up, so place the offer early in the letter or set it off.**

Path on CD-ROM: General Promotion→ Mass Marketing→Promotions—bonuses→Cable Web-1

Event promotion

Meet [Hardware Harry] In Person!

Dear Valued Customer:

This coming [Saturday, May 5], come to [Abe's Hardware] and meet [Hardware Harry, Harry Reeves, renowned home improvement expert and host of the "Around the House" show aired on more than 200 radio stations around the country]!

[Harry] will give an opening speech at [9:30] then be on hand for the next hour to answer YOUR [home improvement] questions and sign copies of [his] classic [*101 Fix it Right! Answers* and his new book, *Harry's Handy, Helpful Hardware*].

Don't pass up this once-in-a-lifetime opportunity to meet [Hardware Harry] in person!

PLUS! Get tickets for our special raffle!

Win [a copy of Harry's books or your very own set of Black & Decker power tools]!

That's [May 5 from 9:30 to 11:00 A.M.] at [Abe's Hardware on Billings Road]. Don't miss out!

Sincerely,

[Name]
[Title]

- **Give brief credentials for the expert in case some readers aren't familiar with him/her.**

- **Be clear about specifically what will happen and what opportunity the customer will have to interact with the expert.**

Path on CD-ROM: General Promotion→ Mass Marketing→Promotions—events→Hardware-1

Event promotion

You're Invited!

[Kids First!] cordially invites you to join us at our [Donor Reception] on [Saturday, March 27] between [10 A.M.] and [2 P.M.]

Come meet our staff, see our offices, and meet other people just as special as you! We plan a special [awards ceremony] at [11:30 A.M.]

Be sure to bring your entire family! We'll have FREE food and beverages, and the [Singalong Kid will be there from 12:30 to 1:00 P.M.]

JUST ANNOUNCED! Family favorite [Jerry the Juggler] will entertain the kids from [10:30 to 11:00 A.M.]

No need to RSVP! Just show up with your kids in tow!

- **Emphasize that the celebration carries on the theme of the organization ("kids first").**

- **Keep the details brief and clear so people can easily mark their calendars.**

Path on CD-ROM: General Promotion→ Mass Marketing→Promotions—events→Charity-1

Promotion response form

Customer Certificate

Yes! Please send me [*Harry's Handy, Helpful Hardware Book* for only $39.95].

Name _____

Address _____

City _____ State _____ ZIP _____

Phone _____

Number of Copies _____ Amount Enclosed _____

Guarantee: If I am not totally satisfied with this book, I understand that I can return it within 10 days for a full refund.

- **This is not a coupon or even an order form, but a more impressive sounding customer certificate. Direct marketers also use member certificates and charter subscription certificates.**

- **The guarantee reminds the reader that this is a no-risk offer.**

Path on CD-ROM: General Promotion→ Mass Marketing→Promotion response form→Publisher-1

MASS MARKETING

Reminder of end of promotion/sale

[Name]
[Company]
[Address]
[City, State ZIP]

Dear [   ]:

Don't tell me you've started cleaning the office yourself!

That's the only reason I can imagine that you haven't yet taken advantage of the offer we made several weeks ago.

Fortunately, it still stands. [MetroMaids Cleaning Service], described as "hard-working, dependable and thorough" by an overwhelming 96% of our current clients in a recent survey, would still like to offer you a trial cleaning at half price.

Just call us at [800-555-5555] us by [date]—that's just 4 days from now!—and we'll set up your first appointment. See for yourselves why our clients are so satisfied with our service!

Sincerely,

[Name]
[Title]

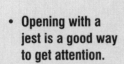

- **Opening with a jest is a good way to get attention.**

- **Remind the reader of the offer and the phone number.**

Path on CD-ROM: General Promotion→ Mass Marketing→Reminders of end of promotion or sale→Cleaning-1

Reminder of end of promotion/sale

TO: [Name@company.com]
FROM: [Name]
SUBJECT: Sale ends soon!

Dear [   ]:

Just a reminder to our best customers: our "Big Names" sale is on now but ends on [date and time].

For the next [number] days only, we're offering all *New York Times* bestsellers at a whopping 60% off the cover price! (You can go there now: [LINK].)

And all Billboard Top 100 CDs are 50% off the list price! (Go there now: [LINK].)

These savings are available only until [date], so act now!

Go to [LINK to homepage] now and start saving on the top-selling books and CDs—only at [musicNbooks.com].

Sincerely,

[Name]
[Title]

- **Remind the reader about the special sale, including dates, items, and percentages.**
- **Provide specific product/category links and a home page link.**

Path on CD-ROM: General Promotion→ Mass Marketing→Reminders of end of promotion or sale→Retailer-6

MASS MARKETING

Reminder of end of promotion/sale

[Name]
[Address]
[City, State ZIP]

Dear [   ]:

Just a reminder: NOW is the time to shop at [company]!

That's because through [date] ONLY, you'll [find/get] amazingly low [prices/rates] on [all/selected] [products/services] in every [area/department/category] of our [store/business/Web site].

Here are just a few of the hundreds of sale [items/services]:

* [item]: [price] ([LINK])
* [item]: [price] ([LINK])
* [item]: [price] ([LINK])

[Come in/call/go to homepage LINK] NOW to take advantage of these tremendous savings—but hurry!

These incredible [prices/rates] are available for just [number] more [days/weeks], and [products/services/ items] are going fast!

Sincerely,

[Name]
[Title]

* **Remind the reader of the scope and effective dates of the sale using an urgent tone.**

* **Provide specific savings on selected items, with direct links (if using e-mail).**

Path on CD-ROM: General Promotion→ Mass Marketing→ Reminder of end of sale or promotion→ Generic-3

Reminder of end of promotion/sale

[Name]
[Company]
[Address]
[City, State ZIP]

Dear [   ]:

If you've been considering providing corporate credit cards to your employees
to help them manage their business expenses, now's the time to do it. And
there's still a chance to take advantage of [company name's] limited-time
introductory offer.

As a reminder, until [date] only, the annual fee for the basic Corporate Card is
only [$] per card, a savings of [$]. For the Gold Card, it's only [$], a full [$]
lower than the usual [$] fee.

These lower fees are only good for [number] more days, so call our Corporate
Accounts Card Services number [number] today.

Sincerely,

[Name]
[Title]

- **Briefly remind the reader of the differences between your various product offerings and include price comparisons between the special offer and the usual price; stress the offer's end date.**

Path on CD-ROM: General Promotion→ Mass Marketing→ Reminder of end of sale or promotion→ Credit card-1

Reminder of end of promotion/sale

[Name]
[Address]
[City, State ZIP]

Dear [   ]:

Time's running out on the opportunity to purchase your [Rugged Adventurer Multi-Sport Rack] at the special introductory price.

Don't forget—this is the [one rack that can carry all your outdoor gear, including bikes, canoes, kayaks, skis, snowboards, camping equipment camping, and other equipment.

But you have to call or e-mail us before [October 1] to get our amazing introductory [40%] discount. Again, the normal retail price for the [Rugged Adventurer Multi-Sport Pack] is[$199.95], but it's only [$119.95 IF you order by October 1].

Call our toll-free number, [800-555-5555], or order online at [www.ruggedadv.com] and refer to promotion code [#AX55], and we'll rush your [rack] to you within 24 hours.

[Ski season's just around the corner. Don't go into it without a Rugged Adventurer.]

Sincerely,

[Name]
[Title]

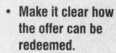

- **Make it clear how the offer can be redeemed.**

- **Reiterate prices and/or discount amounts.**

Path on CD-ROM: General Promotion→ Mass Marketing→ Reminder of end of sale or promotion→ Retailer-1

Reminder of end of promotion/sale

[Name]
[Company]
[Address]
[City, State ZIP]

Dear [   ]:

Don't forget—the [Four Corners Mall] celebration is going on right now!

In honor of the opening of the newest branch of [Bozeman's Fashions], the Mall is open until [10 P.M.] every night this week. We've got live entertainment, free food and drinks, and all Mall merchants are holding special sidewalk sales!

It's fun and it's free, but it's only for a few days!

On behalf of [Bozeman's] and all the [Four Corners Mall] merchants, we look forward to seeing you any night—or every night!—between now and Saturday!

Don't forget!

Sincerely,

[Name]
[Title]

- **The addition of a new store to a mall or downtown business area can generate traffic for the established businesses as well as the new one; reminding (potential) shoppers about the event is critical.**

Path on CD-ROM: General Promotion→ Mass Marketing→ Reminder of end of sale or promotion→Mall-1

Announcing a new Web site

TO: [Name@company.com]

FROM: [Name]

SUBJECT: New Time-Saving Web site

Dear [   ]:

The [your field] department at the [University of wherever], publishers of the field's most prominent journal, [*Your Field Today*], is pleased to announce a new Web site: [www.YourFieldToday.com]. This site, scheduled to launch on [date], will offer the following valuable features:

- lists of upcoming conferences and colloquia

- summaries of feature articles from the journal's vast archives

- lists of [your field] related e-mail lists and Usenet groups

- job and fellowship postings for [region and region and region]

While the site is still under construction, you may click here [LINK] for a preview. We trust you'll find [www.YourFieldToday.com] a valuable addition to your arsenal of research tools.

Sincerely,

[Name]

- **Establish your credentials.**

- **List the key features of the site.**

- **Let the reader know that site isn't yet complete but still offers value.**

Path on CD-ROM: General Promotion→ Web-Internet→Announcing new Web site→Journal-1

Announcing a new Web site

TO: [Name]

FROM: [Name]

SUBJECT: The Most Comprehensive Gaming Site of the Century

Dear [   ]:

Online gaming has just entered a new era. [www.powergaming.com] includes online versions of every game rated in the top 500 by [*Game Magazine Monthly*] and allows you to play online, 24 hours a day. We offer solo play, small-group games, and massive multiplayer versions of virtually every one of the top games of today.

Free membership is limited to the first 1,000 subscribers, so go to [www.powergaming.com] now.

We look forward to having you as a member of the [PowerGaming] community.

Sincerely,

[Name]
[Title]

- **Quickly and dispassionately deliver the vital facts.**

- **Provide incentive for reader to take immediate action.**

Path on CD-ROM: General Promotion→ Web-Internet→Announcing new Web site→Gaming-1

Announcing a new Web site

TO: [Name@company.com]

FROM: [Name]

SUBJECT: Check out [high-ticket items] online!

Dear [   ]:

Last time you visited [our retail store/dealership], you gave us your name and e-mail address, so we hope you won't mind our contacting you now.

We just wanted to let you know that [our company] now has a Web site. You can check out our full line of model-year 2001 [products] without even leaving your home.

Just go to [www.ourcompany.com] and you'll be able to

- see full-color photographs—interior and exterior—of every [item] we have in stock

- arrange for a [demonstration or tryout] of any [item] you choose

- get the latest news on [product-users'] clubs, destinations, and [item] accessories.

Hope to see you soon at [www.oursite.com]!

Sincerely,

[Name]

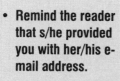

- **Remind the reader that s/he provided you with her/his e-mail address.**

- **Describe features of the site.**

Path on CD-ROM: General Promotion→ Web-Internet→Announcing new Web site→High ticket-1

Announcing a new Web site

TO: [Name@company.com]

FROM: [Name]

SUBJECT: You Can [Help Solve X Problem] NOW!

Dear [   ]:

As a regular contributor to [charity X], you understand how vitally important it is that [suffering victims of cause Y] be given at least a [solution]. And we know you'll be pleased to learn that [our cause] has a new and even more efficient way of reaching its contributors and helping those [victims] who need [X's] aid most desperately.

Thanks to our new Web site, [charity X] has a presence on the Internet. Our site, [www.charityX.com], will be updated daily, providing you and our other supporters with breaking news about regions of the world must urgently needing donations. The Web site will also allow our loyal supporter base to make immediate contributions via a secure credit-card ordering system.

Won't you take a moment—right now—to visit [www.charityX.com] and consider making a much needed donation to [the area/cause] of your choice? Just click on our name [link]. Thank you so much for your continuing support.

Sincerely,

[Name]

P.S. Please click on [link] now. To delay may mean to forget.

- **Establish empathy and gratefully acknowledge the importance of the reader's prior support.**

- **Clearly explain the content of the site.**

- **Encourage and remind the reader to visit the site.**

Encouraging customers to order through Web site

To: [   ]

From: [   ]

Subject: [Office supplies]

[Last month] you ordered [office supplies] from our print catalog. We are inviting you to see how easy it is to place your order online.

Visit our online catalog at [www.officecall.com] and check out our latest specials and inventories. Check the items you want and enter your customer code (printed at the bottom of this message). [You will automatically receive an additional 10% discount—even on sale-priced items].

We will deliver your items to your home or business within [5] days. Guaranteed. We will bill your account at the low, discounted rates available now.

This special offer expires [January 10]. Don't wait. Check our Web site and place your order now. [Don't forget to add your customer code for an additional 10% discount].

- **E-mail pitch highlights introductory, online discount, and ease of ordering.**

- **Last sentence is a positive statement, presuming the customer will place an order.**

Path on CD-ROM: General Promotion→ Web-Internet→Encourage customers to order over Web→Office-5

Encouraging customers to order through Web site

TO: [Name]

FROM: [Name]

SUBJECT: Who Needs Crowded CD Stores?

Dear [   ]:

You love music. And you're one of our most loyal customers, so we know you love buying CDs at [Palace Music]. But even we have to admit that shopping in our University District store can be a hassle—either you're too busy studying to get to the store before closing time, or when you do have some down time, our prices and selection are so great that the shop's mobbed with all the other students from the U.

So let us make a suggestion—stop shopping at [Palace Music].

We don't want you to stop being a customer. We just want to tell you something you might not know. You can order any CD in [Palace's] inventory online. Same prices, same selection, no hassle. You can use your Student Discount Card online, just like in our store. Best of all, you can even listen to any CD you're considering buying—online—just like in our store.

[www.palace.com] uses the same technology as all your other favorite online stores, so you already know how easy the experience will be. Just click here [link] and start shopping.

Sincerely,

[Name]
[Title]

- **Lay out the obstacles that the reader currently encounters with your traditional business.**

- **Describe the features and benefits of the online alternative.**

- **Relate your (new) site to other similar sites that the reader is presumably already comfortable with.**

Announcing changes in Web site

TO: [Name@company.org]

FROM: [NAME]

SUBJECT: [Company Name] Site: Better Than Ever!

Because you regularly call on [Company] and/or use our Web site to provide you with [service], we know you'll appreciate the changes we've just made to our site.

The [Company] site, [www.company.com], now lists [service] workers by [region], [cost], [other categorization], and [another categorization]. What's more, because you're a frequent customer, you can establish a [Company] account with us: All you do is type in your account number, and the site automatically provides you with a list of available [service] that fit your industry and [other categorization] profile! Best of all, billing is also done right through the Web site.

Take a look at the new and improved [LINK: www.company.com] right now, and bookmark it for easy access next time you need [service].

- **The reader of this letter already is familiar with your site (the "old" version) so he/she should be happy to learn about any improvements you've made; this doesn't have to be a hard sell.**

- **List changes you've made that make the site easier or better for the reader, not just for your self-image.**

- **Provide a link.**

Path on CD-ROM: General Promotion→ Web-Internet→Changes in Web site→Generic-1

Announcing changes in Web site

TO: [Personnel Managers and Small-Business Owners]

FROM: [NAME]

SUBJECT: [Temps-R-Us] Site: Better Than Ever!

Because you regularly call on [Temps-R-Us] and/or use our Web site to provide you with temporary office help, we know you'll appreciate the changes we've just made to our site.

The [Temps-R-Us] site, [www.tempsrus.com], now lists available office temp workers by city and state, industry, occupation, and price range! What's more, because you're a frequent customer, you can establish a [Temps-R-Us] account with us: All you do is type in your account number, and the site automatically provides you with a list of available temps that fit your industry and occupation profile! Best of all, billing is also done right through the Web site.

Take a look at the new and improved [www.tempsrus.com] right now, and bookmark it for easy access next time you need a temp.

- **The reader of this letter already is familiar with your site (the "old" version) so he/she should be happy to learn about any improvements you've made; this doesn't have to be a hard sell.**

- **List changes you've made that make the site easier or better for the reader, not just for your self-image.**

- **Provide a link.**

Path on CD-ROM: General Promotion→ Web-Internet→Changes in Web site→Personnel-1

Announcing changes in Web site

TO: [Name@company.com]

FROM: [Name]

SUBJECT: It's Easier to Help Than Ever Before!

Dear [   ]:

We'd like to thank you for all the support you've given to [charity] over the years. As someone who has himself [experienced X or been close to victims of X], you can truly appreciate the value of our work.

That's why you'll be pleased to know that we've made significant improvements to our Web site, [www.OurCause.com]. Now you can read about the latest [category] advances made and [solutions] available, and with our updated "How You Can Help" section you can make contributions directly, right on the site itself.

Won't you take a moment to visit the new [www.OurCause.com] and consider helping us with a donation in whatever amount you can afford? Just click here, on our name: [www.company.com].

On behalf of millions of [problem] victims and survivors everywhere, thank you.

Sincerely,
[Name]

- **Acknowledge the reader's prior contributions and her personal association with the cause.**

- **Explain why the site revisions benefit the reader.**

- **Politely suggest further support and thank the reader.**

Path on CD-ROM: General Promotion→ Web-Internet→Changes in Web site→Nonprofit-1

Announcing changes in Web site

TO: [Name]

FROM: [Name]

SUBJECT: A Great New Site to Check Out

Dear [   ]:

You love hanging out online and checking out new Web sites. So here's one you've got to see:

The new and improved [www.oldfamiliarsite.com].

OK, so it's not exactly an ALL-new site. But the improvements we've made and features we've added sure make it feel brand new:

- news
- interviews with top [people in the field]
- downloadable [product] demos
- even a chat room, so you can meet fellow [oldfamiliar] fans

We don't want to give too much away—we know you'll want to go to the site and experience it for yourself. You've probably got it bookmarked already, but just in case, simply click here and have fun!

[link to site]

Sincerely,

[Name]

- **Remind the reader of his favorite site's key benefits.**

- **Quickly enumerate some new features but also tease the reader.**

- **Don't give away all the news; tease the reader into going to the site (and provide a link) to get the rest of the site experience.**

Path on CD-ROM: General Promotion→ Web-Internet→Changes in Web site→Portal-1

Announcing changes in Web site

TO: [Name]

FROM: [Name]

SUBJECT: News You'll Be Thrilled to Use

Dear [   ]:

You recognize the power of the Internet as an information source, whether for business or personal use. So you'll be thrilled to know that [U.S. Demographic Information Online] is even more valuable to you than ever before.

You'll want to check out the newly revised [www.usdemoinfo.com] right away. When you do, you'll find an expanded list of demographic databases that will let you make whatever projects you're working on that much more accurate, thorough, and up-to-the-minute.

We've expanded [www.usdemoinfo.com] to now include:

- the latest U.S. Census data, broken out by region, metropolitan area, ethnic background, and income profile
- magazine and newspaper readership data for every major American publication
- ZIP codes and area codes for the U.S. and Canada

I know you'll want to dig into this wealth of information right away, so just click here [link] and start putting our expanded power to work for you now!

Sincerely,

[Name]

- **Acknowledge the reader's appreciation of the Internet's value as a multipurpose information source.**

- **Explain the improvements made to the site.**

- **Invite the reader to an immediate visit and provide a link for easy action.**

Path on CD-ROM: General Promotion→ Web-Internet→Changes in Web site→Research-3

Asking Web customers to revisit

TO: [Name]

FROM: [Name]

SUBJECT: New Titles at e-BOOKS !

Dear [   ]:

Check it out!

We've added TONS of great titles since the last time you were here!

Here are just a few of the latest offerings in the categories you told us interest you. There's some GREAT reading here. I know you'll find something you like.

[TRAVEL ESSAYS] [Title] by [Author].
Just click HERE [link] to go right to [a description of book's content..].

[BIOGRAPHY] [Title] by [Author].
Click HERE [link] for [a description of book's content..].

[ROMANCE] [Title] by [Author].
Click HERE for [a description of book's content..].

And don't forget about the amazing e-BOOKS No-Risk Reads Policy! As always, you can read excerpts and reviews of the books you're interested in before you buy. So there's NO risk!

To get to our home page and read about all our other fantastic NEW titles, just click HERE [link]!

Sincerely,

[Name]

- **Open with a quick news flash.**

- **Acknowledge the reader's own (previously expressed) interests and provide a customized e-mail leading with those. You might also want to throw in one or two (but no more) additional categories as a way of getting the customer to broaden his commitment to your product offerings.**

- **Provide separate links to each category/product.**

- **Remind the reader of a key customer service policy or other benefit of your site/company.**

Path on CD-ROM: General Promotion→ Web-Internet→Ask Web customer to revisit→Bookstore-1

Information about your Web site

Dear Valued Customer:

With the proliferation of e-commerce, consumers like you are naturally concerned about how your information is used by companies like ours. We value our customers' privacy and make the following pledge to you:

1. All information you enter at this site will be treated with the strictest confidence.

2. We will continue to use the latest encryption technology to ensure that your financial information, address information, etc. is totally secure. Click here for details about the systems we use. If anyone does gain access to your information through this Web site, [company] will reimburse all charges made to your account and pay you [$500] for the inconvenience.

3. We will track your personal information for internal purposes only. That is, we will not share ANY information about you or your purchases with any other company without your prior permission.

[Company] is committed to providing you with safe, secure ordering through our Web site. We want you to want to do business with us, so please let us know of any questions or concerns. Just click here to send us e-mail, or call [800-555-5555].

Sincerely,

[Name]
[Title]

Path on CD-ROM: General Promotion→ Web-Internet→Web letters about Web site→Privacy-1

Information about your Web site

Like Our Makeover?

We thought it was time our Web site was a better reflection of our personality—dynamic and fun—so we asked our Webmaster for a complete makeover! We couldn't be happier with the results…and hope you agree! (If not, please let us know!)

You'll still find everything is where you left it, just check out the menu to the [left] to quickly access each of our main screens. But you'll find [a much cleaner look and simpler graphics that make each screen load more quickly].

We're committed to creating the most attractive, easiest-to-use Web site you'll ever visit. So if there's anything you don't like, send us a note or call [800-555-5555].

- On the one hand, customers don't really care about why you've changed the Web site design as long as they find it easier to use. However, there will be some customers who will be confused by the different appearance, so you need to tell them whether it's just a makeover or if more substantial changes were made (as in other examples in this category).

- Even if the changes were just cosmetic, use the opportunity to reinforce your commitment to providing high quality services/ products.

ANNOUNCEMENTS

Announcing a sale or promotion

TO: [Name@company.com]

FROM: [Name]

SUBJECT: [vehicle company's] [year] Lineup

Model-year [year] vehicles are at [our name] dealers now, and since you previously requested information about our vehicles, we hope you don't mind getting this message. We've got dealerships in every state of the country, sales are up, prices are great, and there are amazing deals waiting for you!

Don't miss out on unbelievable CASH REBATES available until [date] during our [year] [name of incentive program] Program.

To learn more, visit [www.ourwebsite.com/cash.htm].

You'll see [$ amount] cash back on all [year/vehicle category], and the savings don't stop there. [Our company] is offering up to [higher $ amount] back on [other vehicle categories X and Y]. That's some cool pocket money!

You can even schedule a test drive at our site—just visit [www.ourwebsite.com/dealer.html] today!

Sincerely,
[Name]

- **Open with a news flash.**

- **Remind the reader that he/she PROVIDED you with his/her e-mail address, thereby legitimizing this communication.**

- **Provide separate links to each of your key site pages/features and encourage a specific direct action.**

Path on CD-ROM: General Promotion→Announcements→Sale or promotion→Car sale-1

Announcing a sale or promotion

[Name]
[Company]
[Address]
[City, State ZIP]

Dear [   ]:

As principals of a startup company, you and your partners have enough on your mind without having to worry about things like benefits, payroll processing, compensation plans, and recruitment. Yes, these elements are crucial to any business, but you need to focus your attention on core functions like developing your company's vision and executing business plans.

That's where we come in. We're [company name]. We provide outsourcing support for everything from benefits packages to policy writing. It's not a waste of our time—it's what we DO. And since we're trying to build our client base, we're doing it for less—for a limited time.

Take a look at the [enclosed/attached] brochure explaining what we do and how we can do it for your company. Then call [name] at [number] and ask [him/her] to tell you about our special pricing for new clients. Then get back to focusing on what you do best— and let us do what we do best.

Sincerely,

[Name]
[Title]

- **You may need to educate your reader on the range of services your company supplies and why the reader should even consider using a company such as yours in the first place.**

- **Provide the name and number of an individual who handles the reader's business.**

Path on CD-ROM: General Promotion→Announcements→Sale or promotion→Outsourcing-1

ANNOUNCEMENTS

Announcing a sale or promotion

Dear Skier:

The snow's melted and the flowers are blooming—what better time to buy skis!

That's right—it's [SuperSlalom's] annual postseason ski sale! Prices on every item in every [SuperSlalom] store have been drastically reduced to make room for next season's lines.

Every pair of this model year's skis, both downhill and cross-country. Every pair of boots. Every set of poles. Every helmet, parka, ski rack, pair of goggles, ski jacket, hat, pair of gloves—you get the idea. Everything's on sale until everything's gone! It's that simple.

Come in to your nearest [SuperSlalom] store now for the greatest selection. We look forward to seeing you soon.

Sincerely,

[Name]
[Title]

- **Postseason sales offer a great opportunity to move merchandise at terrific prices. But since most of your customers will no longer be thinking about your product once the season is over, you must make the sale attractive enough to bring them into the store. Be bold.**

Path on CD-ROM: General Promotion→Announcements→Sale or promotion→Ski shop-1

Announcing a sale or promotion

TO: [Name@company.com]

FROM: [Name]

SUBJECT: SALE at [INSTOFILM]!

Dear [   ]:

Now sharing your favorite photos with family and friends is easier—and cheaper—than ever when you send your film to [InstoFilm] for developing.

Here's how it works: Simply print this e-mail and enclose the coupon below with your next roll of film. Check the box on your mailer to order Internet notification. As soon as your photos are developed, we'll send you an e-mail telling you that your photos are ready to view online. From there it's easy to e-mail friends and family your latest shots.

Best of all, through [date], we'll take [%] off our already low film development costs— and we'll post your photos on our Web site at no charge! For more information about this special offer and all the other great [InstoFilm] products and services, go to [www.instofilm.com] or call our toll-free customer service number, [number].

We look forward to developing your photos and helping you share them with your family and friends—just don't forget to get your film to us no later than [February 1]!

Sincerely,

[Name]

- **Open with an appeal to sharing with friends and family.**

- **Clarify which service is discounted and which (other) service is free.**

- **Provide a link and a customer service phone number.**

Path on CD-ROM: General Promotion→Announcements→Sale or promotion→Film-1

Letters to increase traffic

[Name]
[Company]
[Address]
[City, State ZIP]

Dear [   ]:

[Four Corners Mall] is pleased to announce the opening of our newest store: [Bozeman's Fashions]!

Yes, this well-known purveyor of high-end designer fashions is opening a branch in the [Four Corners Mall] [next Wednesday]. To celebrate this prestigious addition to the Mall, and welcome the newest member of the [Four Corners] retail community, the Mall will be open [until 10 P.M. on Wednesday, Thursday, and Friday nights]. We'll have live entertainment, free food and drinks, and all Mall merchants will be offering special sidewalk sale merchandise!

On behalf of [Bozeman's] and all the [Four Corners Mall] merchants, we look forward to seeing you next week!

Sincerely,

[Name]
[Title]

- **The addition of a new store to a mall or downtown business area can generate traffic for the established businesses as well as the new one.**

- **Create an event around the new store's opening and invite customers.**

Path on CD-ROM: General Promotion→Announcements→Letters to increase traffic→Mall-1

Letters to increase traffic

[Name]
[Company]
[Address]
[City, State ZIP]

Dear [   ]:

It's really true when we say it's the best sale of the year. So don't miss [Summer Free Days], when you'll be able to buy one of many items and get another one of the same item absolutely free!

We really appreciate your business, and that's why we're offering this great sale opportunity from [3 P.M. to 5 P.M. every Tuesday in May]. In addition to the free items, you'll also [be able to take in a fashion show, meet the author of *Home for the Summer*, and enjoy many pleasant surprises].

Mark your calendar now for these great events. You'll be glad you did.

Sincerely,

[Name]
[Title]

- **Make the promotion extend over several weeks to try to bring people in several times.**

- **Mention the fun and the savings planned for the event.**

Announcing a contest

[Date]
[Name]
[Address]
[City, State ZIP]

Dear [   ]:

To say thank you for your continued support of [A-1 Photo's] custom services, we want to make you feel like you are truly [one in a million]. We would like to invite you to visit our store to enter our [One in a Million] contest.

To enter, just purchase any one of our custom services between now and [December 31]. We'll do the rest. We'll enter your name in our drawing for one of dozens of prizes, including [100 free color reprints, 5 antique photo touch-ups, and our grand prize of free custom services for a year!]

Join us at our [One in a Million Celebration] on [January 22 at 1:00 P.M.]. where the winners will be drawn from eligible entries. You don't have to be present to win, but we'd love to see you there!

Sincerely,

[Name]
[Title]

- **Get potential clients into your place of business by announcing a drawing.**

- **Give highlights of prizes to encourage entries.**

Path on CD-ROM: General Promotion→Announcements→Sale promotion→Photography-1

Announcing a new or expanded catalog

[Date]
[Name]
[Company]
[Address]
[City, State ZIP]

Dear [   ]:

[Art Experts] has been shaping and promoting [affordable original art] since [1988]. Our commitment to unique [designs and original artwork] is constantly renewed through additions to our collection, brought to you exclusively through our catalog.

This particular catalog features a selection of products that [spans the century, from the roaring twenties through the technologically savvy nineties]. We're sure you'll find just the [original art piece] you've been searching for.

Remember, if you join the [Art Guild] now, you'll receive [10% off] of every purchase in our catalog. Call us any time. Our trained experts are on call [24 hours a day] to help you.

Sincerely,

[Name]
[Title]

- **Presents the unique features of the catalog and provides insight into how the catalog is organized.**

- **Offers an additional discount program.**

Path on CD-ROM: General Promotion→Announcements→New or expanded catalog→Fine art-1

ANNOUNCEMENTS

Announcing a new or expanded catalog

[Date]
[Name]
[Company]
[Address]
[City, State ZIP]

Dear [   ]:

It's the holiday season. Time to deck the halls, trim the tree, light the candles, and wrap the gifts. Make merry! Celebrate! And there's no better way to launch the festivities than with a trip to the [Glad Tidings holiday] catalog.

We've crisscrossed continents, sought out the finest materials, and worked with master crafters to make sure your season sparkles. Quality tops our list in everything we bring you, from [hand-painted ornaments on page 12] to the [sparkling champagne flutes on page 22].

And this [new holiday] catalog also marks a renewed commitment to [more detailed product descriptions and more accurately portrayed colors]. And, as always, we know you'll find our service to be excellent.

Sincerely,

[Name]
[Title]

- **Announces improvements made to the catalog.**

- **Pulls out key products to get customers into the catalog.**

Path on CD-ROM: General Promotion→Announcements→New or expanded catalog→Generic-2

Announcing a new or expanded catalog

[Date]
[Name]
[Company]
[Address]
[City, State ZIP]

Dear [   ]:

Welcome to the [20th] edition of our [Spring] catalog! Over the years we have grown from a [small company in the owner's garage] to a [rather large company housed in two buildings]. Our growth has forced some changes for us, including [more conventional means of production].

But never fear! The folks here at [Avid Sportswear] are still committed to bringing you the best in the business. We are proud to announce the addition of [The Stitchery] as one of our suppliers. They share our vision of [sustainability and fair pay for workers].

You can continue to count on [Avid Sportswear's] commitment to [comfort, community, and service]. Look inside for [dozens of] new products. You know your satisfaction is 100% guaranteed with [Avid]. Thanks for shopping with us!

Sincerely,

[Name]
[Title]

- **Announces changes at the company but lists benefits of those changes.**

- **Stresses the company's philosophy.**

Path on CD-ROM: General Promotion→Announcements→New or expanded catalog→Sportswear-1

ANNOUNCEMENTS

Announcing a new or expanded catalog

[Date]
[Name]
[Address]
[City, State ZIP]

Dear [   ]:

Here is the latest edition of our chef's catalog, especially designed for restaurants, hotels, catering services, and other food service businesses. As you know, [company] has provided the best in cookware, utensils, cutlery, and kitchen equipment for many years.

We hope you will be pleased with our newest selections and choose several additions to your well-stocked kitchen. [To show our appreciation to our most loyal customers, we have enclosed a 10 percent discount certificate to use with your next order].

Take a moment now to look through the current issue of our catalog. Share it with your top staff. Then pick out the items that will most enhance your kitchen operation. Take advantage of this opportunity to get some great gadgets and equipment at an excellent price.

Thank you for your business.

Sincerely,

[Name]
[Title]

- **Endeavor to make the repeat customer feel like he belongs to the inner circle in your industry.**

- **Express appreciation for the reader's patronage.**

Path on CD-ROM: General Promotion→Announcements→New or expanded catalog→Cookware-2

Corrections

[Date]
[Name]
[Company]
[Address]
[City, State ZIP]

Dear [   ]:

[Art Experts] has been shaping and promoting [affordable original art] since [1988]. Our commitment to unique [designs and original artwork] is constantly renewed through additions to our collection, brought to you exclusively through our catalog.

Because [Art Experts] offers many [original pieces], it is common for us to sell out of items listed in the catalog. This is the case with the [hand-blown vase] on page [16]. The [artist] will not be making any more of these pieces.

If you have your eye on a particular [art piece], do not hesitate to order! We have a limited quantity of all of our pieces! Our trained experts are on call [24 hours a day] to help you.

Sincerely,

[Name]
[Title]

- **Presents the unique features of the catalog as a benefit.**

- **Creates a sense of urgency for their products.**

Path on CD-ROM: General Promotion→Announcements→Corrections→Artwork-1

Corrections

[Date]
[Name]
[Company]
[Address]
[City, State ZIP]

Dear [   ]:

Here at [Golden Deer], we're here to make your holiday shopping easier, quicker, and much less stressful. We have something for everyone on your list, including many items you won't find at the mall.

One quick note from our latest catalog. You'll notice that the [2] items pictured on page [34] have erratic descriptions. It seems in our final layout the identification letters for these items were switched. Just read the opposite description for each item and all will be well! And we're sorry for any confusion this may have caused.

As always, a substantial portion of our profits supports the [Community Foundation to benefit children in the community]. Thank you for shopping with us—and happy holidays!

Sincerely,

[Name]
[Title]

- **The correction keeps the same upbeat attitude that the letter and catalog have.**

- **Describes other benefits of ordering, like offering a reason to buy rather than just for the profit of the company.**

Path on CD-ROM: General Promotion→Announcements→Corrections→Generic-5

First pre-event mailing from event organizer

[Date]
[Name]
[Title]
[Company]
[Address]
[City, State ZIP]

Dear [   ]:

A new coalition of [textile industry leaders] is forming. [Silk Threads, Perfect Plaids, and Welcome Woolens] have already signed on as members of the group, which hopes to form partnerships and efficiencies of scale.

Representatives from these [three] groups and others will be on hand the [weekend of June 22 in Washington, D.C]. The goal of the meeting will be to set a vision for the group. In a few days you will receive more details of the gathering from [John Koehn]. In the meantime, if you would like more information, please don't hesitate to call me.

Sincerely,

[Name]
[Title]

- **Use a two-step approach to overcome objections or to explain a complicated product.**

- **In the first letter, explain the big picture.**

Path on CD-ROM: General Promotion→Event-Related Campaigns→1st Preshow from organizer→Trade group-1

Second pre-event mailing from organizer

[Date]
[Name]
[Title]
[Company]
[Address]
[City, State ZIP]

Dear [   ]:

Several days ago you received a preliminary letter regarding the upcoming [textile industry group] meeting in [June]. Enclosed you will find a brochure with the details of the goals and sessions of the gathering, which will be held at the [Hotel Mont Marc].

We hope that you will be able to send a representative from your company to the event. Please feel free to call me if you have any questions.

Thanks for considering supporting your peers in the [textile] industry.

Sincerely,

[Name]
[Title]

- In the second letter, provide details, perhaps in an accompanying brochure.

- Ask for a commitment.

Path on CD-ROM: General Promotion→Event-Related Campaigns→2ndpreshow from organizer→Trade group-1

Event follow-up by event organizer

[Date]
[Name]
[Title]
[Company]
[Address]
[City, State ZIP]

Dear [   ]:

Thanks for joining us in [D.C]. for the [textile industry leaders] group! It was a terrific meeting, with lots of great ideas about how to [strengthen our whole industry] and [secure jobs for American workers]!

[Serita Juarez] has volunteered to coordinate the working groups that we discussed at the meeting, and she'll be contacting everyone within the next month. We hope you'll sign up to help out.

We're also working on establishing a Web site where we can share ideas and promote our industry to the world!

Thanks again for coming. If you have any questions, don't hesitate to give me a call!

Sincerely,

[Name]
[Title]

- In the third letter, recap highlights of the meeting and any developments since the meeting.

- Describe how the person can continue to be involved.

Path on CD-ROM: General Promotion→Event-Related Campaigns→Follow-up from organizer→Trade group-1

EVENT CAMPAIGNS

First pre-event mailing from a vendor

[Date]
[Name]
[Company]
[Address]
[City, State ZIP]

Dear [   ]:

I hope you've got the dates for the [Northeast Business Publishers Convention] on your calendar! It's going to be on [date] at [city/hotel].

You won't want to miss this convention. [Allison Printing and Bindery] plans to have our biggest booth ever showing the latest in printing technology. We'll be demonstrating our [direct-to-press technology, the latest ink formulations for brilliant full-color jobs, and our image management database].

[Allison Printing and Bindery] is one the oldest printing companies in the business. We've been around for decades because we're dedicated to staying out in front! Our staff is continually being trained in the latest technology, and are known for their outstanding prepress support.

And you can meet them at the [Northeast Business Publishers Convention]. We'll have our top reps on hand to discuss your printing needs!

So let's make a date to meet in [city] on [date]!

Sincerely,

[Name]
[Title]

- **Compare this letter from a printer with the one from a book publisher, both related to the same conference. This letter emphasizes the company's credentials.**

Path on CD-ROM: General Promotion→Event-Related Campaigns→1st Preshow from vendor→Printer-1

First pre-event mailing from a vendor

[Name]
[Address]
[City, State ZIP]

Dear [   ]:

The weather outside may be frightful, but there is nothing more delightful than visiting [The Golf Shanty] at the [Winter Sports and Fitness Show]. Come and see us in booth [#148] at the biggest show of the year!

With more than [250] booths, how do you decide where to spend your time? We'll make it easy for you by inviting you into our space. We will have demonstrations of [new clubs, high-loft balls, and several tools to help you improve your swing]. With so many great products to try for yourself, why spend your time anywhere else?

Mark your calendar now for [January 30-31] and think about how great it will be to enjoy [your favorite summer sports in the middle of winter]!

Sincerely,

[Name]
[Title]

- **Provides an incentive to visit the booth by having a chance to try before you buy.**

- **Takes the customer out of the current situation to a better sounding place and time.**

Path on CD-ROM: General Promotion→Event-Related Campaigns→1st Preshow from vendor→Golf retailer-1

First pre-event mailing from a vendor

[Date]
[Name]
[Company]
[Address]
[City, State ZIP]

Dear [   ]:

Every business executive is feeling the pinch these days. But the pressures to increase effectiveness, reduce overhead, and improve customer satisfaction is nowhere greater than for financial executives!

That's why you should stop by the [Casey Leadership, Inc.] booth at the upcoming [Financial Executives Meeting] scheduled for [dates] in [location].

[Casey Leadership, Inc.] has been helping executives gain both the business and personal skills they need to stay on top of their jobs. Come to our booth and we'll prove it!

- You can watch videos from prior training sessions.

- Hear testimonials from prior [Casey] banking, insurance, and other financial executives to hear how they've used what they learned.

- Speak with our trainers and executive coaches. We think they know what they're talking about since all have prior managerial experience, but you can come by and judge for yourself!

If you want to stay on top of the game, come see us at the [Financial Executives Meeting] in [location]! You'll find us at booth [372].

See you there!

Sincerely,

[Name]
[Title]

- **This opening is the same as the one used in the "organizer" version of this letter because the need is similar (trying to provide incentive for the reader to attend the show).**

- **Explain what the person can get by coming to a show that they can't get in other ways (e.g., by going to your Web site).**

Path on CD-ROM: General Promotion→Event-Related Campaigns→1st Preshow from vendor→Training-1

First pre-event mailing from a vendor

Meet the authors!!!

[Date]
[Name]
[Company]
[Address]
[City, State ZIP]

Dear [   ]:

I hope you've got the dates for the [Northeast Business Publishers Convention] on your calendar! It's going to be on [date] at [city/hotel].

You won't want to miss this conference. [BookPub, Inc.] plans to bring [10] of our most popular authors to the show. PLUS, we've invited representatives from the companies who purchase the most business books to be on hand.

That means you'll get to meet both the people who make the books possible AND those who purchase them! What better way to build your own distribution capability than by knowing your suppliers and customers better!

Look for [BookPub, Inc.] at the [Northeast Business Publishers Convention] on [date] at [location]. We'll be looking for you!

Sincerely,

[Name]
[Title]

- Give the who, what, where right away.

- Provide strong incentives to come to the show AND to visit your booth.

Path on CD-ROM: General Promotion→Event-Related Campaigns→1st Preshow from vendor→Publisher-1

Second pre-event mailing from a vendor

**Tour the [Allison Printing & Bindery] plant
at the [Northeast Book Publishers Convention]!**

[Date]
[Name]
[Company]
[Address]
[City, State ZIP]

Dear [   ]:

Wondering what to do at the [Northeast Book Publishers Convention] for extra fun? Sign up for a tour of the [Allison Printing & Bindery] plant. You'll see where it all happens, from high-resolution scanning to prepress layout to plate production and printing. Our facilities are state-of-the-art, and we have some of the most innovative production control processes in the business. You can also view our new [docu-text] printers for small printing runs!

Tours will take place from [1 P.M. to 5 p.m]. on Saturday. No preregistration is required, just come to our booth [#123] and we'll put you on a shuttle. The entire tour should last a little over an hour, including traveling time to and from our facility.

This offer is only available to attendees of the [Northeast Book Publishers Convention].

If you have any questions about the tour, call [800-555-5555] or go to our Web site at [www.allisonprinting.com]. See the future of printing, traditional and electronic, at [Allison Printing & Bindery].

Sincerely,

[Name]
[Title]

- **Here the incentive to come to the show is a chance to tour the facility (something few people would do in the normal course of their jobs but which they might be curious about).**

- **Be clear about how people can sign up for the course.**

Path on CD-ROM: General Promotion→Event-Related Campaigns→2nd Preshow from vendor→Printer-1

Second pre-event mailing from a vendor

**Reserved your tee time yet at the [Winter Sports and Fitness Show]?
[January 30–31] at [location]**

Dear [   ]:

The [Winter Sports and Fitness Show] is just around the corner! And we here at [The Golf Shanty] are teeing up for a great show! We hope you're planning to come by booth [#148]. As promised, we'll have all the latest golf clubs, high-loft balls, and lots of other equipment you can try out for yourself.

JUST ANNOUNCED! We've arranged to have our VirtualGolf Indoor Driving Range set up! Come experience the latest in high-tech ways to measure and improve your game!

Mark your calendar now for [January 30-31]!

Sincerely,

The Golf Pros at Golf Shanty

- **Headline should give the show dates and location for ease of reference; other important messages can be highlighted through other text effects.**

- **Reiterates the initial incentive and describes an additional incentive for coming to the booth.**

- **Clearly displays the name, date, and location of the show and of the vendor's booth.**

Path on CD-ROM: General Promotion→Event-Related Campaigns→2nd Preshow from vendor→Golf retailer-1

Second pre-event mailing from a vendor

[Date]

Dear Financial Executive:

JUST ANNOUNCED! [Casey Leadership, Inc.] has arranged to have [famous business executive] appear at the [Financial Executives Meeting] on [dates] in [location].

You can meet [him/her] at a special reception scheduled for [Tuesday evening] in the [Grand Suite] of the [Hyatt Hotel] or at our booth (#[372]) from [10 A.M. to 11:30 A.M.] on [Wednesday].

We expect a big turnout, so please call [800-555-5555] to register for the reception (it's free!), or stop by our booth early on [Tuesday] to see if space is still available.

See you in [location] on [dates]!

Sincerely,

[Casey Leadership, Inc.]

- Use the follow-up postcard to provide extra incentive for people to come to the booth.

- Reinforce dates and locations.

Path on CD-ROM: General Promotion→Event-Related Campaigns→2nd Preshow from vendor→Training-1

Second pre-event mailing from a vendor

Come to the [BookPub, Inc.] Hospitality Suite at the [Northeast Book Publishers Convention]

[Date]
[Name]
[Company]
[Address]
[City, State ZIP]

Dear [   ]:

Have you signed up for the [Northeast Book Publishers Convention] yet? If not, here's what you'll miss out on at the [BookPub, Inc.] hospitality suite to be held on [date] from [4 P.M. to 7 P.M.].

As we promised in a previous letter, the authors of our most popular titles will be on hand, PLUS at least [50] representatives of companies who purchase business books in volume!

FLASH! More authors added!

We now have arrangements with authors of 16 of our most popular titles to be on hand for the hospitality suite.

Send your registration in soon so you won't miss out on this exciting event.

Be sure to drop by booth [#123] to see the full [BookPub, Inc.] catalog, and stop by our hospitality suite for free drinks and refreshments on the afternoon of [date].

See you in [city]!

Sincerely,

[Name]
[Title]

- **A special invitation provides a strong reason for doing a second mailing.**

- **Build up the event to entice the reader.**

Path on CD-ROM: General Promotion→Event-Related Campaigns→2nd Preshow from vendor→Publisher-1

EVENT-RELATED CAMPAIGNS

Follow up by vendor

Don't worry...you didn't miss out!

Dear [   ]:

If you missed getting your SIGNED copy of [*Coaching to Win*] at the recent [Sports Expo]—don't worry! We've still got a LIMITED supply of auto-graphed copies left!

Act now and you can get one of these unique gifts by calling [800-555-5555]. Or log on to [www.coachingcenter.org].

Here's what some readers of [Coaching to Win] have to say:

- [I've been coaching for 15 years, but this book taught me a lot about how to work better with my kids.—[Name], [Coaching position]]

- [I'm in my first year of coaching [sport], and this book gave me the confidence I need to be more effective—[Name 2], [Coaching position 2]]

- [We coaches are so busy that we rarely have time to sit down and share experiences. When reading this book, I felt I was talking with [famous coach] face to face. It's terrific!—[Name 3], [Coaching position 3]]

If you want to become a better coach, you owe it to yourself to purchase [*Coaching to Win*]! And if you order today, you can get an autographed copy for no extra cost!

To order, call [800-555-5555] or go to [www.coachingcenter.org].

Sincerely,

[Name]
[Title]

- **Opening sets up presumption that the reader would have gotten a copy of the book at the show if they could have.**

- **Include quotes to build credibility.**

- **A call to action is included both at the beginning and end of the letter.**

Path on CD-ROM: General Promotion→Event-Related Campaigns→Follow-up from vendor→Coaching-1

Follow up by vendor

[Name]
[Company]
[Address]
[City, State ZIP]

Dear [   ]:

I was sorry that we didn't get a chance to meet at the recent [American Printer's Convention]. I was looking forward to finding out more about your [convention and digital printing needs] in the year to come.

If you're considering any major printing jobs, I invite you to log on to [www.printingcompany.com] to check out our latest capabilities. You'll be amazed at how easily we can achieve eye-popping effects—at a very affordable cost!

Hope to see you at next year's convention!

Sincerely,

[Name]
[Title]

- **Express regret for not catching up with the person at the event.**

- **Briefly describe an attractive capability.**

- **Tell the person how they can get more information (either include a brochure or, as done here, provide your Web site address).**

Path on CD-ROM: General Promotion→Event-Related Campaigns→Follow-up from vendor→Printer-2

Follow up by vendor

[Name]
[Company]
[Address]
[City, State ZIP]

Dear [   ]:

On behalf of the other conference organizers, [Amazing Booksellers] would like to thank you for attending the [25th Annual Book Expo and Publisher's Conference]. We had a fabulous time and hope you did, too.

Thanks to the participation of great people like you, the conference once again proved why its one of the most prestigious [book publishing] events in the country! [Amazing Booksellers] is proud to sponsor this important conference.

We look forward to seeing you at the show! And in the meantime, please feel free to contact [Amazing Booksellers] to meet all your [publishing and distribution needs].

Sincerely,

[Name]
[Title]

- **As before, the primary goal is to build your corporate image, not sell a particular product or service.**

- **By selling the importance of the conference, you increase your own prestige as a sponsor.**

Path on CD-ROM: General Promotion→Event-Related Campaigns→Follow-up from vendor→Publisher-1

Did you get YOUR questions answered?

[Name]
[Address]
[City, State ZIP]

Dear [   ]:

What a crush at the recent [Lawn and Garden Show]! We know there were a lot of [Green Lawns] customers who didn't get a chance to talk with our owner, [George Greenthumb], to get their questions answered.

If you're one of those people, we hope you'll call us at [800-555-5555] or log on to our Web site ([www.greenlawns.com]) to get practical, simple lawn and garden-care advice. We want to make sure that you get all the answers you need! This service is offered FREE to [Green Lawns] customers.

[Green Lawns]. [Motto].

Sincerely,

[Name]
[Title]

- **Emphasizes company's dedication to meeting each customer's needs.**
- **Delivers the message that extra service is a perk of being a customer.**

Path on CD-ROM: General Promotion→Event-Related Campaigns→Follow-up from vendor→Lawn care

Current/Former Customers

If you've ever read anything about the companies who have won the Malcolm Baldrige National Quality Award, you know that they put a lot of energy into building and maintaining their customer base. They know with great specificity who their customers are and what they want…and they go to great lengths to retain every customer. Like you, they don't want to lose any customer. These companies know that paying attention to customers is critical for any business that wants to thrive.

While some companies have thousands and thousands of customers, others may have just a handful. That's why the letters in this chapter cover a broad range of customer communication, everything from wishing an individual client "Happy Birthday" to sending announcements of new products to your entire mailing list.

The goal of such letters is to make it clear that you care personally about the individual reader, about what they want from your product/service, and about what they are trying to accomplish in their workplace.

There are several ways to accomplish this goal:

1. Mention something specific about that customer: when they last purchased, what particular challenge they were facing in their job, a personal detail. Minimally you should customize each of these letters to personalize them to your customer.
2. Link the information you are conveying to the reader's individual needs. For example, if announcing a new product, describe how the product meets a specific need you know that customer has.

3. Be sure to reference any previous, relevant contact with the person. For example, if they had contacted your company about the matter before, you have to show that that contact was noted and remembered, and that you are following up. Any time a customer has to repeatedly give the same information to your company, they get the message that no one is paying attention.
4. Use a friendly, informal style. A dry, standard business style will communicate subtly that there is nothing special about the reader, that they are just a member of the pack. "Informal" in a business context doesn't mean using slang or inappropriate language, but rather trying to sound conversational.
5. Use common courtesy. For example, thank the person for contacting your company or purchasing your product/service.

Accompanying a catalog

[Name]
[Address]
[City, State ZIP]

Dear [   ]:

We haven't heard from you for a while! You used to be one of our best customers and, frankly, we miss you. We're not sure what we might have done wrong, but we'd like to make things right. Perhaps offering you a special incentive might help.

Our new catalog is enclosed. Flip through it and you'll see that we're still offering the most exciting selection of [types of clothing] available, at quite competitive prices.

Since we haven't done any business together for some time, we're going to offer you [20%] off any or all items you care to order from the new catalog. That's right—[20%] off, with no minimum order required. You can get a $300 parka for just $240. Or select an $8.00 pair of socks and it's yours for $6.40.

Just look through the catalog; jot down what you'd like to order; call, fax, or e-mail us; and we'll take [20%] off your total purchase! We hope to hear from you soon.

Sincerely,

[Name]
[Title]

P.S. You can also place orders on our Web site. Look for the "special offer" box and enter [code #12345] to get your 20% discount!

- **Open by acknowledging the customer's long absence.**
- **Maintain a friendly tone throughout.**
- **Make the special offer as clear as possible; provide examples of how the offer would work and mention every available way to order.**

Path on CD-ROM: Current and Former Customers→Lapsed or Lapsing Customers→Accompanying a catalog→Clothing-1

Accompanying a catalog

[Name]
[Company]
[Address]
[City, State ZIP]

Dear [   ]:

Our records show that it's been [over 9 months] since your last order from [Inclusive Office Supplies]. We know we offer small and medium-sized businesses the area's widest selection of office supplies, at the most competitive prices, and with the most personalized customer service—so we can only assume we've done something wrong.

We still value your business. So we decided to add value to our own offerings.

We're going to make you a special deal in the hope of winning you back. Look through our new catalog (enclosed). Place an order. Buy up to [$100] of merchandise and we'll take [10%] off our regular price. Order between [$101 and $200] worth of supplies and the discount increases to [15%]. An order between [$201 and $200] gets [20%] off. And any order [over $300] will be discounted by [25%].

We won't even require you to place your order this minute. This special will be available to you for the life of the [2001] catalog. That's right—you can take advantage of this "we want you back" deal through [the end of this year].

We hope you'll take us up on this offer.

Sincerely,

[Name]
[Title]

- If you have a working relationship with the customer, make the letter more personal.

- Convey how important the customer is to you.

- Spell out the terms of the offer, including end date.

Path on CD-ROM: Current and Former Customers→Lapsed or Lapsing Customers→Accompanying a catalog→Office-1

Renewal letters

[Date]
[Name]
[Company]
[Address]
[City, State ZIP]

Dear [   ]:

We have missed you! Your membership to our audio book club for mystery lovers ended several months ago, and we invite you to take another look at our latest tapes.

We are especially excited about the new mysteries we are offering this month, including the latest titles from [Tony Hillerman, Sue Grafton, and Dick Francis]. We did not want you to miss them, so we have enclosed our most recent catalog. We invite you to make your selections and take advantage of our special reintroductory offer.

Slip the tapes into the player in your car, your Walkman, or other player and enjoy the newest tales from the best writers in the business, just as you have done so many times before.

Welcome back.

Sincerely,

[Name]
[Title]

- **Describe what the former customer is missing.**

- **Remind the reader how much he or she enjoyed your product.**

Path on CD-ROM: Current and Former Customers→Lapsed or Lapsing Customers→Renewals→Audio club-1

Renewal telemarketing script

Hello. This is [Name] calling about your subscription to [Fundraising Alert].

Your subscription is ending soon, and we want to make sure that it has met your needs.

Has your copy of [*Fundraising Alert*] arrived promptly each month?

What kinds of [fundraising] topics are of most interest to you?

Do you plan to renew your subscription to [*Fundraising Alert*]?

A) IF THE RESPONSE IS "NO," SAY: May I ask why not?

FOLLOWED BY: Is there someone else in your organization who may better benefit from a subscription to [*Fundraising Alert*]?

CLOSE: Thank you for your time and honest comments.

B) IF THE RESPONSE IS "YES," SAY: Would you like to renew your subscription now? We can bill you at a later date and you will ensure that your subscription to [*Fundraising Alert*] will continue uninterrupted.

CLOSE: Thank you for your thoughtful comments and subscription renewal.

- **This letter ensures that the customer understands that his feedback about the product is important.**

- **Even a negative response can garner useful information for the publisher/ business owner.**

LAPSED OR LAPSING CUSTOMERS

Offer to lapsed customer

TO: [Name@company.com]

FROM: [Name]

SUBJECT: LOWER PRICES!

Our records show that you haven't purchased anything from [elexonline.com] for quite some time.

We just want to let you know that there couldn't be a better time to come back to [www.elexonline.com] for your consumer electronic needs because we've just lowered prices on major purchases throughout our online store. Just to give you a few examples: we've slashed prices on desktop computers, high-end stereo components and systems, digital cameras, big-screen TVs, telephone/answering machine systems, and even kitchen appliances!

Best of all, this isn't a sale. It's part of our new—and continuing—policy of offering top-of-the-line equipment at lower-than-normal prices because we want you back! So click here [LINK] and start shopping at [www.elexonline.com] again!

Sincerely,

[Name]
[Title]

- **With constantly falling prices in electronics categories— and new online retail competition increasing—a permanent lower-price policy may be worth considering as a way of getting former customers back into the franchise.**

- **Provide a link to encourage easy, immediate reader action.**

Path on CD-ROM: Current and Former Customers→Lapsed or Lapsing Customers→Offers to lapsed customers→Retailer-1

Offer to lapsed customer

[Name]
[Address]
[City, State ZIP]

Dear [   ]:

Our records show that it's been [number] years since you closed your [bank name] checking and savings accounts. We valued your years as a [bank name] customer, and we think we may be able to interest you in coming back. Here's why:

For starters, we've just lowered our interest rates on a wide range of loans including residential mortgages, home equity loans (second mortgages) and all-purpose debt-consolidation loans. If you're considering purchasing a new home or vacation residence, our new home loan rates might make such a decision easier than ever. And with the economy healthy and inflation under control, this may be the best time ever to get a handle on your credit cards and other bills with a debt-consolidation loan at a terrific new low rate.

We've also added a whole new selection of checking accounts with interest and high-yield CDs and other savings products.

Take a look at the enclosed brochure which describes in detail all our checking, savings and loan products, new rates, and new easy payment plans. Then, when you're ready, call any of our lending officers at [number]. They'll be happy to welcome you back and answer any questions you may have.

Sincerely,

[Name]
[Title]

- **Lower interest rates on loan products and higher rates on retail accounts can help set a financial institution apart from its competitors and possibly win back former customers.**

- **Provide just an overview of your new products/services, then direct the reader to a separate brochure and a conversation with a loan officer.**

Path on CD-ROM: Current and Former Customers→Lapsed or Lapsing Customers→Offers to lapsed customers→Bank-1

LAPSED OR LAPSING CUSTOMERS

Offer to lapsed customer

[Name]
[Address]
[City, State ZIP]

Dear [   ]:

As a former [frequent/regular] customer of [business], you probably recall our [product/service/selection/superiority], even though it's been [number of years/months] since you [shopped here/bought product/ subscribed to service].

We want to let you know that there's never been a better time to come back to [company]. That's because we've lowered our [prices/rates] on [all/selected] [products/services] in every [area/department/category] of our [store/business/Web site].

This is no mere sale—these [price/rate] reductions are just part of an ongoing [program/policy] to offer our [clients/customers] the most competitive [prices/rates] in the [category] business. [Reason] is the reason we can offer lower [prices/rates] to you.

[Come in/call/go to link] now and take advantage once again of the tremendous savings these new [rates/prices] provide. We'll be thrilled to have you back.

Sincerely,

[Name]
[Title]

- **Acknowledge that the reader is a former customer, but don't induce guilt.**

- **Tempt the reader to give you her/his business again with big news (savings, new products, etc.).**

- **Provide a number or link for easy access and immediate action.**

Path on CD-ROM: Current and Former Customers→Lapsed or Lapsing Customers→Offers to lapsed customers→Generic-1

Offer to lapsed customer

[Name]
[Company]
[Address]
[City, State ZIP]

Dear [   ]:

Our records show that your employees are frequent fliers on the [city A] to [city B] route. They also show that you've practically stopped flying [our airline], meaning you must be using our competitor for your flights to and from [B].

We value your company's business, and we want it back. So we're going to make you a special offer. If you're willing to commit to choosing [our airline] for your employees' flights to [B], we'll let you lock in a terrific per-flight rate through the rest of the calendar year. We'll give you and your employees a [%] discount off the normal weekday fare—each one-way ticket will cost you only [$z] for travel in either direction.

How can you resist?

Just call our Special Corporate Reservations Desk at [number] and refer to offer number [number]. One of our Special Corporate Reservationists will give you all the details.

We look forward to seeing your employees again on their next [our airline] flight to [B]!

Sincerely,

[Name]
[Title]

- **If your product/ service is identical to the competition's, price may be the only way you can distinguish yourself.**

- **Provide valid dates and price comparisons, along with a special reservations number.**

Path on CD-ROM: Current and Former Customers→Lapsed or Lapsing Customers→Offers to lapsed customers→Airline-1

LAPSED OR LAPSING CUSTOMERS

Offer to lapsed customer

[Name]
[Company]
[Address]
[City, State ZIP]

Dear [   ]:

We thought we had a good thing going. We catered ten of your company holiday parties and picnics, and then suddenly—nothing.

We'd like to get back together with you. And with the holiday season approaching, what better way than to hire us to cater your company Christmas party?

To make amends for whatever we may have done wrong, we'd like to make you an unusual offer:

Hire us to cater your Christmas party and we'll take [percentage] off our usual per-person food charge and [percentage] off the usual per-person bar charge. Just give [name] a call and she'll fill in all the details.

It will be our way of saying "happy holidays" and "great to see you again!"

Sincerely,

[Name]
[Title]

- **Make a special offer to a former customer if it means the chance for ongoing business.**

- **Provide the name of a contact person if it's someone other than you.**

Path on CD-ROM: Current and Former Customers→Lapsed or Lapsing Customers→Offers to lapsed customers→Catering-1

Personal thank-you note

[Name]
[Company]
[Address]
[City, State ZIP]

Dear [   ]:

I happened to attend the [name of conference/tradeshow] last week and heard the nice things you said about [company] and our [products/services]. On behalf of everyone here, I'd like to express our appreciation of the kind words. We greatly value your business, and if you ever have a question or concern, I hope you'll let me know.

Kind regards,

[Name]
[Title]

- **Mention what prompted the note.**

- **Thank the customer.**

- **Express appreciation for their business.**

- **Open the door for them to contact you with questions or comments.**

Path on CD-ROM: Current and Former Customers→Relationship Maintenance→Personal note of thanks→Generic-1

Personal thank-you note

[Name]
[Title]
[Organization]
[Address]
[City, State ZIP]

Dear [Name]:

Thank you for awarding us the [retail] portion of your account.

I know that you were considering several other leading [advertising agencies] in addition to [R&W] for this business, so it's particularly pleasing to be the one selected. As we said during our pitch, we're convinced that our approach to your [retail] communications challenge will help you grow your business, not only in the short term but for years to come.

All of us at [R&W] are thrilled to be working with you on this exciting project, and we're all looking forward to next week's kick-off meeting. Thanks again for the vote of confidence.

Sincerely,

[Name]
[Title]

- **Thank the new client right at the start.**

- **Acknowledge your awareness that you weren't the only candidate, and remind the client of the relationship between her/his concerns and your company's ability to address them.**

- **Communicate your enthusiasm for the work about to begin.**

Path on CD-ROM: Current and Former Customers→Relationship Maintenance→Personal note of thanks→Account-1

Congratulatory note

[Date]

[Name]
[Company]
[Address]
[City, State ZIP]

Dear [   ]:

Congratulations on your new job! We'd like to help you celebrate by scheduling a free sitting for your media portrait. Let's face it, people whose careers are growing need a great publicity photo on hand.

To further show our enthusiasm for your success, we'll give you a free 8 x 10 when you purchase pictures from the sitting.

Give us a call by [deadline] to set up a time for your free shoot. We look forward to seeing you.

Sincerely,

[Name]
[Title]

- **Offer the person something free and special in honor of the occasion.**
- **Show how both the job and your offer are steps up in the world.**

Path on CD-ROM: Current and Former Customers→Relationship Maintenance→Congratulations→Promotion-5

Congratulatory note

[Name]
[Company]
[Address]
[City, State ZIP]

Dear [   ]:

I just spotted your engagement announcement in the paper and couldn't be happier for you!

Please come into [my business] any time between now and the wedding and take [x%] off [item or service] as our way of saying congratulations and thanks for all your years of being a loyal customer.

Best wishes, [name]! I'm looking forward to seeing you and hearing all about your wedding plans!

Sincerely,

[Name]

- Express your excitement about the good news.

- Offer an incentive to purchase that's tied to the announcement.

- Close on a personal note.

Path on CD-ROM: Current and Former Customers→Relationship Maintenance→Congratulations→Engagement-1

Birthday note

[Name]
[Title]
[Organization]
[Address]
[City, State ZIP]

Dear [Name]:

Your loyalty and support have been critical to the success of my consulting practice over the past three years. And just because we're both insanely busy, it doesn't mean we can't take some personal time out to celebrate special occasions together.

I know your birthday is coming up later this month, and I'd like to say both "Happy birthday" and "Thanks for everything" to you. Let's pick a date during your birthday week and have a fabulous lunch or dinner, on me, at Chez Jacques. It'll be the least I can do for such a special customer.

I'll call you later this week so we can make plans.

Sincerely,

[Name]
[Title]

- **Acknowledge the reader's personal and professional support to you.**

- **Link the special occasion to your ongoing appreciation and suggest a way to celebrate.**

- **Commit to an action step.**

Path on CD-ROM: Current and Former Customers→Relationship Maintenance→Holiday or birthday notes→Birthday-1

RELATIONSHIP MAINTENANCE

Holiday note

[Name]
[Company]
[Address]
[City, State ZIP]

Dear [   ]:

On behalf of [spouse] and myself, and the entire staff of [ethnic product shop], we would like to extend to you, [spouse's name and the children, if any] our best wishes for a healthy, happy, and prosperous New Year.

Please stop by any time before Rosh Hashanah eve or after Yom Kippur so that we can wish you Happy New Year in person—and have a [ethnic product] or two on the house. It'll be wonderful to see you again and catch up on all the latest.

L'shanah tovah!

Sincerely,

[Name]
[Title]

- **Extend holiday greetings from yourself (and your own significant other) to the customer and his/her significant other and family.**

- **Suggest an opportunity for a visit to your place of business; tie it to a token offer or freebie.**

Path on CD-ROM: Current and Former Customers→Relationship Maintenance→Holiday or birthday notes→Holiday-2

Thanks for a referral/recommendation

[Name]
[Address]
[City, State ZIP]

Dear [   ]:

You may recall that the last time you called me to place a buy order, I asked you if any of your coworkers might be interested in taking me on as their broker. You suggested that I call [Nancy Brenner].

Well, [Kim], I can't thank you enough. I gave [Nancy] a call right after I hung up with you, and she told me that she'd just gotten a stock tip that she'd wanted to follow up on. I gave her some background information and she immediately placed an order—the timing couldn't have been more perfect!

So I wanted to thank you for referring me to [Nancy]. We've spoken a few more times since that initial conversation and I think she's going to be a terrific client!

I'd like to say "thank you" in a more tangible way, so I'll give you a call in a few days to see when we might be able to get together for drinks or a meal, on me. Maybe [Nancy] can come along, too. It would be my pleasure to take TWO of my favorite clients out to dinner together!

Thanks again, [Kim]!

Sincerely,

[Name]
[Title]

- If a current client turns you on to a potential new (additional) client, be sure to show your gratitude.

- You may wish to offer a token thank-you gift to both the reader and the new client, possibly at the same time if appropriate.

Path on CD-ROM: Current and Former Customers→Relationship Maintenance→Thanks for referral→Broker-1

Thanks for a referral/recommendation

[Name]
[Address]
[City, State ZIP]

Dear [   ]:

Thank you for sharing one of your client's names with me.

As you suggested, I did call [Joan Ramsay] to see if she was looking for an interior designer. Knowing that you just completed [construction] on her new house and having some of the details was a big help!

As it happens, [Joan] had not yet started shopping around for a designer, and she said she'd be happy to meet with me. She and I have an initial meeting scheduled for [next week]. We haven't signed a contract yet, but I have a good feeling about this one.

No matter how it goes, I wanted to thank you for the contact. I'll keep my ears open for referrals I can send your way, too.

Thanks again, [Pete]!

Sincerely,

[Name]
[Title]

P.S. While Joan and I were talking, she happened to mention how thrilled she was with the work you and your team have done on her house. Just thought you'd like to know that!

- **Make a habit of sharing referrals with colleagues in related fields, and be sure to thank your colleague when a referral pans out.**

- **Let the reader know how things with the new prospect are going.**

- **If you've heard anything from the prospect about the reader, pass it along.**

Path on CD-ROM: Current and Former Customers→Relationship Maintenance→Thanks for referral→Designer-1

Thanks for a referral/recommendation

[Name]
[Title]
[Organization]
[Address]
[City, State ZIP]

Dear [Name]:

I just wanted to thank you for referring [person's name] to me for her [financial planning].

As you can imagine, starting a [financial planning] practice in a new location is often quite challenging, so it's tremendously flattering—and quite helpful—to get such a ringing endorsement from a current client. It's especially flattering in light of the number of [planners] your business has used over the years.

Thanks for thinking of me.

Sincerely,

[Name]
[Title]

- **Mention the name of the person who made the referral.**

- **Acknowledge that the client could have gone with another source and show your appreciation for his/her picking you.**

Path on CD-ROM: Current and Former Customers→Relationship Maintenance→Thanks for referral→Financial-1

RELATIONSHIP MAINTENANCE

Thanks for a referral/recommendation

[Name]
[Address]
[City, State ZIP]

Dear [   ]:

It was great seeing you at the [Johnsons' holiday party last month].

When we spoke, you mentioned that your friend [Jim] was looking for a new ad agency. So, on your advice, I called him last week, and he's invited my firm to give him and his colleagues an initial credentials presentation. I'll let you know how it goes.

No matter the outcome of the presentation, I'd like to take you out to dinner as my way of saying "thank you." I'll give you a call later this week to set a date.

Sincerely,

[Name]
[Title]

- **Thank the person who gave you the tip.**

- **Let him/her know how things are progressing.**

- **You may wish to offer the reader a token thank-you gesture such as a meal or drinks.**

Path on CD-ROM: Current and Former Customers→Relationship Maintenance→Thanks for referral→Ad agency-1

Asking for a testimonial or referral

[Name]
[Company]
[Address]
[City, State ZIP]

Dear [   ]:

We hope you've enjoyed your [Web page/Internet service] as much as we enjoyed [designing it/providing service] for you.

If you've been pleased with [the service we've provided you so far], would you be willing to share your impressions with other potential customers?

We're about to update our own Web site and would like to include brief testimonials from satisfied customers on the "What Our Customers Have to Say About Us" page. If you'd be willing to add a sentence or two to that page, we'd be just thrilled. And we'll give you [$x or x%] off [your next month's bill] as our way of saying thanks.

When you have a moment, click on [LINK]. You'll see a form with a few short questions asking for your opinions about specific elements of our service. (You'll also see that your privacy will be protected; if we do quote you, we'll mention only your initials, unless you'd rather have us use your full name. It's your choice.)

Thanks again for your continued business, and for sharing your opinions about us with other future customers.

Sincerely,

[Name]

[Title]

- **Explain exactly how/where the customer's testimonial will be used.**
- **Provide a token incentive.**
- **Assure the customer that his/her privacy will be protected.**

Path on CD-ROM: Current and Former Customers→Relationship Maintenance→Referral or testimonial→Web designer-1

Asking for a referral or recommendation

[Name]
[Address]
[City, State ZIP]

Dear [   ]:

On behalf of everyone here at [House The Homeless], I'd like to thank you for your continued support of our worthy cause.

As part of our [2001 Outreach Campaign], we're trying to identify other caring individuals like you who are concerned about the plight of [homeless members of our community]. And we'd like to ask for your help.

If you have any friends, family members, or business associates that you feel would be interested in supporting [House The Homeless], we'd be most appreciative if you'd refer us to them. I've enclosed a simple form on which you can list the names and phone numbers and/or addresses of people you know who you think might be potential supporters.

Won't you take a moment to fill it out and send it back to us in the enclosed postage-paid envelope? Widening our base of caring contributors means we can provide [shelter for that many more members of our community].

Thanks again for all your help.

Sincerely,

[Name]
[Title]

- **Acknowledge the supporter's ongoing contributions.**

- **Touch on emotional benefits of the reader's contributions and link those to the request for additional prospects.**

- **Provide an easy way for the reader to provide referrals.**

Path on CD-ROM: Current and Former Customers→Relationship Maintenance→Referral or testimonial→Charity-1

Thank-you promotions (telemarketing script)

Good morning. Is [CUSTOMER] in?

As a valued customer of [Henry's Department Store], you are eligible for a [Henry's] charge account, available only to regular patrons.

[With your new Henry's card, you will receive a free T-shirt and a customer certificate, giving you an additional 10% off your first credit card order. In addition, whenever you use your card, you automatically will receive a 5% regular customer discount on all purchases.]

May I send you a [Henry's] charge card? You will activate your [Henry's] credit account when you first use your new card.

(YES)

Wonderful. I will put it in the mail today. Have a great day.

(NO)

I am sorry to hear that. [Henry's] still appreciates your business, and if you should change your mind, just call us at [444-4444]. Have a great day.

- **Script gets to the selling points as quickly as possible.**

- **Even a negative response receives a positive close.**

Path on CD-ROM: Current and Former Customers→Relationship Maintenance→Thank-you promotions→Dept store-1

RELATIONSHIP MAINTENANCE

Thank-you promotion

[Name]
[Company]
[Address]
[City, State ZIP]

Dear [   ]:

We'd like to thank you for being such a loyal customer for so many years. And, naturally, we'd like you to think of us first when you start planning your company Christmas party.

So we'd like to make you an offer you won't be able to refuse:

Hire us to cater your Christmas party this year and we'll take [percentage] off our usual per-person food charge and [percentage] off the usual per-person bar charge. Just give [name] a call and she'll fill in all the details.

It's our way of saying happy holidays and to thank you for all your business over the years.

Sincerely,

[Name]
[Title]

- Tie the special offer in with a thank-you or happy holidays message if you're talking to a regular, loyal customer.

- Provide the name of a contact person if it's someone other than you.

Path on CD-ROM: Current and Former Customers→Relationship Maintenance→Thank-you promotions→Catering-1

Follow-up and cross-sell

Special Offer to Loyal [Company] Customers

[Name]
[Address]
[City, State ZIP]

Dear [Name]:

You've used [company's] leading product, [product], for years, so you know how [effective/reliable] products from [company] can be. As a valued customer, you deserve an opportunity to preview [company's] latest [product], made with today's [consumer type] in mind. It's made with the same great [materials/craftsmanship] as our well-known [existing item], yet it's [more than twice as powerful] and [available at the same low price.]

The new [product] features [improved performance and reliability]. Come into [our showroom] or call [800-555-5555] to get our new catalog sent to you free of charge.

Don't you deserve the best?

Sincerely,

[Name]
[Title]

- Soft sell approaches avoid hyperbole; just state the facts.

- Don't forget the hook that will make them call or bring them into a store.

- Leverage the reader's loyalty to the existing product, and therefore to the company, in order to provide incentive for trial of the new item.

Path on CD-ROM: Current and Former Customers→Relationship Maintenance→Follow-up, cross sell→Product-1

RELATIONSHIP MAINTENANCE

Follow-up or cross-sell

[Name]
[Company]
[Address]
[City, State ZIP]

Dear [   ]:

As a hard working business owner, you appreciate the high-quality service you get from [Speedy Delivery]. For [##] years, we've made sure your packages get down the street or across town, intact and on time.

So you'll be happy to know that we're introducing a new [Value Package] service. Just send [10] or more packages a week using [Speedy Delivery] and you'll receive a 10% discount.

With [Value Package], you get the same guaranteed, on-time delivery you've always trusted from [Speedy Delivery]. You get the same courteous, professional drivers who treat your package with the care it deserves. Only now you get an even better value the more you use [Speedy Delivery].

Best of all, your business automatically qualifies for [Value Package]. We'll keep track of how many packages you send each week and automatically credit the 10% discount on our monthly statements. You need do nothing except send your packages the safest way possible!

Thanks for being a loyal customer.

Sincerely,

[Name]
[Title]

- **Remind the reader that they're already doing business with you.**

- **In this case, the reader doesn't have to do anything new to qualify; make it clear he or she gets this extra value just for being a customer.**

Path on CD-ROM: Current and Former Customers→Relationship Maintenance→Follow-up, cross sell→Delivery-1

Follow-up or cross-sell

[Date]
[Name]
[Company]
[Address]
[City, State ZIP]

Dear [   ]:

It was really a pleasure researching your new market. I am excited that you have been able to run with several of the ideas included in my proposal. We make a great team!

Because of this I want to follow up with you about another project we had discussed: [project]. As with our first project, I am confident I could provide you with more ideas you can use—and the supporting research as well!

I'll give you a call next week to see if you are interested in proceeding.

Sincerely,

[Name]
[Title]

- **Use this kind of follow-up letter to encourage future business with the same client.**

- **Note the success of your previous work together.**

Path on CD-ROM: Current and Former Customers→Relationship Maintenance→Follow-up, cross sell→Generic-4

RELATIONSHIP MAINTENANCE

Follow-up or cross-sell

To: [   ]

From: [   ]

Subject: [Advanced graphic design seminar]

In [February], you graduated from our seminar, [Beginning Graphic Design]. Now, we are offering [Advanced Graphic Design] in your city on [June 17] and thought you would want to attend.

Now that you have become skilled in [using your company's graphic programs, learn to use your natural sense of style and design. Learn how to catch the reader's eye and get the response you want from all your company's printed materials. Produce reports, newsletters, and brochures that get rave reviews from your customers, shareholders, and industry colleagues.]

The [one-day] seminar will be held at [Lincoln Towers, from 9 A.M. to 4 P.M. Cost: $127 or $97 per person for groups of two or more].

To reserve your spot in [Advanced Graphic Design], simply e-mail the names of all participants along with the name, address, and telephone number of your company to [www.alltrain.com].

We will register you for this valuable seminar and mail an invoice to you. Our no-risk policy allows you to substitute or cancel up to the day before the seminar.

Take your [design] skills to a whole new level in [one seven-hour day]. Mark your calendar for [June 17] and e-mail your response today.

- **Message provides all the key information— what, when, where, and, of course, why and how much.**

- **Guarantee removes the risk of customers changing their mind.**

Path on CD-ROM: Current and Former Customers→Relationship Maintenance→Follow-up, cross sell→Seminar-1

Damage control

[Name]
[Address]
[City, State ZIP]

Dear [   ]:

I was just made aware that you had an unpleasant experience the last time you [visited our store/talked to an employee]. Obviously, I am deeply pained that any of our customers would be treated that way. [Company] has long prided itself on our commitment to customer service, and we regret any departure from our [values].

On behalf of [company], I hope you will accept my heartfelt apology, and my assurances that such an incidence will never recur. Though I know nothing can fully compensate you for your treatment, I hope you will accept the enclosed [coupon/gift] as a token of our respect.

Thank you for giving us your business. I hope that you will consider [coming back/purchasing from us again].

Sincerely,

[Name]
[Title]

- **Make the apology quickly and state the obvious (that it is not a corporate value you endorse).**

- **If possible, offer a token gift/ discount/coupon.**

Path on CD-ROM: Current and Former Customers→Relationship Maintenance→Damage control→Rude employee-1

Damage control

[Name]
[Title]
[Organization]
[Address]
[City, State ZIP]

Dear [Name]:

On behalf of [writer's company], I wanted to write and thank you for sticking with us during our recent merger with [company]. It got a bit hectic around here at times, and I know that [writer's company's] sometimes fell short of our goals to provide our customers with trouble-free [type of service].

As an expression of our appreciation, our [CEO, name,] has authorized me to offer our customers a discount of [dollar amount or percentage discount] off your [July] invoice.

I also wanted to assure you that everything here is back up to speed, so you shouldn't encounter any more [type of problem] problems in the future.

Thanks again!

Sincerely,

[Name]
[Title]

Path on CD-ROM: Current and Former Customers→Relationship Maintenance→Damage control→Support-1

Making contact

TO: [Name@company.org]

FROM: [NAME]

RE:

[Sally]:

I don't know if you get a chance to read the [*New York Herald*] regularly, so I'm sending the attached article from this morning's online Business section. It talks about new developments in the plastics business that might have some relevance for your own engineering and design groups—even if it's not directly applicable for our upcoming plans, it's a pretty fascinating piece in its own right.

See you at Friday's presentation—you're gonna love what we have to show you!

Until then,

[Name]

- **Mention the source and topic of the article.**

- **Touch briefly on the article's contents as well as its potential relevance to the reader and/or the business you're working on together.**

- **Refer to an upcoming meeting or issue.**

Path on CD-ROM: Current and Former Customers→Relationship Maintenance→Making contact→Sending article-2

RELATIONSHIP MAINTENANCE

Making contact

TO: [Name@company.org]

FROM: [NAME]

RE: Can we reschedule?

Sharon:

I hate having to do this, but I need to ask you if we can reschedule the meeting that's currently set for next Tuesday.

We just reviewed the presentation internally and, frankly, we're not there yet. We're close, but, in all candor, we need a few more days to bring the work to a level that's worthy of presentation to you and your team. If we moved the meeting back to Thursday or Friday, I could assure you that we'd have a top-notch presentation to give you.

I'll give you a call later today to see which other day next week would work for your schedule. Again, my apologies for having to do this, but I think the end result will be worth the slight delay.

- **No client wants to hear that a meeting has to be postponed. Make this "bad" news more palatable by letting the client know about the delay as far in advance as possible.**

- **Make clear that the reason for the delay is to improve the quality of the work.**

- **Briefly apologize and offer to call to reschedule.**

Path on CD-ROM: Current and Former Customers→Relationship Maintenance→Making contact→Reschedule-1

Making contact

TO: [Name@company.org]

FROM: [NAME]

RE: [Confirming [event]]

Tom:

I just wanted to confirm that we're on for [event] this [day, date, time of day].

I made reservations at [place] for [time] for [number of people]. Please let me know if that works for you—and if you want to bring any of your team along, just let me know and I'll change the reservation.

I look forward to seeing you on [day] night.

- **Socializing with clients can be a critical part of the business relationship.**

- **Even though the social occasion may be informal, written confirmation is always a good idea; miscommunication of dates, times, or places is never helpful.**

- **Depending on the event, you may want to invite the reader to bring colleagues along.**

RELATIONSHIP MAINTENANCE

Making contact

[Name]
[Company]
[Address]
[City, State ZIP]

Dear [   ]:

It's been three months since you purchased your [high-ticket item] from [store/business name]. We just wanted to check in and make sure everything's running smoothly.

Should you encounter any problem with your [item], please don't hesitate to give me a call.

I look forward to helping you again when it comes time for your next [category] purchase.

Sincerely,

[Name]
[Title]

- **Merchants selling high-ticket items can turn a retail customer business into one with more of a client service orientation by treating customers like clients; envision an ongoing relationship that includes regular contact and servicing.**

- **Letting the customer/client know that your interest in him doesn't end when he leaves the sales floor with his purchase is important. This sort of follow-up letter, though brief, can encourage repeat business.**

Path on CD-ROM: Current and Former Customers→Relationship Maintenance→Making contact→After purchase-1

Making contact

TO: [Name@company.org]

FROM: [NAME]

RE: How can we help?

Dear Donna:

How have you been?

We haven't spoken in a while or had a project assigned by you or anyone on your team in quite some time. I know you've all been busy getting out the spring product line, and I'm sure we could be of some assistance right about now.

Since the agency doesn't have any specific assignments right now (but we're still on retainer!) we've had a chance to start putting together some business-building concepts for your company that we'd like to present to you some time this month. I think several of the ideas will spark some thoughts for the fall campaign and the coming year that could really take the company into new growth areas.

I'll call you later this week to see about setting a time to get together. I'm looking forward to seeing you again.

Sincerely,

[Name]

- **Use a subject line that shows the person you can help them solve a problem.**

- **This letter doesn't "give" something to the client, but it does let the inactive client know that you've been thinking about her business and may even have done some (unpaid) work as an incentive to reactivate the relationship.**

- **Close by promising to call to set a meeting.**

Path on CD-ROM: Current and Former Customers→Relationship Maintenance→Making contact→Dormant client-2

Ticklers

[Name]
[Company]
[Address]
[City, State ZIP]

Dear [   ]:

I've moved!

Yes, it's true. I finally left the city and bought a house in the suburbs. I love the space and the peace and quiet.

I know you live in the same part of the county. I'd love to have you [and your spouse] over for dinner or a barbecue some time this summer. Give a call next time you're in the neighborhood.

Sincerely,

[Name]
[Title]

- **Use personal (but not intimate) news of your own as an excuse to write.**

- **Touch on a common point, such as your location being near the client's.**

- **Suggest a social get-together.**

Path on CD-ROM: Current and Former Customers→Relationship Maintenance→Ticklers→Share news-1

Ticklers

[Name]
[Company]
[Address]
[City, State ZIP]

Dear [   ]:

I ran into Jerry at the mall this weekend. He asked how you were doing, and I realized that I didn't know the answer to that question either!

How are you doing? It would be great to catch up one of these days. Give me a call or drop me an e-mail when you get a moment.

Sincerely,

[Name]

[Title]

- **Turn the fact that you haven't been in touch with the customer into a reason in itself for contacting him/her.**

- **Ask the reader straight out how s/he's doing, and suggest that s/he contact you.**

Path on CD-ROM: Current and Former Customers→Relationship Maintenance→Ticklers→Encounter-1

RELATIONSHIP MAINTENANCE

Responding to complaints

[Name]
[Company]
[Address]
[City, State ZIP]

Dear [   ]:

Thank you for sharing your concerns about [our company's] work. While I'm never happy to hear such comments from our clients, I'd much prefer to be made aware of the issues while there's a chance to address them.

First, let me state that I understand your position. The work we've done for you on [recent project/assignment] admittedly did not [perform as well / get the same results] as some of our previous [projects/ assignments]. There are a number of factors operating here that need to be looked into in more depth, and I'd prefer to discuss them with you in person when we get together for [meeting/social occasion] on [date], if not before.

I also want to spend some time talking with you about some of the other concerns you raised. I agree that there may be some [staffing/personnel] issues operating; some may be simple personality clashes, while others may go deeper than that. At any rate, I want to hear everything you and your team have to say on this point.

I'll call you later today to see when we might get together—this week or next, hopefully—to iron out the situation.

Sincerely,

[Name]
[Title]

- **Do not get defensive in writing; if there is an undeniable, factual problem, acknowledge it but do not admit that you or your company are directly to blame.**

- **Propose an in-person meeting to discuss delicate issues and to bring your side of the story to the table. Again, do this in person, not on paper.**

- **Make clear that you are LISTENING.**

Path on CD-ROM: Current and Former Customers→Relationship Maintenance→Responding to complaints→Agency-3

Responding to complaints

[Name]
[Address]
[City, State ZIP]

Dear [   ]:

I was very upset to learn about your unpleasant evening at [Chez Jacqueline].

I pride myself not only on our food but on the professionalism of my wait staff, so I was rather dismayed to hear that one of my waiters was less than perfectly gracious to you and your [spouse]. I have spoken to my staff and can assure you that such an incident will not be repeated.

In order to express my apology and hopes that you will continue to patronize [Chez Jacqueline], I would like to invite you and your family to dinner at the restaurant—on me—any night this month that is convenient for you.

Please call me directly and we'll reserve a special table for you.

Sincerely,

[Name]
[Title]

- **Small businesses cannot afford to offend customers.**

- **Acknowledge the complaint and assure the customer that the problem was an anomaly that will not be repeated; if possible, offer the customer a return visit to your establishment at no charge.**

Path on CD-ROM: Current and Former Customers→Relationship Maintenance→Responding to complaints→Restaurant-1

RELATIONSHIP MAINTENANCE

Buck sheet

[HEADLINE: Check Our References]

Here is a sampling of the many comments we have received on this valuable business seminar:

["I just wanted to let you know that your seminar was the most valuable that I have ever attended. The instructor covered vague questions I had only half formed. She seemed to know what I was going to ask next." —[name]]

["Thank you for an outstanding workshop. It met my training needs 100 percent. After taking it, I am much better prepared to succeed in my new position." —[name]]

["What a terrific workshop! Our instructor provided just the right balance between practical guidance and theory. The pace of the class was fast but not so demanding that I felt overwhelmed. I learned a great amount of solid information in two short days." —[name]]

["I am so glad that my company sent me to your workshop. I learned enough new knowledge and leadership skills to practically guarantee that our department will reach its goals this year." —[name]]

["Your seminar provided practical strategies, advice, encouragement, and insight to those of us working in the trenches of our profession on a daily basis. It helped me to form new job goals for the remainder of the year and definitely enhanced my professional skills. Thank you." —[name]]

- **Use a buck slip in place of a lengthier brochure and focus on one theme on each side of the dollar-bill sized sheet.**

- **Get permission from customers to reprint excerpts from their letters, solicit testimonials from loyal customers, or ask reviewers for permission to quote from their comments on new products.**

Path on CD-ROM: Current and Former Customers→Relationship Maintenance→Buck sheets→Seminar-1

Firefighting urgent issues

[TO:]

[FROM:]

[SUBJECT:]

[DATE:]

The good news: We're on track to go live with [your company's] new Web site on [Monday at 8:00 A.M.]

The bad news: We still haven't received a copy of your [revised company logo].

[Since the logo is featured prominently on the home page and we will be creating several variations on it throughout the site], I need to get a copy of it by [this Thursday night at the latest] or I'm afraid we'll miss our [Monday morning launch time].

Please [e-mail the logo] to me as a [file type] file as soon as possible—and get psyched for an awesome site launch on Monday!

- The good news/ bad news approach can make an urgent client memo a little friendlier, as can an excited (not panicky) closing.

- Explain why you're asking for as much lead time as you are.

- Be specific about how the art can/should be transmitted to you.

Path on CD-ROM: Current and Former Customers→Relationship Maintenance→Urgent issues→Web developer-1

Firefighting urgent issues

[TO:]

[FROM:]

[SUBJECT:]

[DATE:]

I need to bring a pressing media-related issue to your immediate attention. (I left a voice-mail message earlier but need a response quickly, so I'm following up with this fax.)

We just got a call from [the local TV station]. They're planning on doing a feature on [the best Web sites of 2001 and their designers] on their [6:00 P.M. news broadcast tomorrow night] and they want to include the site we designed for you, [along with interviews with our site designers].

How would you like us to handle this request? Would you like to speak to the [TV station] or be otherwise involved with the segment? Do we have your permission to discuss [the site/design] on the broadcast?

Please call me as soon as you get this note. Thanks.

- **When you're being brought into a situation that involves client business and potentially confidential information, alert the client immediately.**

- **Lay out the basics, then cover details in the phone call you're requesting.**

Path on CD-ROM: Current and Former Customers→Relationship Maintenance→Urgent issues→Press issue-1

Firefighting urgent issues

[TO:]

[FROM:]

[SUBJECT:]

[DATE:]

This will confirm the date, time, and location of the [catalog shoot] we will be doing for [your 2002 product line].

We will be shooting at [9:00 A.M. this Friday at our studio].

In order to set up the lighting and props and be able to start right on time [on Friday morning], we will need to get [three copies of each product] delivered [to our studio] no later than [Wednesday morning]. Receiving product later than [Wednesday morning] will require us to go into overtime in order to be ready for [Friday's] shoot; this could increase your production budget considerably given the number of crew members we have hired for this job.

Please messenger [the products] to [person at address]. Thank you.

- Explain the complexity of the job in order to quell any potential objections about the request.

- Make clear that a delay in receipt of product translates to additional cost to the client; this often can be your most powerful motivator!

- Note that the urgency here is not stated directly; you're simply stating the facts without panic.

Firefighting urgent issues

[TO:]
[FROM:]
[SUBJECT:]
[DATE:]

Thank you for your recent [gift] order from [AllToys.com].

We have just received word from [credit card company] that your purchase was not approved. Would you please reply to this e-mail before [tomorrow morning] authorizing purchase with a different credit card? This will allow us to fill and ship your [gift] order in time for [Christmas].

Simply hit "reply" and return this letter to us with the blanks below filled in. Thank you again for ordering from [AllToys.com], and have a wonderful holiday.

- **Thank the customer for his/her order.**

- **State the problem and then move directly to a solution.**

- **Avoid embarrassing the customer (even in an online communication).**

Path on CD-ROM: Current and Former Customers→Relationship Maintenance→Urgent issues→Credit card-1

Firefighting urgent issues

[TO:]

[FROM:]

[SUBJECT:]

[DATE:]

We've received your order and will be happy to send you the [parts] you ordered via [overnight delivery], as requested.

In order to make this shipment to you, we need to receive a down payment [of at least xx% of the total invoice amount]. You may then pay the balance within [10 days] of receipt and inspection of the shipment.

Please call or fax us at [800-555-5555] as soon as possible with a credit card authorization or send us your corporate card account number and expiration date via e-mail.

If we receive your card information by [4 o'clock this afternoon], we should have no problem in sending out [your parts] tonight. If the information reaches us later than [4:00], the shipment will go out tomorrow and you will receive your order the following day.

Thank you for your business and your prompt response.

- **While urgent action is required on the part of the reader, the note is unfailingly cheerful and cordial.**

- **Provide specific deadlines and payment amounts that the reader must attend to in order to receive the shipment when s/he wants it.**

Path on CD-ROM: Current and Former Customers→Relationship Maintenance→Urgent issues→Down payment-1

Changes in policy

[Name]
[Company]
[Address]
[City, State ZIP]

Dear [Name]:

I must bring a seemingly small but ultimately costly issue to your attention.

As you know, our contract with you stipulates that we will pay for all routine shipping costs from our office to yours. Unfortunately, however, requests by members of your team for overnight delivery services has become routine, even for the shipping of nonurgent materials and letters. The constant use of such suppliers is cutting significantly into our operating budget and is threatening our profitability in serving your business.

We're sorry to have to do this, but we can no longer afford to cover your overnight shipping costs. We will bill back to you all shipping expenses for overnight delivery requested by your team. We will, of course, be happy to cover the cost of nonovernight delivery, as we have been doing, and will continue to fax and/or e-mail all urgent letters or memos to you so that overnight delivery will become practically unnecessary.

I hope you understand the need for us to institute this policy. Please call me if you would like to discuss this matter in more detail.

Sincerely,

[Name]
[Title]

- **There is often a thin line between providing client service and endangering profits. When that line is crossed, say something.**

- **Diplomatically explain the problem and show what you will do to solve it in a way that serves all parties needs.**

Path on CD-ROM: Current and Former Customers→Announcements→Change in sales policy→Shipping policy-1

Price increase

Dear [Parent]:

Yes, this is the letter we hate writing (and you no doubt dread receiving) every year.

In order to keep pace with escalating expenses, your child's tuition and fees will be increased by approximately [x%] for the coming academic year. Per-semester tuition and fees have been set at [$x,xxx]. We also estimate that on-campus housing will increase by about [x%], books about [x%], and on-campus dining by [x%]; actual increases will be determined within the next month.

As you know, even with these increases, the costs borne by students and their parents do not even come close to covering the actual expense of a top-quality education. We are supported by government grants and private donations and even with that additional help usually do not break even.

Thank you for your understanding and continued support.

Sincerely,

[Name]

- **A little levity to relieve the tension of a tuition rate hike may not be a bad idea.**

- **Explain the need for the increases as well as the shortfalls you face even with higher fees.**

Path on CD-ROM: Current and Former Customers→Announcements→Price increase→Tuition-1

Price increase

[Name]
[Address]
[City, State ZIP]

Dear [   ]:

In order to offset [expenses/costs of doing business], [company] will be raising [price/rate] by [$ amount/% amount], effective [date].

Your individual rate increase may vary. A detailed [insert] explaining all increases by [region/category] [is enclosed/will be provided separately].

We hope you understand [reason for increase] and will continue to choose [our company] for your [category needs]. If you have any questions about the increase, please call [department] at [phone number] or visit our Web site [www.website.com/prices].

Thank you for your continued [patronage/support].

Sincerely,

[Name]
[Title]

- **Provide key facts: reason for increase, amount, effective date.**

- **If there are individual variations, explain them. Provide a separate document with details.**

- **Provide a customer service phone number and/or Web site address.**

Path on CD-ROM: Current and Former Customers→Announcements→Price increase→Generic-1

Price decrease

[Name]
[Address]
[City, State ZIP]

Dear [   ]:

In light of the continually decreasing costs of operating telecommunications networks, [cellular company] is happy to announce that we will be DECREAS-ING the cost of certain of our services starting next month.

If you're currently part of our [plan name] plan, your monthly base rate will decrease from [$x] to [$y] for [number] minutes. Additionally, all home-area calls beyond the initial [number] minutes will be billed at [number] cents per minute, a [%] per-minute savings compared to the current home minute rate. And calls to numbers outside the home area will also cost less: only [number] cents per minute, [%] less than the current long-distance rate.

You also have the option of switching to one of our [number] other monthly plans for even greater per-minute and per-call savings. A brochure detailing all plans and new costs is [enclosed/attached] for your convenience.

Thank you for choosing [cellular company] as your wireless communication provider.

Sincerely,

[Name]
[Title]

- **Increased competition in the wireless phone category will require competitive pricing and inventive service plans.**

- **Given the confusion surrounding pricing plans in the category, provide particularly clear explanations for base-rate and per-minute costs and changes.**

Path on CD-ROM: Current and Former Customers→Announcements→Price decrease→Wireless-1

ANNOUNCEMENTS

New ways to contact you

TO: [Name@company.com]

FROM: [Name]

SUBJECT: New! Contact us on our Web site!

Dear [Name]:

You can now contact us at [Metropolitan Light & Power] through our Web site, 24 hours a day, 7 days a week.

Just go to [www.metlightpower.com] to

- ask questions about your account;
- check your billing status;
- learn about ways to cut down on your utilities usage to save energy and money;
- even pay your monthly utilities bill.

Getting in touch with [Metropolitan Light & Power] has never been so simple!

Sincerely,

[Name]

P.S. If you prefer, you can still speak with a customer service representative Monday to Friday from 8 A.M. to 6 P.M. Just call our toll-free number: [877-989-0098].

- **Let the reader know that your Web site is a means of contact.**

- **Give the URL and list some of the key contact functions your site provides.**

- **If you offer another means of contact (such as a customer service phone number), mention it; not every customer is comfortable with the Web.**

Path on CD-ROM: Current and Former Customers→Announcements→New ways to contact→Web site-1

New contact

[Name]
[Address]
[City, State ZIP]

Dear [ ]:

Allow me to introduce myself. My name is [Dave Volkman], and I'll be your new [firm name] personal financial advisor. I am taking over all accounts previously handled by [Diane Young], who recently left the company.

Before leaving, Diane did have a chance to take me through your portfolio and briefly explain your objectives. While I have a good handle on what you and Diane had been trying to accomplish, I would still like to get together with you at your convenience to review your current investments, determine whether your objectives have changed, and tell you about some innovative and very successful investment strategies I developed during my [number] years as Senior Portfolio Manager at [my previous firm].

Please give me a call and let's set something up. I look forward to working with you and helping you meet your financial goals.

Sincerely,

[Name]
[Title]

- **Introduce yourself as the new contact person and immediately allay any possible concerns the reader may have about your credentials, experience, or familiarity with his/her account.**

- **Suggest a in-person meeting to establish your own relationship with the reader.**

Path on CD-ROM: Current and Former Customers→Announcements→New contact→Financial advisor-1

ANNOUNCEMENTS

New contact

[Name]
[Company]
[Address]
[City, State ZIP]

Dear [ ]:

As you may know, [your current contact] recently left [company name] to pursue [reason for leaving]. I have assigned [new person], who's been with [company] for [time period], to be your new [contact function/title].

[New person] will be calling you [day/date] to set up a meeting with you and [your colleagues] at [your corporation]. [New person] will review the [products/services] that [your corporation] currently [uses/buys] and will tell you about some new [product/service options] that we're offering that you may want to consider [buying/using/selling].

In the meantime, please feel free to call me if you have any questions or if I can help in any way.

Sincerely,

[Name]
[Title]

- **Use a somewhat routine personnel transition to offer new products/ services; empower the new contact person by having him/her bring them to the client.**

- **Let the reader know you're available if he/she has any concerns.**

Path on CD-ROM: Current and Former Customers→Announcements→New contact→Generic-3

Changes at your company

[Date]
[Name]
[Company]
[Address]
[City, State ZIP]

Dear [   ]:

Recently I got my business card reprinted to reflect my new title: [Senior Sales Associate].

You may think, "Oh no! What happened to [name] being [sales manager]?" At first glance, the change may look like a step down; in reality it's a great change for me, for the company, and for you.

I've always loved being a [sales associate]. I love to [meet with clients, discover their needs, and find appropriate solutions]. As [sales manager], I was [tied to my desk too often], and I was really missing doing what I do best: [helping customers directly].

So if you see a new spring in my step, you'll know why. I'll give you a call next week to catch up and to help you find good solutions to your current needs.

Sincerely,

[Name]
[Title]

- **Explain background for the demotion.**

- **Show how the change will only benefit the client.**

Path on CD-ROM: Current and Former Customers→Announcements→Changes at company→Demotion-1

ANNOUNCEMENTS

Changes at your company

[Date]

[Name]
[Company]
[Address]
[City, State ZIP]

Dear [   ]:

I told my managers they had to hire someone really good as my replacement because that person would have to take really good care of you. Fortunately, they came through.

I'm really pleased with their choice of [name]. [S/he] has the same commitment to serving customers as I do. Plus, you'll benefit from tapping into [name]'s extensive knowledge of [area].

I'm going to miss meeting with you, [prospect]. I'd like to say good-bye and introduce you to [name] personally over lunch sometime in the next two weeks. I'll give you a call very soon to find out your schedule.

Sincerely,

[Name]

[Title]

- Show that the new person has the same commitment to clients.

- Suggest a personal meeting.

Path on CD-ROM: Current and Former Customers→Announcements→Changes at company→Salesperson-2

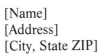

New distribution channels

[Name]
[Address]
[City, State ZIP]

Dear [   ]:

[Serious Stereos] are now at [Bullseye Electronics Stores]!

Yes, you can now find the industry's most highly rated CD players, tuners, and speakers at a [Bullseye] store near you. The same high-end equipment that was once sold only in exclusive stereo boutiques in a limited number of cities is now available practically everywhere, and at prices that more audiophiles can afford.

Check out the selection of [Serious] equipment at the [Bullseye] store at [1627 West Main St.] or any other [Bullseye] location in the metropolitan area.

Sincerely,

[Name]
[Title]

- **Expanding distribution within an existing channel category can greatly increase your (potential) consumer base; announce the expansion in a way that's consistent with your brand/ company image.**

- **If you can customize the letter to include specific locations/ addresses, do so.**

Path on CD-ROM: Current and Former Customers→Announcements→New distribution channel→Manufacturer-1

New uses for Web site

Unhappy with our [products/services]?

Is there something you don't like about doing business with us?

Do us a favor and TELL US!

Just click here!

[Company] is serious about providing our customers with the best service they can find. And we're serious about constantly improving what we do.

So if there's anything you're unhappy about, please let us know. We respond to every complaint.

If we can't solve your problem with our [products/services], you'll get an immediate refund. No questions asked.

Thanks for doing business with [Company].

- **Use the solicitation of complaints to build a corporate image of a company that cares about serving its customers better.**

- **Tell the customer whether they will or won't get a personal response, and don't promise anything you can't deliver!**

- **Thank them for caring enough to take the time to provide their feedback.**

Path on CD-ROM: Current and Former Customers→Announcements→New uses for Web site→Complaint-3

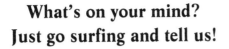

New uses for Web site

What's on your mind?
Just go surfing and tell us!

Dear [Name]:

We'd like to know what you think! Do you have ideas about how we could improve our [products/services]? Are there new [products/services] you think we should add to our line-up? Want to give us a tip on what our competition's up to?

If you've got 5 minutes, we'd like to hear about it!

That's why we've developed a new online survey you can fill out any time you have an idea you want to share.

Just go to [www.company.com] and click on SURVEY.

You can lodge a complaint, share your ideas on how we can improve, tell us about an idea for a new product or service—whatever is on your mind! It won't take long to complete, and we'd be very grateful for your time.

Thanks for your help!

Sincerely,

[Name]
[Company]

- You can't be quite as telegraphic in a letter as you are on the Web or in an e-mail. In written form, you need to make sure all your sentences and thoughts are complete.

- Highlight the Web address.

- Indicate it won't take long for the customer to complete the survey.

- Thank them for their input.

Path on CD-ROM: Current and Former Customers→Announcements→New uses for Web site→Comments-2

Opening of new business/location

[Name]
[Company]
[Address]
[City, State ZIP]

Dear [Name]:

As you are probably aware, I left [McDougal and McCormick] earlier this year to pursue the opportunity to start my own legal practice. I am happy to announce that the dream has become a reality. As of [date], [Andrew McFarland, L.L.P.] will be open for business in beautiful new downtown offices at [1627 W. Main Street].

This letter will serve as both an announcement of the opening of my firm as well as a hearty thank you to all of you who I was privileged to represent while at [M&M].

I hope to see you at some point in the near future. Thank you again for all your support over the years.

Sincerely,

[Name]
[Title]

- In situations where a partner or employee leaving a firm to open his/her own may be constrained from taking his/her former clients along to the new business, a letter of this sort should not resemble business solicitation.

- If this is NOT an issue, however, encourage the reader to contact you for counsel (or mention which areas of specialty you will be offering that do not compete with those your former employer offers).

- Simply announce the opening of the firm and thank people who have supported you.

Path on CD-ROM: Current and Former Customers→Announcements→New retailers→Lawyer-1

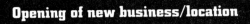

Opening of new business/location

[Name]
[Address]
[City, State ZIP]

Dear [Name]:

Forgive me for not being in touch with you for the past few [months]—I just wanted to wait until all the pieces had fallen into place before sharing my good news. As of [date], [Jane Bogart Management Consulting] is open for business!

I'd like to acknowledge and thank all of my former clients and colleagues who were so supportive during my many years on the management team at [Norris and Churchill Advertising].

And since I'm sure this question is on all of your minds, let me address it right from the start: I'm happy to report that while I will be offering advertising and marketing consulting services, my firm will not be competing with [N&C], nor will we be attempting to steal business away from my esteemed former employer. Indeed, my partners and I will be offering services intended to complement or augment those offered by most ad agencies, tackling projects with a fresh eye and a perspective not always possible when working on a longer-term, retainer-based basis.

This could even mean that I might work for current [N&C] clients and/or collaborate with [N&C] staff on certain projects, should the situation arise, and it would not represent a conflict of interest for any party. In fact, I'd welcome such an arrangement!

You can take a look at the enclosed brochure if you'd like to read more about the types of services we'll offer and projects we hope to tackle. In the meantime, though, I want to invite you to a little Opening/Office-Warming Party my partners and I are throwing to inaugurate the business. Please join us on [May 4 at 5:30 P.M. for cocktails and hors d'oeuvres].

I look forward to seeing you on the [4th]. Thanks again for all your support, and perhaps we can work together again!

Sincerely,

[Name]

- **When opening your own business, make clear to former clients whether you will be competing with your former employer; it is not always wise to put clients in a position of having to choose.**

- **Use a letter of this sort as an introduction and thank-you; save details for an enclosure.**

- **Provide some tangible thank you, whether it's a party, a discount, or other sort of gift.**

Path on CD-ROM: Current and Former Customers→Announcements→New retailers→Consultant-1

ANNOUNCEMENTS

New ways to pay

[Name]
[Address]
[City, State ZIP]

Dear [   ]:

Tired of writing checks to [Harlowton's] each month?

[Harlowton's] is thrilled to announce that you can now pay your charge account bill through our Web site. Once you've signed up with our online payment system, you'll be able to go to [www.harlowtons.com/accounts] and enter your [Harlowton's] charge account number. You'll see your latest purchases and credits, minimum payment, and total balance information. Just indicate how much you wish to pay, and we'll deduct the amount from your checking account or bill the major credit card of your choice, whichever option you've signed up for. (And while you're visiting our site, you'll also be able to find out about upcoming sales, new merchandise, and exclusive online-customer-only events.)

For more information, or to sign up for online bill-paying today, go to [www.harlowtons.com/signup] or call [1-888-555-6111]. And for any other customer service needs, just call our Customer Service Center at that same number: [1-888-555-6111].

Thanks again for being a loyal [Harlowton's] customer!

Sincerely,

[Name]
[Title]

- **Identify the problem, then provide your solution.**

- **Briefly list or describe key features and provide an information phone number where customers can get greater detail.**

- **Close with a thank you.**

Path on CD-ROM: Current and Former Customers→Announcements→New ways to pay→Online-1

New ways to order

TO: [Name@company.com]

FROM: [Name]

SUBJECT: Subscribe Online!

Thank you for your continued support of [theater] in [city].

In order to make it easier for you to order individual event tickets or season subscriptions, we've added a page to our Web site. Just go to [www.citytheatre.com/season] to read about upcoming [plays]. Then, to place your ticket order, season subscription order, or current subscription renewal, click the "orders" button and follow the simple instructions.

(Of course, if you'd prefer, you can also place orders by mail or phone. Just call our ticket office to place an order directly or request a brochure.)

We look forward to seeing you again during what promises to be an outstanding season!

Sincerely,

[Name]

- **Ordering tickets via the Web is now common enough that detailed explanation in this letter is probably not necessary.**

- **Provide alternative means for ordering as well (phone or mail).**

Path on CD-ROM: Current and Former Customers→Announcements→New ways to order→Season tickets-1

Introduction to new contact

[Name]
[Company]
[Address]
[City, State ZIP]

Dear [Name]:

Congratulations!

I learned about [your company's] decision to add a [Director of Corporate Investments] to its executive staff and figured I would introduce myself.

My name is [name], and I'm the [title] of [financial company]. I've been working with [your boss, boss's name] for over [number] years, handling a number of [your company's] corporate investments. While [your boss] is a terrific person to work with, his role as [CEO] doesn't allow him the luxury of focusing as much attention on [company's] portfolio as he might like, so I was thrilled to hear that he'd added you to the staff.

I would like to meet with you at your earliest convenience to review with you the various investments [your company] currently has with [my firm] and also tell you about a few new products I'm sure you'll be interested in. I'll call you in a few days to determine a time when it might be convenient for me to come by your office.

I look forward to working with you.

Sincerely,

[Name]
[Title]

- When a new title/position is added to a client's staff, there's always the risk that the new person will be looking to bring in her/his own suppliers.

- Remind/advise the new person of the value of the current relationship with your company.

- Offer an in-person visit to update the new person on current issues and new opportunities.

Path on CD-ROM: Current and Former Customers→Changes at client→Introductions→New position-1

Potential product sales opportunity due to change at customer

[Name]
[Company]
[Address]
[City, State ZIP]

Dear [Name]:

Congratulations on the opening of the second [Chez Michel] restaurant!

Now that you'll be serving over [300] diners a day, you'll need a lot more napkins and tablecloths! The good news is your increased customer volume will definitely qualify you for our quantity discount rates on all of our [restaurant linens].

We should get together very soon and work out the exact numbers you expect to be dealing with once the second restaurant is operating at full capacity. I can then put together an estimate for you and offer you some very attractive pricing.

I'll give you a call later this week so we can schedule a meeting. Again, congratulations and my best wishes for continued success!

Sincerely,

[Name]
[Title]

- **An expansion of a client's business can give you the opportunity to offer greater quantity at sharper per-unit prices .**

- **Notice that this letter takes an assumptive position—the writer is assuming (or pretending to assume) that the incremental business is already his/hers. This approach carries with it some risk, but if your current relationship with the client is strong, it should pay off (and may even go unnoticed).**

Path on CD-ROM: Current and Former Customers→Changes at client→New product→Supplier-1

Potential service sales opportunity due to change at customer

[Name]
[Company]
[Address]
[City, State ZIP]

Dear [Name]:

Congratulations on taking the leap! [Your company's] recent announcement that you will be adding an e-commerce division to your existing retail operations is not only exciting but could also be quite profitable.

As we've been your key Web site design and maintenance supplier for the past [number] years, I want to let you know that we can also be your e-commerce supplier. Our company instituted an e-commerce division over [18] months ago, and since that time we've developed entire e-commerce operations for a number of large [retailers, banks, and telecommunications] companies with tremendous success. We can do everything from mapping out your e-commerce business plan, to setting up customer interfaces, to identifying and working with order-fulfillment and tracking services. The programming, the design, the operations—you name it and we do it.

I realize that you may have already begun your review process for an e-commerce business developer, but I'm hoping that we'll have a chance to be a part of that process in light of the terrific work (if I may be so bold!) we've done to date on your current Web site and the great working relationship we've built over the years.

Please give me a call or send me a note and let me know when we can talk about this further. It would be very exciting if we could deepen our relationship in this way.

Sincerely,

[Name]
[Title]

- If you have a good relationship with a current client in one area of business and have the credentials and capabilities to expand the relationship, pursue the opportunity.

- Remind the client of the great work you've done for them, but focus more on the new area of capability—how you've demonstrated your abilities in that area for other clients, results you've achieved, etc.

Path on CD-ROM: Current and Former Customers→Changes at client→New service→Web designer-1

Potential service sales opportunity due to change at customer

[Name]
[Company]
[Address]
[City, State ZIP]

Dear [Name]:

If the rumors in the press have any validity, [your company] may very well be facing litigation from [plaintiff] in the near future.

While this likely situation is not a pleasant one, you can take some comfort in the fact that our Litigation department is among the best in the country. Although to date we've only provided [your company] legal counsel for fairly standard corporate issues, we are prepared to handle any litigation-related work that may come up on this or any other matter.

It would be wise for us to speak about your potential litigation needs and our capabilities as soon as possible. Please call me at your convenience.

Sincerely,

[Name]
[Title]

- If you've only provided one area of service to a client, and suspect that the client will soon be needing a different area that you can provide, jump on the opportunity before it's lost.

- Assure the client that your firm has the expertise necessary for the situation and ask the client to call you before the situation gets out of hand.

Path on CD-ROM: Current and Former Customers→Changes at client→New service→Law firm-1

Prospecting

Prospecting is a specialized form of marketing. Here, you are contacting specific people you believe have reason to be interested in your company and its products or services. Prospecting isn't like general promotion because you have specific knowledge of the person to whom you're writing; yet it's not like contacting known customers, either, because you have no personal knowledge of them. So you need to walk a line between treating the person formally (since you don't know them), but not so formally that you sound like you know nothing about him or her.

Prospecting is also a specific process: you want to make contact with the person, address his or her questions and needs, then end up with someone who is now a customer. This process is common in companies where it takes a lot of time to cultivate customer relationships. Often, too, the relationships involve a degree of formality not seen in retail transactions—such as requiring your company to complete an RFP, or signing a contract to confirm a specific transaction.

The letters in this chapter cover the full range of activities involved in such relationships, from the actual prospecting, to developing contracts (if the client relationship requires such formality), then welcoming the new customers to your company after their first purchases.

There are several common elements to include in any prospecting letter:

1. Be sure to mention how you learned about the person. People are more likely to read a letter, e-mail, or fax if they have reason to believe that it really is targeted at them personally (as opposed to being sent to a mailing list, for instance). Put the source of the reference in the e-mail subject line or in the opening of the letter or fax.
2. Succinctly describe *why* and *how* you think your company (and its products or services) can be of benefit to the reader. Avoid going into too much depth. Remember that generally the purpose of prospecting letters is to generate further contact, such as a phone call or request for information—the purpose is NOT to anticipate every possible question the person might have.
3. Much more so than any other type of communication, the primary goal of prospecting letters is to lead to further action. So you must *always* include information that makes it easy for the customer to take the next step—or plan on taking the next step yourself and say so in the letter ("I'll call you on Friday...").
4. Use the letter to document questions, actions, and decisions, particularly if you are involved in an RFP or negotiation process ("In our phone call today, we decided that ..."). This helps both parties keep track of who knows what.

The last subset of letters in this chapter—contact with new customers or clients—reminds us that our job isn't done just because we've signed up a new customer. Showing your appreciation for their business signals can kick off the relationship on a very positive note, proving to the customer that you *are* paying attention to them.

People you've met

[Name]
[Company]
[Address]
[City, State ZIP]

Dear [   ]:

It was a pleasure meeting you [and spouse] at [location/event] on [date].

I'm writing you because you spoke about [service/product] you're [interested in/considering purchasing/in need of]. I think I can help. I'd be happy to [speak with you/meet with you] in more detail at [my office/your office/your home].

Please give me a call if you think you might be interested in meeting to discuss [my business/service/product]. In the meantime, I encourage you to visit [my/our] Web site, at [www.web-address.com] to get a better idea of the sort of [work/service/product] I/we have [done/provided] for other [clients/customers/applicants].

I look forward to hearing from you. [OR: I'll call you [within short time period].]

Sincerely,

[Name]
[Title]

- **Remind the reader of the circumstances of your meeting and the fact that you spoke about a product or service you can provide.**

- **Suggest that the reader phone you to set up a meeting at your office; meanwhile, direct him/her to your Web site to see examples of your work.**

- **If you prefer, close with a promise that you'll make the first call.**

Path on CD-ROM: Prospecting→Prospecting→People you've met→New→Generic-4

People you've met

[Name]
[Company]
[Address]
[City, State ZIP]

Dear [   ]:

It was a pleasure meeting you [OR you and your spouse OR you and your family] at [event/location] on [date].

I didn't [mention/go into detail] at the time but I wanted you to know that I offer [product/service]. [I/my firm/we] offer a wide range of affordable, [traditional/family-oriented] [products/services] that provide [adjective: large, traditional] families like yours with [emotional/functional benefit].

If it's all right with you, I'd like to [call/visit/follow up with] you [OR you and your spouse] to hear about your concerns and talk to you about how [my company/I] can help [provide solutions/provide answers] to [problem/need]. There's no obligation, of course.

I'll phone you later this week. I look forward to seeing you again.

Sincerely,

[Name]
[Title]

- **Remind the reader of the circumstances of your meeting and mention the product or service you can provide.**

- **Bearing in mind the nature of the "believer" target, point out the traditional/ dependable attributes of your product or service.**

- **Offer to call to set up a meeting at your office at no obligation to the reader.**

Path on CD-ROM: Prospecting→Prospecting→People you've met→New→Generic-5

PROSPECTING SPECIFIC PEOPLE

People you've met

[Name]
[Company]
[Address]
[City, State ZIP]

Dear [   ]:

I'm so glad we bumped into each other while picking up our children from their 4-H Club meeting last week.

I was very pleased and proud to notice that you're still driving the car I sold you nine years ago—it's great to see that Detroit can still make 'em like they used to! But I couldn't help thinking that you might be able to use something a little more roomy now that the kids have gotten bigger and you're driving them around so much—maybe a minivan?

We have a terrific assortment of American-made vehicles, new and used, and I'm offering some terrific year-end incentives right now to help clear out some of the current year's inventory. If you think this might be the right time to trade in the current [brand], give me a call or stop into the dealership.

In any case, I'm sure we'll run into each other again soon at church or a PTA meeting! Until then,

Sincerely,

[Name]
[Title]

- **Open with a reminder of your recent (unplanned) meeting with the reader.**

- **Link an observation about the reader's current product ownership status with a solution you can provide, bearing in mind the target's preference for dependable, practical products and no-nonsense sales approaches.**

- **Suggest that the reader call or visit your place of business.**

Path on CD-ROM: Prospecting→Prospecting→People you've met→Old→Car dealer-2

People you've met

TO: [Name@company.com]

FROM: [Name]

SUBJECT: Great to meet you [last week]!

Dear [   ]:

I enjoyed meeting you at the [Combined Insurers Meeting] and thought about our lunch conversation [on the plane flight all the way home].

Yesterday I approached our president about having our independent agency handle your policy for equipment maintenance insurance in our state. He agrees that our business customers would be very interested in your policy. They would appreciate the opportunity to buy one insurance policy in place of the myriad service and repair contracts for equipment such as copiers, computers, and telephone systems.

We would like to schedule a conference call with you and the head of your division to discuss the next steps in a partnership to promote your policy here. Would the afternoon of [Friday the 18th] work for you? Please call to confirm a time or suggest an alternate date.

Sincerely,

[Name]
[Title]

- **Introduction demonstrates that the reader made quite an impact on the writer.**

- **Close is a request to proceed to the next step.**

People you've met

[Date]
[Name]
[Company]
[Address]
[City, State ZIP]

Dear [   ]:

Thank you for stopping by our booth at the recent [Midwest Ultimate Internet Show].

As promised, I am enclosing information on how [N-TICED] redesigned the Web sites for [three] businesses that are very similar to yours. While they differ in size, each appeals to computer-savvy Gen X professionals and their children.

You can see these sites for yourself at [www.company1.com], [www.company2.com], and [www.company3.com].

We could easily design and maintain your Web site, providing an interactive and attention-getting way to explain and sell your products to this audience. Your new sales likely would more than cover the costs of redesigning your site. That is what happened in all [three] of the enclosed cases.

If you would like our company to develop a proposal for redesigning your Web site—a proposal in your price range—please call me at [800-555-5555].

We would enjoy working with you to make your Web site more customer friendly and interactive.

Sincerely,

[Name]
[Title]

- **Opening maintains the personal interaction begun at the show.**

- **Case studies help explain how this company could help the prospect.**

Path on CD-ROM: Prospecting→Prospecting→People you've met→Conference follow-ups→Web designer-1

People referred to you

[Date]
[Name]
[Company]
[Address]
[City, State ZIP]

Dear [   ]:

A colleague sent me an e-mail message today and mentioned that [she] is a member of your board of directors, which is seeking a facilitator to lead a retreat for directors and officers. My colleague also reported that [she] had recommended my services to you.

For many years I have led strategic planning retreats around the country and have written several articles on the topic, which have appeared in leading business publications. My active client list includes [company], [company], [company], and [company], as well as corporations in other industries.

I am interested in learning more about your needs. If you think that I can help, please call me at [555-5555]. I would be pleased to send you a detailed resume.

[Enclosed is my most recent article, which appeared in *Business Planning Today* just last month.]

Sincerely,

[Name]
[Title]

- **Explain the source of your information.**
- **Provide a brief overview of your services; entice the reader with an offer of additional information.**

Path on CD-ROM: Prospecting→Prospecting→To referrals→Facilitator-1

People referred to you

TO: [Name@company.com]

FROM: [Name]

SUBJECT: [Contact's name] suggested I write

Dear [   ]:

My colleague, [contact's name], sent me an e-mail message today mentioning that [she/he] is a member of your board of directors. [She/he] said you are seeking a facilitator to lead a retreat for directors and officers and that [she/he] had recommended my services to you.

I've led strategic planning retreats around the country and have written several articles on the topics. You can find samples of these online at my Web site, [www.me.com]. My active client list includes [company], [company], [company], and [company], as well as corporations in other industries.

I'd love to hear more about what your needs are because I enjoy working with organizations like yours. Could you contact me at this e-mail address or phone [555-5555].

Sincerely,

[Name]
[Title]

- With so much junk e-mail around these days, you can usually get through by just mentioning the contact's name in the subject line.

- Explain how you know the contact, then quickly get to the purpose of the e-mail in the first paragraph.

- The style of this e-mail is a little briefer and less formal than the letter.

Path on CD-ROM: Prospecting→Prospecting→To referrals→Facilitator-2

People referred to you

[Name]
[Title]
[Organization]
[Address]
[City, ST ZIP]

Dear [Name]:

I know what it's like to work hard to start up your own business. I think that's why our mutual friend and I discovered we had so much in common when we bumped into each other last week. [S/he] said you were in a bind because your business was going great, but you were run ragged having to do everything yourself. [S/he] thought my company [Associated Accounting] might be able to help.

[Associated Accounting specializes in the accounting needs of small businesses. We can streamline your purchasing, accounting, and payroll record keeping, saving you time and money in the process. I started the company [##] years ago and built it from the ground up. Everyone I hire has worked in small companies as well, so we know what you're going through. Our experienced professionals have an unsurpassed reputation for helping small businesses like yours, and we have the references to prove it.]

Perhaps we could meet over breakfast or lunch to discuss your accounting needs. I'll call in a few days to try to set up something, or you can reach me at [Associated Accounting, 555-5555]. If nothing else, I'd be happy to give you a few pointers that may make your life easier!

Looking forward to meeting you.

Sincerely,

[Name]
[Title]

- **The first paragraph provides the justification for writing; the second paragraph spells out the credentials.**

- **The actual benefit from relationship building may not appear for months or years down the road, so the closing offer to give the reader pointers leaves the door open for you to establish a personal relationship even if nothing comes of a professional relationship right away.**

Path on CD-ROM: Prospecting→Prospecting→To referrals→Accounting-1

PROSPECTING SPECIFIC PEOPLE

People referred to you

[Name]
[Company]
[Address]
[City, State ZIP]

Dear [   ]:

[George Birch], one of my favorite clients, just called to tell me that he was leaving the [Happy Toy Company] to pursue an exciting new business opportunity of his own. He also mentioned that you'll be taking over his old spot. Congratulations!

As I'm sure George mentioned, my firm has been supplying the [ball bearings] to [Happy Toy] for over twenty years, and the relationship between our two companies has been a most productive one. Since [Happy] is one of our most important customers, I know we both want to make this transition a smooth one.

I'm sure you'll want to be brought up to speed on our product line once you've settled into the new post. I'll give you a call in a couple of weeks to schedule a time for us to meet. I look forward to working with you in your new position.

Sincerely,

[Name]
[Title]

- **When a client leaves, you may have to resell yourself to his successor.**

- **If the relationship with the old client was positive, state that in your letter; make it difficult for the new (potential) client to even consider replacing you.**

Path on CD-ROM: Prospecting→Prospecting→To referrals→Manufacturer-2

Cold letters to targets

[Name]
[Company]
[Address]
[City, State ZIP]

Dear [   ]:

As a former employee of your company, I still keep in touch with many current staff members and was interested to hear about plans for constructing the addition we had first discussed a year and a half ago. Now that I operate my own carpentry and remodeling firm, I would be interested in learning more about your ideas for the addition.

Since leaving the company I have completed additions for [company], [company], and [company], as well as several remodeling projects for other businesses.

I would appreciate the opportunity to provide an estimate for your addition and will phone you in a few days to discuss the possibility.

Sincerely,

[Name]
[Title]

- **Keep in touch with former employers and clients as sources of future projects and referrals.**

- **Provide an update on your experience since leaving your former employer.**

Path on CD-ROM: Prospecting→Prospecting→Cold letters to targets→Construction-2

Cold letter to targeted person

[Date]

[Name]
[Title]
[Company]
[Address]
[City, State ZIP]

Dear [   ]:

Welcome to [Mercury City!] We hope you will be very happy living and doing business here.

I'm enclosing several things I think you might find interesting as a newcomer to the area: [a detailed street map, a chamber of commerce newsletter, and a card for a free introductory subscription to the *Hometown Press*].

I'll give you a call sometime soon to see if I can take you to my favorite [Mercury City] restaurant for lunch. In the meantime, if I can be of any help to you as you get settled, please give me a call. Again, welcome!

Sincerely,

[Name]
[Title]

- **Focus on welcoming not selling.**

- **Offer help getting settled, and say you'll follow up with the prospect soon.**

Path on CD-ROM: Prospecting→Prospecting→Cold letters to targets→Potential client-1

Cold letter to targeted person

TO: [Name@company.com]

FROM: [Name]

SUBJECT: Interested in Wellness?

Dear [   ]:

Your purchase of our other wellness publications prompts me to forward to you information on a new book, [*Wellness the Easy Way: 97 Tips for Improved Health*]. The author, [Dr. Miles K. Jones, teaches at [Name] university hospital and explains what he has learned about making healthy living a part of your normal lifestyle—without extra effort].

There is no need to spend your precious dollars and time scouring health food stores or organic food markets. [Dr. Jones provides simple suggestions anyone can use at the grocery store, doctor's office, and even on the job to improve your lifestyle. Dr. Jones addresses questions like: How to prevent weight gain as you get older? Do good athletic shoes have to be expensive? and Can you control your own blood pressure?]

[Dr. Jones's] advice can help you stay well and save on all of the costs associated with not operating at your best—including stress and dissatisfaction as well as doctors' bills, prescriptions, and processed foods.

For more information, e-mail [wellnessdoc@healthscan.com] or phone [800-888-8888].

- **The e-mail promotion is brief and to the point.**
- **The e-mail promotion is not a hard sell.**
- **The e-mail message is targeted to people who previously have indicated an interest in this type of product.**

Cold letter to targeted person

[Date]
[Name]
[Company]
[Address]
[City, State ZIP]

Dear [   ]:

The Web content you create is terrific—the Web sites I program also are outstanding. Let's work together to provide clients a seamless team, and to make ourselves some additional profit.

Here's what I propose:

If it's your client originally, you'll be the point person for all the administration. You hire me to do the HTML work and mark up my services. This way you'll make money on an additional piece of these projects.

In turn, if it's my client originally, I'll be the point person for all the administration. I'll hire you to develop the content and mark up your services. This way I'll make money on an additional piece of these projects.

Are you interested? We could certainly develop my initial proposal further and run it by our lawyers before we formalize it. It seems like a potential win-win situation to me. I'll give you a call next week to follow up.

Sincerely,

[Name]
[Title]

- **Show what the professional has to gain from the deal.**

- **Use flattery gently to soften the beginning of the letter.**

Path on CD-ROM: Prospecting→Prospecting→Cold letters to targets→Web design-1

Hello. Is [CUSTOMER] in?

My name is [NAME] and I am calling to invite you and your company to participate in our [Community Foundation Scholarship Auction] on [April 19]. This is the [seventeenth] year that our auction will raise funds to help [three local high-school seniors attend the college of their choice].

Are you familiar with the auction?

(YES)

Good. I am hoping you will donate [a basket of gourmet foods and wine from your wonderful inventory of specialty food and beverages]. Your gift is tax deductible, and we will list your company in all of our publicity for the auction. [As a donor, you will receive two free tickets to the auction at Macy's Restaurant on the 19th.]

Do you think you can donate a [basket] to help our students?

(YES)

Wonderful. May a member of our volunteer auction committee stop by to pick up your [basket on Monday]?

Thank you very much. The volunteer will also deliver a letter to document your tax deduction and [your two complimentary tickets to the auction].

(NO)

I am sorry to hear that. If you change your mind, please call me at [333-3333]. And have a great day.

- **The first question is designed to lead the donor into providing positive responses to the caller. (A no response to the first question would provide an opportunity to describe the event in greater detail.)**

- **Close reminds the donor of the personal advantages resulting from the gift.**

Trial or charter offer

[Name]
[Company]
[Address]
[City, State ZIP]

Dear [   ]:

All over the world, college administrators are getting smarter about money. They're educating themselves about financial planning because they must improve their know-how to help their institutions survive.

It hasn't been easy, until now. [*Fundraising Alert*] is a newsletter created to help you improve your college's bottom-line financial stability without compromising academic quality. It's designed to get beyond financial planning theory to practical ideas that have worked on other campuses.

You are one of roughly 1,000 administrators selected to receive TWO FREE ISSUES of this new valuable resource. You have an opportunity to test [*Fundraising Alert*] for FREE.

You soon will receive a Subscription Continuation Certificate inviting you to subscribe to the next 12 monthly issues at the charter subscription rate of [$99]. Whether or not you continue your subscription, the first two issues are yours to keep.

Or, you can begin saving immediately by subscribing now: Send money with your order and pay only [$89].

Don't miss this opportunity to subscribe to [*Fundraising Alert*] and increase your worth to your institution. Subscribe today while you're thinking about it.

Sincerely,

[Name]
[Editor and Publisher]
P.S. If after reading the enclosed free issue you believe [*Fundraising Alert*] will not help you be more effective in your job, please pass it to a colleague who may find it more useful.

- **Marketing research has shown that adding a postscript often boosts a letter's response rate.**

- **The close gets to the point: it asks for the order.**

Path on CD-ROM: Prospecting→Prospecting→Trial offers→Fundraiser-1

Trial or charter offer

[Name]
[Address]
[City, State ZIP]

Dear [Name]:

Pop quiz: When was the last time your living room was really neat? How many dust bunnies do you have hiding under your bed? Are your windows a little less than crystal clear?

If so, give [Neat-n-Clean] a call today! We'll stop by, vacuum cleaner in hand, and give you a FREE TRIAL DEMONSTRATION. That's right! Pay nothing and get one room cleaned FOR FREE!

How long has it been since you cleaned UNDER your refrigerator? Do you have handprints on the hallway walls from when your kids were in kindergarten? Don't you think you should get them off before they graduate from high school?

[Neat-n-Clean]. Your friendly, FAST, and professional home cleaning service. Call today, and breathe easy tomorrow knowing your home has never been so clean! Dial [555-5555] now!

Sincerely,

[Name]
[Title]

P.S. Don't forget that FREE IN-HOME DEMONSTRATION. We even do windows! Call [Neat-n-Clean] at [555-5555] now!

- **Repeat the company name and phone number three times, and even more often if you can fit it in.**

- **Use the P.S. to really push the kicker—the free demonstration.**

Path on CD-ROM: Prospecting→Prospecting→Trial offers→Cleaning-1

Follow up to initial contact

[Date]
[Name]
[Company]
[Address]
[City, State ZIP]

Dear [   ]:

Thank you for letting me know you ordered your new [photocopier] from another company.

It is unusual for customers to let a salesperson know exactly where they stand. I really am grateful to you for telling me.

I know that [Multiples Inc.] can meet your future needs. I'm sending you information about our [copier toner recycling program and also Multiple copier model 8530, which has the reduction and enlargement capabilities you were considering but chose not to purchase this time].

If you have any questions about the products and services [Multiples] offers, please don't hesitate to contact me.

Thanks again for the opportunity to serve you. I hope we can do business in the future.

Sincere regards,

[Name]
[Title]

- **Use this letter to "keep the door open" with this potential customer.**

- **Show your strong interest in doing business in the future.**

Path on CD-ROM: Prospecting→Prospecting→After initial contact→Lost sale-1

Follow up to initial contact

[Date]
[Name]
[Title]
[Company]
[Address]
[City, State ZIP]

Dear [   ]:

Earlier this week I was going through our files and realized we had not followed up with you on our letter inviting you to buy [Sure-Pump replacement parts] from us.

I realize that several months have gone by since we originally talked, so I am attaching the original information we had discussed. Please take the time to look it over. We are confident that these [parts will last longer than those made by other manufacturers]. In addition, our prices are extremely competitive.

I will call you next week after you have had time to review the information. I would be glad to set up an appointment at that time or to answer any questions you may have.

Thank you.

Sincerely,

[Name]
[Title]

- **Take responsibility for the long time with no contact; do not blame the contact!**
- **Send information and say when you'll follow up.**

Path on CD-ROM: Prospecting→Prospecting→After initial contact→Cold prospect-1

Getting an appointment

[Date]
[Name]
[Company]
[Address]
[City, State ZIP]

Dear [   ]:

What's the main reason you haven't invested in time management training for your employees? Is it …

- a lack of time?

- a lack of commitment from management?

- a lack of ability to pull employees from their regular duties?

What if I told you that I provide a time management training that wouldn't cost you anything up front, make management put up a red flag, or take away from employees' work time? Would you call me?

Please do. I promise I'll only take five minutes of your time to explain how [company]'s training is ideal for you. Only if you're still interested after five minutes will we keep talking.

Sincerely,

[Name]
[Title]

- **Recognize and respond to the potential problems faced by training managers.**

- **Make a deal about how long you get to pitch before the trainer gets to say yes or no.**

Path on CD-ROM: Prospecting→Prospecting→Cold letters for appointment→Training-1

Getting an appointment

[Name]
[Address]
[City, State ZIP]

Dear [   ]:

I just read in [trade journal] that you've been appointed [Media Supervisor] on the [Snowblaster Snowmobiles] account. Congratulations!

Since you'll be a critical media-planning decision-maker on this major piece of business, you and I really need to talk.

As you may already know, you can't plan an ad campaign for [snowmobiles] without making [*Snowmobiling Monthly*] the cornerstone of your plans, so I know our book will be a crucial part of your print effort.

What you might not be aware of, however, is the amazing array of merchandising options that we at [*Snowmobiling Monthly*] can put together for our advertisers: merchandising and promotion packages that make your client's product visible everywhere in the world of [snowmobiling], banners on our own Web site that are seen by every devoted [snowmobiler] in the United States, and more. All of which will let you bring innovative ideas to your management and client and really make [Snowblaster] stand out from the pack.

I'd like to spend just 15 minutes taking you through some of the innovative added-value packages we've put together for other advertisers in the category—and start brainstorming some original ideas for [Snowblaster]. If your schedule is too crazy to meet in the office, we can do it over lunch—my treat, naturally. I'll call you later this week to set a time.

I look forward to meeting you.

Sincerely,

[Name]
[Title]

- **Use a specific hook, such as congratulating the prospect on a recent appointment or promotion, to get your foot in the door.**

- **Show how your product/service/ publication will make the prospect's professional life better and enhance his/her reputation.**

- **Propose options for a first meeting (in the prospect's office, over lunch, etc.).**

Path on CD-ROM: Prospecting→Prospecting→Cold letters for appointment→Sales-1

Requesting an RFP

[Name]
[Title]
[Organization]
[Address]
[City, State ZIP]

Dear [Name]:

A friend of mine, whom I believe you know—[name]—informed me that your company is in the process of securing bids for a new [management] training program you hope to get started in the spring. I would like to receive a copy of the RFP and get any additional information you have about your training needs.

[Casey Training] is a [xx-year old] firm specializing in [custom] training programs for companies of all sizes. [We cover a broad range of managerial skills, including planning, budgeting, communication, coaching, decision-making, data analysis, trend analysis, and problem solving. Our experienced trainers are supported by a team of talented instructional and graphic designers, writers, and computer specialists. This allows us to produce high-quality, dynamic programs tailored to your company's needs.]

Please send a copy of the RFP to me at the address shown in our letterhead, or you can fax it to me [201-555-5555]. I'd like to call and speak with you about [writer's company] and our capabilities in the near future if I may.

Sincerely,

[Name]
[Title]

- **You'll have a better chance of getting in the door if you develop a personal relationship with the decision-makers, so follow up the letter with a phone call (unless the RFP specifically says no calls).**

- **Though the company isn't going to make a decision based on infor-mation you put in the letter, it doesn't hurt to provide a little background to help make your and your company's names familiar.**

- **Include some way for the company to follow up—a business card, phone number, Web site address, brochure, etc.**

Path on CD-ROM: Prospecting→Prospecting→Requesting RFP→ Training-1

Requesting an RFP

[Name]
[Title]
[Organization]
[Address]
[City, State ZIP]

Dear [Name]:

Thanks for taking the time to talk with me over the phone today. Sounds like you have a lot going on with starting up your new business!

I spoke with our management team after our conversation, and everyone is very excited about the possibility of having [PayTime] handle your [payroll] needs. Our client representatives have all been in the business at least five years and know the ins and outs of how to establish a comprehensive, accurate, and easy to use payroll accounting system. I'm sure [company] can benefit from [PayTime's] expertise!

I look forward to receiving the RFP you've developed. I'll try to give you a call early next week to clear up any questions my team might have and to make an appointment when we can meet in person.

It was a pleasure speaking with you earlier, and I look forward to getting a chance to get better acquainted with [company].

Sincerely,

[Name]
[Title]

- **This letter confirms a previous phone call and provides additional information.**

- **Mentioning the RFP is a way to gently remind the reader to send it to you.**

Path on CD-ROM: Prospecting→Prospecting→Requesting RFP→ Payroll-1

PROSPECTING SPECIFIC PEOPLE

Responding to customer inquiry about proposal

[Name]
[Title]
[Organization]
[Address]
[City, State ZIP]

Dear [Name]:

Thanks for [sending the e-mail yesterday] asking if it would be possible for us to shorten the turnaround time for [project type] from [6 months] to [4 months]. While we are hesitant to cut corners because we don't want to compromise our quality, I pulled together our [design team] and did some quick brainstorming—and I think we have a solution!

[As you are probably aware, the communication back and forth between client and vendor is one of the most time-consuming aspects in a project like this. What we propose is that we send our design team to your location for two solid weeks at the start the project, followed by another two-week period where your people come work with us here. We think this close collaboration will benefit the project greatly and allow us to reach workable solutions to your challenges in a very timely manner.]

I'll be very curious to see how you react to this somewhat unorthodox proposal—our team is very enthusiastic about having the opportunity to get to know our customers up close and personal! I'll call you in the next day or two to describe a little more about what we have in mind and answer any questions you might have. In fact, if you want to raise this issue with your team, I'd be glad to schedule a conference call [early next week] when all the key players could discuss this idea at the same time.

I look forward to speaking with you soon.

Sincerely,

[Name]
[Title]

- **Thank the client for giving you an opportunity to revise a bid; after all, they could have just gone with another supplier.**

- **Keep the description of your proposed solution fairly brief, then follow up with a phone call to provide additional details.**

Path on CD-ROM: Prospecting→Prospecting→Customer queries→Timeline-1

Responding to customer inquiry about proposal

[Name]
[Address]
[City, State ZIP]

Dear [Name]:

Thanks for calling today to inquire about [company's] ability to customize our training to your needs. We are more than willing to do so, and have several options I'd like to discuss with you:

- First, the proposal we sent you [last week] includes what we like to call a "tailoring" level of customization. This is an approach where we use our standard [training materials] but work with the client to insert your own case studies and examples wherever appropriate. That way, the participants can more easily relate the materials to their own jobs.

- Second, we can, if you like, develop a fully customized training program where all of the course topics and materials are designed especially for your company. Typically, we start again from our standardized programs, toss out anything you feel doesn't pertain to your employees, develop entirely new modules for topics that may not be there already, and incorporate as many examples from your company as possible. The whole package is then evaluated by our instructional designers who will recommend a particular design and sequence for the course as a whole.

The fully customized approach naturally adds to the expense and to the up-front time (though it can happen in as little as [a month] if we coordinate our resources). But many of our clients feel the investment was well worth it since their employees get exactly the training they need in a manner that makes it easy for them to translate that training into on-the-job skills and abilities. In fact, I'd be happy to give you the names and phone numbers of several of our clients who have chosen the customization route so you could talk with them about their experiences.

I'll call you soon to follow up. Until then, feel free to call or e-mail me at any time.

Best regards,

[Name]
[Title]

- **However, if the client asks for a substantial change in the timeline or process, you don't want to say an unqualified, immediate yes because you don't want to give the impression that you were holding back on the initial proposal (e.g., "If you knew you could do it in one month, why did you say two in your proposal?"). So in your response allude to the extra effort or special accommodations you've made to ensure you could do what the client wants.**

Path on CD-ROM: Prospecting→Prospecting→Customer queries→Customization-2

Cover letter with proposal

[Name]
[Company]
[Address]
[City, State ZIP]

Dear [   ]:

We are submitting the enclosed proposal to [provide total quality management training to administrators of the Western Region Firefighters Association in response to your recent RFP #8714. We can offer on-site instruction by an experienced team of TQM facilitators who have worked with scores of organizations over the past decade].

As the proposal demonstrates, we have established an excellent record in [facilitating continuous improvement processes in diverse organizations, including more than a dozen security and firefighters associations. Post-training surveys of participants have shown that most rate our instructors at the A or A+ level and indicate they can easily apply what they have learned to their work situations.]

[We strengthen the on-site training experience with PowerPoint and video presentations, and manuals including all graphic materials are available for participants who miss a session or two. Participants report that the manuals are also a useful reference in later applying the TQM tools they have learned in our workshops.]

We are eager to meet your administrative staff members and begin putting our knowledge to work for the [Western Region Firefighters Association].

Sincerely,

[Name]
[Title]

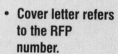

- **Cover letter refers to the RFP number.**

- **Letter summarizes key selling points of the proposal.**

Path on CD-ROM: Prospecting→Prospecting→Cover letter with proposal→Training firm-1

Questions about the RFP

FAX

Page 1 of 1

[Name]
[Company]
[Address]
[City, State ZIP]

Dear [   ]:

We recently received a copy of your RFP #[01-AC12] to secure [process improvement training]. It is unclear to us exactly how many employees you plan to put through this training. Is it just your main facility in [location], or do you plan to train employees at your other locations as well. If you are training at all sites, do you prefer that it be done simultaneously, or can the training be spread out over several months?

Thank you for your assistance in helping us answer these questions. We look forward to submitting our bid in the near future.

Sincerely,

[Name]
[Title]

- If you have just a few questions, keep the fax short and to the point.

- If you have a lot of questions, you may want to list them on a separate page then call the potential client to work through the questions one by one.

Path on CD-ROM: Prospecting→Prospecting→Questions about RFP→Training firm-1

Revising your proposal

[Name]
[Company]
[Address]
[City, State ZIP]

Dear [   ]:

Thanks for calling me on [day or date] to let me know about the changes you'd like in our proposal. As I understand it, [company] now plans to do the [mid-manager communication skills training] in-house and contract out only the [executive coaching and leadership development] portions of your plan.

Accordingly, we have revised our bid to account for only the [five 3-day training sessions] and [4 days per month of one-on-one coaching] for your top [five] executives. [I've left the timelines as they were in the original proposal, and stated that all the training would be held in your home office. If the plans to hold a special strategic planning retreat go through, let me know and I'll send you a separate proposal to have us coordinate and facilitate the event.]

Thanks again for letting [writer's company] bid on your project. I've enjoyed our conversations and look forward to working with you in the future.

Sincerely,

[Name]
[Title]

- **Put in writing your understanding of the reason for the change in case there is any question later on.**

- **Be clear about what has changed and what hasn't.**

Path on CD-ROM: Prospecting→Prospecting→Revising proposal→Consultant-1

Follow up on proposal

[Date]
[Name]
[Company]
[Address]
[City, State ZIP]

Dear [   ]:

It was a pleasure meeting with you last week. I would like to thank you for giving [XYZ Web Construction Co.] the opportunity to submit a design for your upcoming Web site.

We here at [XYZ] are enthusiastic about your interest in a simple, easy-to-use design that also offers a lot of valuable information.

At our meeting we agreed that [XYZ] would send you a thumbnail design and cost proposal as soon as you send us the detailed specifications for your Web site. We projected that, all told, our proposal would be completed and in your office within [four weeks].

I'll follow up with you when I receive the specifications. At that time, I'll let you know exactly when you can expect our proposal.

If you have any questions, please contact me. I'm here to help in any way I can. Thanks again for this opportunity to work with you.

Sincerely,

[Name]
[Title]

- **Be sure to say thank you for the opportunity to meet.**

- **Be enthusiastic about the project and make sure to invite the potential customer to give feedback.**

Path on CD-ROM: Prospecting→Prospecting→To proposal or bid→Web designer-1

Follow up on proposal

[Name]
[Company]
[Address]
[City, State ZIP]

Dear [   ]:

As we discussed on the phone [last week], the news that [company] is going to [merge] with [company 2] isn't just a rumor any more! The [official merger] will take place on [date].

We're very excited about the change here at [company]. Being closely aligned with [company 2] will make us better able to [describe enhanced capability].

I also wanted to take this opportunity to reaffirm that the merger does not affect [company's] ability to meet the projections in the proposal we recently submitted to [client's company]. We will have the same [staff/production capability], so the conditions outlined in the proposal are unchanged. In fact, we're very hopeful that the merger will allow us to realize even greater [efficiency/effectiveness] so that we are able to serve you better.

Please feel free to call any time if you have questions or concerns. You can reach me at [612-555-5555]. I hope we will hear back about the proposal soon.

Regards,

[Name]
[Title]

- **A letter like this should be preceded by a phone call so the client gets a personal reassurance that everything is still a go with the proposal. The letter is a formality to put the news in writing.**

- **Sound excited about any major changes underway.**

- **Assure the client that, minimally, you are still capable of meeting your proposal or, preferably, that you're in an even better position now to serve them.**

Path on CD-ROM: Prospecting→Prospecting→To proposal or bid→Generic-2

Letter with direct mail package

[TO:]

[FROM:]

[SUBJECT:]

Dear [Name]:

Thank you for visiting our Web site.

Since you visited our site, we hoped you might be interested in finding out more about [WebMagic Ltd.]. We figured the best way for you to learn about what we can do for you is to start by seeing what we've done for other companies like yours. So here's a brief list of the solutions we offer to small businesses, accompanied by links to sites we've designed and/or e-commerce solutions we've come up with for some of our clients:

E-COMMERCE: For [XYZ Inc.], we built an e-commerce model from the ground up. See it in operation at [LINK to www.xyz.com].

WEB DESIGN: [WXY Limited] came to us with a simple desire: develop a new image for the company with a cutting-edge Web site. Check out our response at [LINK to www.wxylimited.com].

ONLINE ADVERTISING: [MegaCom] wanted more than just mere banner ads. Take a look at the online advertising we developed for them at [LINK to site containing ads].

If you like what you see, just imagine what we can do for you. E-mail us at [e-mail address] or call [number].

Sincerely,

[Name]
[Title]

- **If your product/ service is Web-related, use the Web as your direct-mail medium.**

- **Be sure to keep your list of links/examples short and focused, yet cover each area of expertise you offer.**

- **Provide various ways for the prospect to contact you.**

Path on CD-ROM: Prospecting→Prospecting→With direct mail→Web consultant-1

Letter with direct mail package

[Name]
[Company]
[Address]
[City, State ZIP]

Dear [Name]:

You may run the best [sales force] in the world. But even top-level [sales] professionals can only stay on top by staying fresh, keeping up with new techniques, and being put to the test and rising to the challenge.

One of the best ways to keep your high-performance [sales force] ahead of the competition is regular training. And that's probably something that you yourself don't always have time for.

Let us help. We're [Sales Training Associates]. We'll come to your offices and give your team a one-, two-, or three-day seminar covering everything from [sales approaches in the Internet age] to [motivational psychology]. We offer large-group meetings as well as individual tutoring. We're all former [sales reps and sales managers] ourselves, so we know what your people are up against every day.

Not sure a training seminar's the way to go? Take a look at the enclosed videotape. You'll see segments filmed at a variety of actual recent seminars we've given and hear comments from top sales managers who've benefited from our training. Our customers range from [one-person start-ups to Fortune 500 companies]. They all have two things in common: They're in the sales business, and their sales results have improved dramatically after working with us.

Watch the tape and see for yourself. I'll give you a call next week. Thank you.

Sincerely,

[Name]
[Title]

- When selling a performance-oriented service, let the prospect see the performance in action and see/hear comments from satisfied customers.

- Include enough information in the letter to pique the reader's interest, but let the tape do most of the selling.

- Follow up with a phone call after the reader's had ample time to view the tape.

Path on CD-ROM: Prospecting→Prospecting→With direct mail→Training firm-1

Follow up on indication of interest

[Name]
[Company]
[Address]
[City, State ZIP]

Dear [ ]:

Thank you for allowing me to introduce [Better Business Travel]. We are a full-service travel agency specializing in satisfying the unique needs of the business traveler.

As the owner and founder of [Better Business Travel], I have several years experience [arranging corporate travel]. Whether it's [an emergency visit to a key account or a conference involving hundreds of participants coming in from across the world], I've done it before. Now I would like to do it for you.

With more business people hitting the road every day it's tough to find the best deals or a hotel that's where you need it to be. Even a seasoned road warrior hits a snag now and again. Let us take the hassle and stress out of making your travel arrangements.

Isn't it frustrating spending more time on the phone arranging a trip than you'll spend on the plane? That happens because most agencies don't take the time to know their customers. Our proprietary system remembers what you want—the lowest possible airfare, a hotel in midtown, an executive car waiting when you arrive, or never to fly on a specific plane or airline. You won't have to tell us twice!

We offer monthly billing (credit approval required) with an itemized statement tailored to meet your company's accounting requirements. And twice a year we'll provide a summary of your travel and make recommendations on how to save you money.

Your business is special and we know it! Please call us at [(603) 555-1233] and find out how ours is special, too.

Call us the next time you need to travel for business and we'll show you that we mean business! We guarantee your total satisfaction.

Sincerely,

[Name]
[Title]

Path on CD-ROM: Prospecting→Prospecting→To indication of interest→Travel agency-1

PROSPECTING SPECIFIC PEOPLE

Follow up on indication of interest

[Date]

[Name]
[Company]
[Address]
[City, State ZIP]

Dear [   ]:

Thank you for requesting information about [Light Right's window blinds]. I'm happy to enclose our current general brochure.

Would you send me information about your company? I would like to provide you with information more specific to your needs.

I will call you early next week to answer any questions you may have. Thanks again for your interest.

Sincerely,

[Name]
[Title]

- **An exchange of information can be an excellent sales strategy.**

- **Because you are enclosing materials, don't give too many product details in the letter.**

Path on CD-ROM: Prospecting→Prospecting→To indication of interest→Window-1

Follow up on indication of interest

[Date]
[Name]
[Title]
[Company]
[Address]
[City, State ZIP]

Dear [   ]:

Thanks for visiting our store last week. I enjoyed showing you our line of [dining room sets].

To help you in your decision, you might like to read the following Q&A about the features and benefits of the sets we offer.

[What woods are available?]
[Most designs are available in teak, oak, cherry, and maple.]
[What designs are available?]
[Queen Elizabeth, Princesa, and Classic Line.]
[What makes these tables stand out?]
[These tables are hand crafted, made to your exact dimension specifications.]
[How long will delivery of our order take?]
[Most table orders can be completed in six to eight weeks.]

You will almost certainly have more questions. Please feel free to call me at [555/555-2833] or stop by the showroom. I'll be glad to help you.

Thanks again for your interest.

Sincerely,

[Name]
[Title]

- Use a question and answer format to make the letter easy to read and to get the potential customer thinking about the product.

- Offer to answer additional questions.

Path on CD-ROM: Prospecting→Prospecting→To indication of interest→Furniture-1

PROSPECTING SPECIFIC PEOPLE

Follow up on indication of interest

[Name]
[Company]
[Address]
[City, State ZIP]

Dear [   ]:

Thank you for your response to our advertisement in the [*Wall Street Journal*]. Our outdoor trips for women offer busy professionals like yourself an opportunity to relax while enriching your life through camping, hiking, skiing, snowshoeing, canoeing, and kayaking experiences across the United States.

You indicated that you want to take a vacation in [August] and have always wanted to explore the [Boundary Waters Canoe Area of northern Minnesota]. We have a [canoe trip scheduled for August 15 through 22 in cooperation with Grand Marais Outfitters that would give you an entire week to explore the waters and wildlife of this area. This trip is for both experienced and inexperienced paddlers, with two guides and a naturalist to point out features of the terrain, water birds, and other animals.]

A somewhat different experience is set for [Aug. 23-30], when another group leaves from [Grand Marais on a sea kayaking trip on Lake Superior]. This trip requires previous kayaking experience.

Enclosed are brochures covering the details on both of these trips, as well as a list of all trips planned for [August]. If you have questions about any of these trips or would like to reserve your space on one of the above [Minnesota] trips, please write or call [800/999-5555].

I appreciate your interest in outdoor trips for women.

Regards,

[Name]
[Title]

P.S. I am looking forward to meeting you on one of our canoeing or kayaking journeys soon.

- **The letter zeroes in on the customer's specific interest areas.**

- **The postscript personalizes the communication.**

Path on CD-ROM: Prospecting→Prospecting→To indication of interest→Outdoors trip-1

Arranging a tour or visit

[Date]
[Name]
[Company]
[Address]
[City, State ZIP]

Dear [   ]:

How secure is your store? Do you worry about break-ins during off hours? Can someone climb into your back windows or pry the emergency exit door open? How long has it been since you've taken a good hard look at your burglar alarms, fire alarms, or closed-circuit TV monitors?

You may not know the real answers to these questions, or even how to answer them. But we do.

We're [Securi-T Safety Systems], the [tri-state area's] most dependable security company, providing the highest quality security equipment and installations available for over [20] years. We've just opened a [downtown] location, and as our way of getting to know our new neighbors, we're offering FREE, no-obligation security consultations this month.

With your agreement, one of our lead security consulting teams will spend about 15 to 30 minutes with you, walking through your store, inspecting your current alarm system, and pointing out "danger zones" within the building such as open windows, faulty locks, and other chinks in your security armor. Should you decide, after the free consultation, that you'd like to sign on with [Securi-T], we'll custom-design a security system for your business that will let you sleep easier. If you decide not to hire us, that's fine, too—this is truly a no-obligation offer.

I'll call you later this week to determine a good time for one of our bonded security consulting teams to visit.

Sincerely,

[Name], [Title]

P.S. Remember, there's no obligation to purchase anything, so why not find out just how secure your current system truly is—at no cost to you?

- **When your business can only be done by visiting customers' premises, a strong introductory letter is key.**

- **Without being exploitative, point out ways that the prospect's current situation might be flawed, leaving the door open for you to make a sale after the proposed visit.**

- **End with a reminder that the visit is without obligation and has value in and of itself.**

Path on CD-ROM: Prospecting→Prospecting→Tours or visits→Security-1

Arranging a tour or visit

[Date]
[Name]
[Company]
[Address]
[City, State ZIP]

Dear [   ]:

Welcome to the neighborhood!

I'm [name], and I provide custom carpentry services. Many of the families in this elegant old neighborhood have hired me to do various woodworking projects to make their homes as beautiful on the inside as they so clearly are on the outside.

If it's all right with you, I'd like to arrange a time to meet with you and take a walk with you through your house. We can talk about the sort of work the house could use and how I could help provide it, whether it's cabinets, trim work, decking, remodeling, or even custom furniture. I provide expert craftsmanship at very competitive prices.

I realize you're still settling in, so I'll give you a call a bit later this month to see when we might be able to get together. I live right down the street myself, so perhaps we'll bump into each other in the meantime!

I look forward to meeting you.

Sincerely,

[Name]
[Title]

P.S. Since I've done work for so many of your neighbors, I'll be happy to provide references, either before or after our initial meeting.

- **Staying on top of potential new prospects is critical.**

- **Be friendly, offering your services and help rather than trying to sell something.**

- **If appropriate, allow a bit of time to lapse after your letter; this is OK if you've said you would wait a while before calling. (Just don't forget to call!)**

Path on CD-ROM: Prospecting→Prospecting→Tours or visits→Carpenter-1

Arranging a tour or visit

[Date]
[Name]
[Company]
[Address]
[City, State ZIP]

Dear [   ]:

If you're considering an off-site meeting, planning session, or seminar for your top executives and selected clients, you owe it to yourself to visit [Westchester Corporate Retreats].

Our facilities are superior to those of most inns, ballrooms, or hotel meeting rooms because they were designed specifically for the purpose of hosting executive-level meetings. Each room comes equipped with the latest presentation equipment, speaker phones, fax machines and computers, and audio and video components. All of our seminar rooms are also equipped with all the "old-fashioned" basics including easels, large-size pads, cork-boards, push pins, markers, pads, pens, and pencils. We provide on-premises catering and, should you require it, overnight accommodations. There's even a tennis court and swimming pool for activity breaks between sessions.

I'd like to invite you to come to [Westchester] so that I can personally give you a tour through our facilities and show you the wide variety of room styles and sizes we can offer you, for any gathering from the smallest meeting to the largest all-staff conference. Since you'll need at least an hour to see our place, I'd like to invite you to either lunch or dinner in conjunction with your tour.

I'll call you next week to set a time. If you prefer to make the call, I can be reached at [number] from [8:00 A.M. to 6:00 P.M., Monday through Friday].

I look forward to meeting you and showing you [Westchester Corporate Retreats] very soon.

Sincerely,

[Name]
[Title]

- **Provide enough information about your location to pique the reader's interest in arranging a visit.**

- **Acknowledge that you're asking for a bit of a time commitment, so offer a meal or some other token of gratitude for the reader's trouble.**

Path on CD-ROM: Prospecting→Prospecting→Tours or visits→Seminar center-1

PROSPECTING SPECIFIC PEOPLE

Arranging a tour or visit

[Date]
[Name]
[Company]
[Address]
[City, State ZIP]

Dear [   ]:

Can you believe it's almost Christmas already?

While there are certain Christmas chores that can be put off until the last minute, selecting your tree isn't one of them. So I'd like to invite you to come down to [Barn Hill Trees] this week and take a tour through our beautiful nursery.

We'll escort you through our extensive mini-forests of pine, spruce, fir, and yew. And if you find the perfect tree for your house during your tour, we can give you the option of cutting it yourself or having one of our nursery experts cut it for you.

Please give us a call at [number] to schedule a time for your tour. We're open seven days a week between now and Christmas, from [10 A.M. through 8 P.M.]

Sincerely,

[Name]
[Title]

P.S. Bring this card with you when you come for your tour and we'll take [x%] off the price of ANY tree if you decide to buy that day! Merry Christmas!

- **In this situation, what could be considered the equivalent of a visit to a retailer can be positioned as a tour of the premises; asking the prospect to call for an appointment elevates the visit to a different level.**

- **Use the fact that time is limited to spur a visit in the near future.**

- **Just because the prospect needs to purchase an item in your category within a limited time doesn't mean s/he has to buy it from you; provide an incentive to get the prospect to visit your location.**

Path on CD-ROM: Prospecting→Prospecting→Tours or visits→Nursery-1

Closing letters

[Date]
[Name]
[Company]
[Address]
[City, State ZIP]

Dear [   ]:

Some of my friends refuse to shop discounted clothing retailers. I like to go there and buy name-brand fashions for half the price.

Why won't my friends take advantage of the savings? They are sure that the discounted stores sell lesser quality goods. In fact, they sell only first-rate goods that are leftovers from the even lots the department stores buy.

Moral of the story? A lower price doesn't necessarily mean lower quality.

From our discussions, I'm quite sure that [prospect company] will realize a [amount] savings this year if you choose to buy [product] from [company]. Our [products], while less expensive, are every bit as high quality as those you currently purchase.

The choice is yours—join me in getting name-brands for less. Or spend more for the same product.

Sincerely,

[Name]
[Title]

- **Stress that the product, though less expensive, is of the same quality.**

- **Call for action by giving the prospect a clearly defined choice.**

Path on CD-ROM: Prospecting→Prospecting→Closing letters→Low price, quality-1

PROSPECTING SPECIFIC PEOPLE

Closing letters

[Date]
[Name]
[Company]
[Address]
[City, State ZIP]

Dear [   ]:

Can you believe it is still just regular phone line Web access?

Your research staff couldn't believe the speed they could get when surfing the Internet after our computer jockeys "souped up" a demonstration computer in your office. Sites that once took a minute to load showed up colorful and clear in 20 seconds. Searches that took two minutes to complete punched out the answers in half a minute! Think of the time that will save them—and you.

I'd like to show you what your staff has already seen. There's definitely a reason that they are recommending you hire [company] to work on your computers. I'll call you next week to set up a time for me to personally show you what a "souped up" system can do.

Sincerely,

[Name]
[Title]

- **Use a before and after to demonstrate the reason for buying your product or service.**

- **Offer a personal demonstration to the decision-maker.**

Path on CD-ROM: Prospecting→Prospecting→Closing letters→Before and after-1

Confirming appointments

[Date]
[Name]
[Company]
[Address]
[City, State ZIP]

Dear [   ]:

Thank you for your interest in [company] and our products. As you might know, we are specialists in [specialization] and we can really help your company [achievement].

It would be marvelous to sit down and talk with you as you suggested, [time and date] in your office. I have made careful notes of your areas of interest— [area], [area] and [area]—and will bring the information to our meeting.

You mentioned that you were collecting that data to help [name of decision-maker] make the final decision. May I recommend that you invite [him or her] to this meeting? I'll be providing a lot of information that [s/he] is likely to appreciate hearing first hand.

If you have any questions before the meeting, please feel free to call me. Otherwise, I'll look forward to seeing you and [decision-maker] on the [date]. Thanks again for your interest in [company].

Sincerely,

[Name]
[Title]

- **Explain that you will provide the information being sought.**

- **Suggest that the decision-maker would be happy to be included in this meeting.**

Path on CD-ROM: Prospecting→Prospecting→Appointments→ With decision maker-1

Requesting deadline extension

[Date]
[Name]
[Company]
[Address]
[City, State ZIP]

Dear [   ]:

This morning we received your letter confirming the changes you want to make in the [number, style, and size of the fixtures you want for your new store. The new configurations and added glass will certainly give your store a more upscale and sophisticated look.]

In order to provide you the most precise estimates possible for your revised plans, I am requesting an extension of our deadline. We can submit your bid by [date]. Indeed, we are already working to do so.

Please let me know if the new time frame is acceptable.

We are looking forward to contributing to your business success by [providing our highest quality fixtures for your new store].

Sincerely,

[Name]
[Title]

- **Compliment the requested revisions; do not use a blaming tone or complain about the required changes.**

- **Close with a description of a productive outcome.**

Path on CD-ROM: Prospecting→Prospecting→Deadline extension→Furniture-1

Cover letter with agreement or contract

[Date]
[Name]
[Company]
[Address]
[City, State ZIP]

Dear [   ]:

I am pleased that we have reached such a mutually beneficial agreement to help your company grow to the next level of sales noted in your strategic plan. I have enclosed your signed copy of our contract for business consultation services.

Our team is looking forward to working closely with your staff in establishing new systems and helping your company effectively serve its customers and reach its long-term goals.

Best wishes,

[Name]
[Title]

- **Introduction points to a win-win agreement.**

- **Close reminds the reader of the purpose and promise inherent in the contract.**

Clarifying terms of contract

[Date]

[Name]
[Company]
[Address]
[City, State ZIP]

Dear [   ]:

Thank you for selecting our firm to print your magazine this year. We are excited about producing such a well-respected publication.

As you begin to draft our contract, we want to clarify our terms. [Company] offers [a 2 percent discount on your invoice if payment is received within 30 days of delivery. We hope this policy affords some assistance to your budget.]

We appreciate this opportunity to work with you and will review and return your contract as soon as possible.

Sincerely,

[Name]
[Title]

- Explain your terms in a positive fashion. Some customers are more inclined to pay within 30 days to receive a discount than to avoid an interest charge that begins to accrue after that date.

- Promise to act on the contract as soon as you receive it.

Path on CD-ROM: Prospecting→Contracting→Clarifying contract→Clarifying-1

Confidentiality agreements

[Date]
[Name]
[Company]
[Address]
[City, State ZIP]

Dear [   ]:

This confirms our nondisclosure agreement:

[1. We agree that "confidential information" refers to any company-specific or [product/service]-specific information provided to us by [Company].]

[2. We agree not to use, share, or disseminate any confidential information with vendors, other clients, or anyone else outside our Company.]

[3. We agree to use reasonable care in safeguarding the security of your confidential information.]

[4. We will not publish, copy, or disclose confidential information to any third party and will use reasonable caution in inadvertently disclosing any information to a third party.]

[company]   [name]

Signature _____   Signature _____

Date _____   Date _____

- **Oftentimes a confidentiality clause will simply be included in a contract. But sometimes a customer will want to have one signed before the contract is complete, so it helps to have a standard form available.**

- **All legal documents should be checked by your legal advisor.**

Path on CD-ROM: Prospecting→Contracting→Confidentiality→To client-1

Welcome letter after first purchase

[Name]
[Company]
[Address]
[City, State ZIP]

Dear [   ]:

Thank you for inviting [Cyber World] to redesign your corporate Web site.

Before beginning the task of restructuring your site, my partner and I would like to meet with you [and, if possible, the heads of your sales and product development departments] to discuss your needs from a marketing standpoint. I understand that [a consumer research study you've recently conducted] turned up a number of surprising findings; we'd like to learn more about the study's results as they are certain to be relevant to our site content discussion.

I will call you [later today] to set a time that will work for you [and your colleagues]. We look forward to launching this exciting project.

Sincerely,

[Name]
[Title]

- **Thank the client for his/her business.**

- **Request a meeting with the key contact person and other important members of the client's company.**

- **If there is specific research or other data that will help guide your task, ask that it be shared with you prior to beginning your work.**

Path on CD-ROM: Prospecting→New Client→Welcome and follow-up→Web designer-1

Follow up to first donation

[Name]
[Title]
[Organization]
[Address]
[City, State ZIP]

Dear [Name]:

Thank you for your generous [$100] donation to [Feed the World].

Your selfless contribution represents more than mere generosity on your part. Your donation to [Feed the World] means that five children in the blighted nation of [Franistan] will be provided with three nutritious meals every day for a month.

As you know, the struggle to provide ongoing nutritional care to the children of [Franistan] and other developing countries is an endless one. If you'd be interested in joining our ["Targeted Help 2001"] program, which directs aid to those areas of the world hardest hit by famine and war, please fill out the enclosed form and return it to us in the postage-paid envelope provided. You'll have the option of making one upfront annual contribution, or directing us to automatically bill 12 smaller monthly amounts to the credit card of your choice.

Once again, thank you for supporting the efforts of [Feed the World].

Sincerely,

[Name]
[Title]

- **Thank the contributor for her/his donation.**

- **Give the contributor some specific information about the impact/result of her/his donation.**

- **Provide an easy way for the contributor to upgrade his/ her level of contribution.**

Path on CD-ROM: Prospecting→New Client→Welcome and follow-up→Nonprofit-2

Contact information

[Name]
[Title]
[Organization]
[Address]
[City, State ZIP]

Dear [Name]:

Thank you for selecting [Nationwide Wireless] as your wireless telephone service provider.

We at [Nationwide] are committed to providing our customers with more than simply the nation's highest-quality, most affordable wireless service. We also pride ourselves on having the most helpful and accessible Customer Service team in the business.

Should you need to reach us at any time, just call our toll-free customer service number from anywhere in the U.S. or Canada: [(555) 555-5555]. Or dial [611] from your wireless phone. Either way, you'll be quickly connected to a Customer Service representative who'll do whatever it takes to address your needs.

Thanks again for signing up with [Nationwide].

Sincerely,

[Name]
[Title]

- **Thank the customer for choosing your company.**

- **Briefly mention your company's unique service/product superiority as a confirmation of the customer's wise choice.**

- **Provide specific customer service contact information.**

Path on CD-ROM: Prospecting→New Client→How to contact→Generic-4

Introducing your company

[Name]
[Company]
[Address]
[City, State ZIP]

Dear [   ]:

Thank you for choosing [Safety World] as your homeowner's insurance provider. Your policy is enclosed.

As your agent may have mentioned to you, as a [Safety World] policyholder you're entitled to a free quote on auto insurance. That's right—in addition to insuring your [home], we can also insure your [vehicle]. Your agent will be calling you within [number] days to get the necessary information from you and will then give you [at least two competitive quotes] on a vehicle insurance policy. There's no obligation, but if you decide to insure your [car] with us, you'll automatically get [$ amount] credited toward your next month's home-owner's premium!

Whether or not you choose to go with [Safety World] to insure your vehicle, we're thrilled that you chose us to insure your home. We wish you many years of happiness there and hope you'll turn to us for all your insurance needs.

Sincerely,

[Name]
[Title]

P.S. If you'd prefer, you can even get an auto insurance quote online! Just go to our Web site, [URL], and enter the necessary information. You'll get two free quotes within [15] minutes—with absolutely no obligation!

- **Use a standard "policy enclosed" cover letter to let a new client know about other services you can offer.**

- **Offer a special deal on either the product the customer currently owns or the one you're trying to sell.**

- **Make clear that the customer's business is appreciated whether or not he/she elects to buy the additional service, but make it easy for the customer to buy.**

Path on CD-ROM: Prospecting→New Client→Introduction to company→Insurance-1

NEW CLIENT

Introducing your company

[Name]
[Company]
[Address]
[City, State ZIP]

Dear [   ]:

Thank you for booking your [Rocky Mountains Ski Vacation] with [Rugged Adventure Travel]. We're sure this [ski trip] will be one you'll remember for years, and we're looking forward to meeting you on [date] at [city] airport.

I've taken this opportunity to enclose our complete [2002] catalog along with your [ski trip] confirmation. You might not be aware of this, but [Rugged Adventure Travel] offers a complete range of year-round [outdoor adventure vacations]. We [guide whitewater rafting trips in late spring and early summer], offer [camping and backpacking adventures in early fall], and even have [rock-climbing and mountain-climbing treks in Nepal in November]. All of our trips are designed with the [rugged adventure traveler in mind].

In any event, we hope you're as excited about your upcoming [Rocky Mountains Ski Vacation] as we are. If you have any questions between now and your departure date, don't hesitate to call us at [phone number] any day between [time] and [time]. See you soon!

Sincerely,

[Name]
[Title]

P.S. While on your [ski trip], you can get more information about any of our spring, summer, or fall [adventures] from your guides.

- **Thank the customer and confirm his/her upcoming plans.**

- **Include a catalog and point out highlights in the letter, illustrating the diversity of your offerings.**

- **Close or use a postscript reminding the reader that in-person information will be available.**

Path on CD-ROM: Prospecting→New Client→Introduction to company→Outfitter-1

Thanks for giving us your business

[Name]
[Company]
[Address]
[City, State ZIP]

Dear [   ]:

On behalf of the chef, kitchen crew, wait staff, and management of [Gateway Bistro], thank you for thinking of us as the location for [your parents' 50th anniversary dinner/party] last week.

It was truly a pleasure serving you, your family, and your guests, and we hope to see you again soon, whether for another large affair or an intimate dinner for two.

Sincerely,

[Name]
[Title]

- **This letter thanks the customer after the event has taken place—a perfectly acceptable tactic as long as the letter is sent soon afterward.**

- **Express gratitude and remind the reader that you also offer other services.**

Path on CD-ROM: Prospecting→New Client→Thanks for business→Restaurant-1

Thanks for giving us your business

[Name]
[Company]
[Address]
[City, State ZIP]

Dear [   ]:

Thank you for selecting [Canyon Satellite] as your satellite TV provider.

We know you have a choice of TV operators in the area and that you switched to [Canyon] from another local provider, so we're especially grateful for your business.

We're sure our wide programming selection, crystal-clear reception, and competitive prices will make it difficult to switch away from us! But if you ever have any problem or wish to discuss any aspect of your [Canyon Satellite] service, we want you to know that our customer service specialists are here for you 24 hours a day, 7 days a week. So just give us a call.

Thanks again for choosing [Canyon Satellite].

Sincerely,

[Name]
[Title]

- **Be particularly attentive to customers if your market situation makes it relatively easy to gain and lose customers to competitors.**

- **Reinforce the customer's decision (to switch to your business) by reminding him/her of your superior offerings and service.**

Path on CD-ROM: Prospecting→New Client→Thanks for business→Cable-1

Confirming first service appointment

[Name]
[Address]
[City, State ZIP]

Dear [   ]:

Thank you for asking [ABC Architects] for an initial consultation for your [renovation] project.

In order to help us get to know you even prior to our initial meeting on [date], we would like you [and the other members of your executive committee] to fill out a brief survey. (We've enclosed [ten] copies of the survey for your convenience.) Your filling out the survey in advance will allow us to approach the consultation in a more efficient and helpful manner, as it will familiarize us with your tastes and objectives. Just as important, it will also allow us to rule out various approaches.

Please share the survey with your colleagues and return completed copies to our office by [date]. This will give us approximately [number] days to review it prior to the consultation.

Thank you for your help. We look forward to working with you on this exciting project.

Sincerely,

[Name]
[Title]

- **Thank the client for requesting a consultation.**

- **Confirm the initial meeting date.**

- **Enclose a survey and discuss your objectives—and benefits to the client—in requesting that it be completed.**

NEW CLIENT

Confirming first service appointment

[Name]
[Address]
[City, State ZIP]

Dear [   ]:

Thank you for awarding [JKL Agency] your advertising and public relations assignments. This confirms our "kickoff" meeting date of [date] at [time] at [location].

While we are obviously familiar with [your company's] current [print and broadcast campaign], we often find it helpful to be brought up to speed by new clients on their recent advertising and sales history before beginning our own strategic and creative development. We would therefore like to be able to review the following materials with you at our first meeting:

- [a reel of your past 5 years TV commercials]
- [selected print ads from the past 5 years: an assortment of those you found most effective and least effective]
- [annual reports and other internally developed publications and literature about your company]
- [sales data for the past 5 years]

If you can forward any or all of these materials to us before our first meeting, that would be even more helpful. If not, we'll be happy to go through them together with you at the meeting.

All of us here at [JKL] are very excited about beginning what is sure to be a most productive working relationship. We look forward to seeing you on the [date].

Sincerely,

[Name]
[Title]

- **Confirm time and location of meeting.**

- **Request materials while assuring the client that you already have at least some familiarity with the client's business.**

- **Give the client the option of forwarding the materials prior to the meeting or simply having them on hand at the meeting.**

Path on CD-ROM: Prospecting→New Client→Confirm first appointment→Ad agency-1

Confirming first service appointment

[Name]
[Address]
[City, State ZIP]

Dear [   ]:

Thank you for selecting [our company] to provide benefits administration for
[your company]. As discussed, we will be at [your office] on [date] at [time]
for an initial meeting.

Since you'll be switching from another company to ours, it would be most
helpful to us—and valuable to you—if between now and our meeting date you
could review the highlights of your current plan and be prepared to discuss its
pros and cons with us. Additionally, we'd like you to look through our policy
manual (enclosed) so that you'll be familiar with the various benefit administration packages we offer. These two important steps will make for a much
more productive meeting on [date] and will help us help you put together the
most appropriate plan for [your company].

We look forward to seeing you on [date].

Sincerely,

[Name]
[Title]

- **Confirm date, time, location, and purpose of the meeting.**
- **Ask the clients to be prepared to discuss their current plan and to read through your company literature.**

Path on CD-ROM: Prospecting→New Client→Confirm first appointment→Benefits-1

NEW CLIENT

Confirming first service appointment

[Name]
[Address]
[City, State ZIP]

Dear [   ]:

Thank you for selecting [All-Event Party Planning] to design and cater your [parents' surprise 50th anniversary party]. As discussed, we've booked the [Room] room at the [Hotel] hotel for the night of [date].

A special occasion such as this one requires more than just planning a menu and booking a hall, although, of course, we will be doing those very things. Before we begin making reservations and food choices, my partner and I would like to have a meeting with you [and your sister] so that we can get from you a detailed picture of the sort of party you have in mind. More than that, we'd like to get to "know" your parents, through you, in as much detail as possible—their history, their sense of humor, their taste in food and music, their friends. This will help us design a party that will truly capture who your parents are.

If at all possible, we'd like to have this little information-gathering session during the week of [date]. I'll call you later this week to set a specific date.

Looking forward to working with you on this exciting and rewarding party!

Sincerely,

[Name]
[Title]

P.S. Any personal mementos of your parents—photos, scrapbooks, etc.—that you can bring to the meeting would be terrifically helpful in letting us get to know your mother and father.

- **This letter confirms the date and location of the event but asks for a planning meeting.**

- **Lay out what you hope to learn/ accomplish in the meeting.**

- **Use a postscript to request additional materials that may not be forthcoming.**

Path on CD-ROM: Prospecting→New Client→Confirm first appointment→Caterer-1

Confirming first service appointment

[Name]
[Address]
[City, State ZIP]

Dear [   ]:

This will confirm our appointment for funeral preplanning for [you and your spouse]. The meeting will take place in [the large conference room] at our main office, [address], at [time] on [date].

Although you will most likely not actually be needing our services for many years, this preplanning meeting is a most important one, as it allows [the two of] you to make arrangements now, well in advance of any actual funeral, without the additional stress that event will cause for the surviving spouse.

In order to make this meeting, which can be a difficult one, go as smoothly as possible, we've found that it's best for clients to come to it prepared for the issues that will be discussed. To help with such preparation, we've enclosed a brochure that lays out every possible issue and question surrounding funeral preparations, including cost. We strongly recommend you look through it prior to [date's] meeting.

Thank you for choosing [Woodland Funeral Parlors]. We will see you on the [date].

Sincerely,

[Name]
[Title]

- **Confirm meeting date, time, and location.**

- **Tastefully explain that preparation for the meeting is in everyone's best interest.**

- **Urge clients to read the brochure and begin considering the issues at hand.**

Path on CD-ROM: Prospecting→New Client→Confirm first appointment→Funeral home-1

Hiring Others

Many companies do not have the specialized staff needed to conduct effective sales and marketing campaigns. Their options are to either do the best they can themselves, or to hire an advertising or marketing agency to help them out. The letters here are for those companies who choose the latter option. (The chapter also includes some letters that will help advertising agencies communicate with companies who have little knowledge or background in marketing issues.)

For an advertising campaign to be effective, the agency and client must both understand and agree on the objectives, each other's roles, and their plans. Consequently, the letters in this chapter are about building and maintaining an effective relationship. There are letters about developing proposals, negotiating contracts, keeping each other informed of changes, and even what to do when it's time to end the relationship.

It would be not only extremely unlikely but also undesirable for a business and its agency to conduct business solely via written communication. However, written communication allows you to document key issues, decisions, actions, and responsibilities. This helps ensure that both parties are on the same page and can save costly rework that would result from miscommunication.

RFP to vendor

[Name]
[Company]
[Address]
[City, State ZIP]

Dear [Name]:

After two years of handling all of our Web-related activities internally, [company] has decided to contract with outside suppliers to supply (1) the redesign and routine maintenance of our site, and (2) the management of all functions related to the increasingly important e-commerce segment of our business.

We are inviting several Web site developers and e-commerce consultants to provide information about their services and qualifications as the first phase of our selection process.

We realize that the development and maintenance of a Web site as a whole and the overhaul and management of an e-commerce function specifically are, or may be considered, two separate jobs. We are therefore inviting proposals from both Web developers and from e-commerce experts. While it is conceivable that one supplier may be able to handle both functions, and while such a scenario might offer certain advantages, it is not critical that a firm have expertise in both areas in order to be considered.

We invite you to send information on your firm, including samples of your work and client references, to my attention by [date]. Please clearly indicate which of the two functions your firm is qualified to handle; if your firm has proven expertise in both areas, please make that clear. After reviewing the information you provide, we will invite two or three suppliers for each functional area to present their services at a team meeting.

Thank you.

Sincerely,

[Name]
[Title]

- **In this introductory letter, provide a quick overview of your needs.**

- **If you require a multiplicity of services, make clear whether you require one supplier to handle all of them or if separate suppliers will be acceptable.**

- **State the deadline by which applicants must submit initial materials/letters.**

Path on CD-ROM: Hiring Others→Bidding Process→RFP to vendor→Multiple suppliers-1

RFP to vendor

[Name]
[Company]
[Address]
[City, State ZIP]

Dear [Name]:

[Company] is soliciting proposals from firms interested in preparing our annual report.

Qualified vendors should be able to take the project from start to finish, handling the following list of tasks, which includes but is not limited to:

- overall concept and layout
- writing text
- preparing charts and graphs
- photography of [company] executives, products, plants, etc.
- all phases of print production, including printing

We invite you to send information about your company, samples of previous work including annual reports as well as other long-form printed pieces, and client references.

Our report distribution deadline is fixed at [date]; consequently, we seek initial proposals as of [much earlier date]. Finalists will be notified approximately [one week] after receipt of all proposals as to next steps.

Thank you.

Sincerely,

[Name]
[Title]

- **When soliciting bids for a specific project, feel free to require that bidders have specific prior experience in the subject area.**

- **List the components of the task you expect all suppliers to be able to handle.**

- **Provide key dates.**

Path on CD-ROM: Hiring Others→Bidding Process→RFP to vendor→Specific task-1

Acknowledging proposal

[Name]
[Company]
[Address]
[City, State ZIP]

Dear [Name]:

Thank you for submitting your proposal for [job/project].

While your proposal was impressive, we have received a number of proposals from other bidders whose expertise in the [category] category is far more extensive. Consequently, we will not be asking you to continue with us in our selection process.

With your permission, we will keep your materials on file and keep your firm in mind should any projects arise that are a good match with your qualifications.

Thank you again for your proposal.

Sincerely,

[Name]
[Title]

- **Thank the bidder for the proposal.**

- **Since this is a rejection, be specific but brief about your decision not to proceed with this bidder.**

Path on CD-ROM: Hiring Others→Bidding Process→Acknowledge receipt of proposal→Displeased-1

Asking questions about proposal

[Name]
[Company]
[Address]
[City, State ZIP]

Dear [Name]:

Thank you for submitting your proposal for [job/project].

We have a number of questions about certain elements of your proposal and credentials that we need to have answered prior to proceeding further with our review process:

[Question #1]

[Question #2]

[Question #3]

Please submit your answers to these questions via letter or e-mail by [date].

Thank you for your cooperation.

Sincerely,

[Name]
[Title]

- **Thank the bidder for the initial proposal.**

- **If you are negatively inclined toward the bidder, it is probably best to simply ask your questions without directly suggesting your stance at the moment; keep an open mind and allow the answers to the questions guide your next move.**

- **Be specific about the format/ medium and deadline for the responses; do not invite telephone responses if you do not wish to communicate that way.**

Path on CD-ROM: Hiring Others→Bidding Process→Questions about proposal→Negative-1

Request modification in proposal

[Name]
[Company]
[Address]
[City, State ZIP]

Dear [Name]:

Thank you for submitting your proposal for [project].

We were very impressed by your ideas for [project] and your expertise in the category and have selected you as a finalist.

We are asking all of our finalists to submit an additional element for our consideration.

As specified in our original request for a proposal, our primary marketing objective is [increasing share among mothers of preschoolers]; your ideas for addressing that objective were indeed quite impressive. We are now also considering going after a secondary target, specifically [the senior citizen population]. Therefore, we are asking all finalists to submit an additional section to their proposals, addressing [media, creative, and online] issues relevant to this secondary [audience]. The budget we have allocated for this secondary [element] is [$x].

You may have until [date] to submit this additional section. Either hard copy or e-mail is acceptable.

Thank you for your continued cooperation. We look forward to seeing your revised proposal.

Sincerely,

[Name]
[Title]

- **Asking finalists to submit additional work is not unusual or unreasonable.**

- **Provide clear direction for the new element(s) of the proposal, including budget guidelines.**

- **Give a deadline and acceptable format/medium for the revision.**

Path on CD-ROM: Hiring Others→ Bidding Process→Request modification→Addition-1

BIDDING PROCESS

Request modification in proposal

[Name]
[Company]
[Address]
[City, State ZIP]

Dear [Name]:

Thank you for submitting your proposal for [project]. We were very impressed by your ideas for [project] and your expertise in the category.

Due to an issue that you could not possibly have anticipated, we need to ask that you revise certain elements of your proposal. Our company [or parent corporation] has a strict policy guideline forbidding [the use of television advertising to children]. While [children's TV advertising] was not the primary element of your proposal, it was one of the elements you recommended that we include in our [2001 media plan].

While we regret having to ask you for this additional work, we do need you to revise the [media, creative and target market] sections of the proposal with this [prohibition] in mind, as we would never be able to get a plan that included [children's TV advertising] approved by our senior management.

You may have until [date] to submit your revision. Either hard copy or e-mail is acceptable.

Thank you for your continued cooperation. We look forward to seeing your revised proposal.

Sincerely,

[Name]
[Title]

- **Thank the bidder for the initial proposal; if you were pleased with it, say so.**

- **Provide clear direction regarding the revisions you require; explain your reasons.**

- **Give a deadline and acceptable format/medium for the revision.**

Path on CD-ROM: Hiring Others→ Bidding Process→Request modification→Internal policy-1

Reject proposal

[Name]
[Company]
[Address]
[City, State ZIP]

Dear [Name]:

Thank you for submitting your proposal for [project].

While we were impressed by [your credentials, your efforts and many of the recommendations provided by other clients], we have decided to invite only those [agencies] with direct experience in the [footwear] category to continue to the next round of our review.

With your permission, we will keep your materials on file and will consider you for future projects that might be appropriate. Thank you for participating in this review.

Sincerely,

[Name]
[Title]

- **Thank the bidder for submitting a proposal and, if appropriate, mention some of its high points.**
- **Be clear about the specific shortfall in the bidder's experience base, if that was the crucial factor in the rejection decision.**
- **Close the letter politely.**

Path on CD-ROM: Hiring Others→Bidding Process→Reject proposal→Lacks experience-1

BIDDING PROCESS

Reject proposal

[Date]
[Name]
[Company]
[Address]
[City, State ZIP]

Dear [   ]:

We appreciated your efforts in developing an advertising proposal for [company]. While your presentation to our communications committee was impressive, we have signed a contract with another firm, which has demonstrated more experience in [survey research].

Thank you for your interest in doing business with [company]. We will keep your firm in mind as other opportunities may present themselves.

Sincerely,

[Name]
[Title]

- **Communicate the decision firmly. Do not lead the reader to the mistaken conclusion that reconsideration is possible.**

- **Express appreciation for the reader's interest in developing a business relationship.**

Path on CD-ROM: Hiring Others→Bidding Process→Reject proposal→Generic-2

Cover letter with proposal

[Name]
[Address]
[City, State ZIP]

Dear [Name]:

Thank you for asking [our company] to submit a proposal for [project]. Our response is enclosed.

Please note that we have actually developed two different programs for your consideration. Program 1 is designed to meet the technical and cost guidelines specified in the RFP. We have also developed a second option, Program 2, which is a higher spending program.

While you may be able to achieve your [marketing] objectives by operating at the spending level specified in the RFP, we would be remiss if we did not share our concerns about that budget with you. In our judgment, the budget specified will deliver only [the bare minimum number of impressions against your target audience], hence our motivation for developing, and strongly recommending, Program 2, should you be able to increase your funding for this [campaign].

In any case, we look forward to the possibility of working with you. Please don't hesitate to call me at [number] with any questions or comments.

Sincerely,

[Name]
[Title]

- **Recommending a higher budget than that specified can be a gutsy move; if you do so, make clear the benefit to the (prospective) client.**
- **Be certain that you answer the brief; develop a proposal at the assigned level first.**
- **Close by thanking the reader for inviting your participation.**

Path on CD-ROM: Hiring Others→Bidding Process→Cover letter with proposal→Agency-2

Asking questions of client

[Name]
[Company]
[Address]
[City, State ZIP]

Dear [Name]:

Thank you for inviting [Tom & Joe Advertising] to participate in your review.

As you may know, [Tom & Joe] is a subsidiary of [MegaCom, a worldwide holding company with a diverse roster of communications divisions.] While our agency, acting alone, would not be able to meet some of the specifications of your brief, we do have corporate brothers and sisters in the [PR, Internet media, and health care advertising] industries.

We would like to prepare our proposal to you in concert with these various related entities and, in the event that we are selected as your [agency], we would like to work in concert with them. In effect, the proposal would come from a select group of [MegaCom] companies and, if selected, your business would be serviced by this same consortium.

Our question: Is this acceptable to [your company]?

Please call or e-mail me with your response.

I look forward to hearing from you and, hopefully, continuing with the development of our proposal.

Sincerely,

[Name]
[Title]

- **Let the (potential) client know up front that you wish to work with your affiliates.**

- **Explain how you would cooperate in the proposal process and in servicing the business in the event that you win it.**

Path on CD-ROM: Hiring Others→Bidding Process→Asking questions→Affiliations-1

Cover letter with revised bid

[Name]
[Company]
[Address]
[City, State ZIP]

Dear [Name]:

Thank you for selecting [agency] as one of your finalists.

As outlined in your revised RFP, we have removed the [online] section of the [2003] campaign and brought the total budget down to [$55,000].

Because the [online] section had accounted for only [$7,000] of our initial bid and we needed to decrease the total program by [$10,000], it was necessary to decrease the [packaging] program by [$3,000].

Please let us know if you have any questions about the modified proposal. We look forward to the opportunity to work with you.

Sincerely,

[Name]
[Title]

- **Give an overview of the tactics used to arrive at the total (lower) budget figure.**
- **Describe cuts to both the client-specified item as well as decreases to other items.**

Path on CD-ROM: Hiring Others→Bidding Process→Cover letter with revised bid→Eliminating-1

Cover letter with revised bid

[Name]
[Company]
[Address]
[City, State ZIP]

Dear [Name]:

Enclosed you will find our revised proposal for the [media planning and buying assignment for your company].

As requested in your response to our initial submission, we have reviewed the [sports broadcast portion] of our recommendation and have modified it to [include several pro wrestling programs]. While we [do not endorse this sort of programming from a pure content standpoint, we cannot deny the importance of pro wrestling as an audience delivery vehicle].

The impact of this [programming] change on the budget was [minimal: an increase of $3,000].

Please review the proposal and call me with any questions or comments. I look forward to hearing with you and working with [your company] in the near future.

Sincerely,

[Name]
[Title]

- **When submitting a revision based on a philosophical issue posed by the client, demonstrate that you understand the request even if you do not fully agree with it.**

- **State how the revision affected the budget, if at all.**

Path on CD-ROM: Hiring Others→Bidding Process→Cover letter with revised bid→Philosophical-1

Follow up on bid

[Name]
[Company]
[Address]
[City, State ZIP]

Dear [Name]:

Thanks again for asking [our design firm] to submit a proposal for your [Web site].

Since forwarding our initial proposal [last month], we have taken another look at [our recommended budget]. Based on new suppliers we're working with, we will be able [to trim our proposed programming costs by 15% while still meeting your strategic and timing objectives]. We have therefore revised our [budget page] to reflect this change; with your permission, we would like to submit this new [budget], which replaces and supersedes the one included in our earlier proposal.

We think you'll be pleased with this costing revision. If for whatever reason such a modification to our proposal is not acceptable, please feel free to work with the figures we submitted previously.

Thank you. We look forward to hearing from you.

Sincerely,

[Name]
[Title]

- Lowering a bid/budget after submitting a proposal is a calculated risk; it might make your submission more attractive, although you risk creating the impression that you didn't have your act together when you submitted your initial documents.

- If you choose to make such a move, provide a brief explanation—how your prices were able to decrease and what this reduction will do for the client.

Path on CD-ROM: Hiring Others→Bidding Process→Follow up on bid→Budget-1

Request for agency presentation

[Date]
[Name]
[Company]
[Address]
[City, State ZIP]

Dear [   ]:

Your agency submitted one of the best proposals we received for a promotional campaign for our affiliated restaurants. We particularly liked your idea to [create a cartoon character to attract children and families to our locations].

Since the proposed campaign represents a major commitment and expense for our restaurants, we are inviting your agency to present your proposal in person to our committee [within the next two weeks]. We also are asking [two] other firms to make similar presentations.

We hope your agency will choose to complete this final stage of our selection process. To schedule a date and time for your presentation at our main office, please call [Kenneth Witherspoon at 333-333-3333].

Thank you for your efforts in developing this promotional plan. We are looking forward to hearing more about your ideas and having the opportunity to ask questions about them.

Sincerely,

[Name]
[Title]

- **Request is in the form of an open invitation.**
- **Letter describes the last stage of the selection process and informs the agency of the number of competitors.**

Path on CD-ROM: Hiring Others→Bidding Process→Request for presentation→Generic-2

Withdrawing from process

[Name]
[Company]
[Address]
[City, State ZIP]

Dear [Name]:

Thank you for selecting [our agency] as a finalist in your review.

After lengthy discussion, my colleagues and I regret to inform you that we will have to withdraw from your review process.

While we would have been honored to work with you on [project], we realized that the revised budget specified in the most recent version of the RFP would put us in the position of losing money on the [project] had we been selected as your [agency]. While we do not expect to make tremendous profits on all projects we take on, it is one of our requirements that we at least break even. Unfortunately, we would not have been able to do so on this [project].

Thank you again for considering us. We hope that you will think of us again and invite us to participate in future reviews.

Sincerely,

[Name]
[Title]

- There is nothing wrong with letting (prospective) clients know that their potential project would have been an unprofitable proposition for you.

- You may wish to communicate this decision in person or by phone in addition to this letter.

- End on a positive note, leaving the door open for possible future assignments.

Path on CD-ROM: Hiring Others→Bidding Process→Withdrawing→Budget-1

HIRING / CONTRACTING

Accepting a proposal

[Date]
[Name]
[Company]
[Address]
[City, State ZIP]

Dear [   ]:

After carefully reviewing your portfolio and presentation, [company] has decided to retain your firm's advertising and public relations services. Congratulations!

We selected your firm based on the quality of your past work and the glowing testimonials provided by your other clients.

As we discussed, [company] is interested in an annual contract covering all advertising plans and execution, all press releases, and brochures.

You will receive a draft contract in a few days.

We are excited about working with your creative and talented staff and hope that this marks the beginning of a long and successful business relationship.

Sincerely,

[Name]
[Title]

- Consider using advertising and public relations firms to handle limited projects or provide full-service communications support, including surveys. Telemarketing also can be outsourced.

- Review the type of contract you have in mind.

Path on CD-ROM: Hiring Others→Hiring, Contracting→Acceptance of proposal→Generic-3

Agency confirming terms

[Name]
[Company]
[Address]
[City, State ZIP]

Dear [Name]:

Thank you once again for choosing [our firm] to supply your [annual report development and publication].

Our legal and financial advisers have just completed their review of your draft contract. There were several significant issues that they brought to my attention:

[issue (1): point of disagreement]

[issue (2): point of disagreement]

[issue (3): point of disagreement]

While we are very excited about the possibility of working with [your company], I am afraid that we will not be able to proceed unless and until we work out these important issues.

Please call me at your convenience so that we can set up a conference call with our respective legal and/or finance teams and iron out these points of concern.

Thank you.

Sincerely,

[Name]
[Title]

- If there are serious financial, legal, philosophical, or ethical issues that are revealed in the client's proposed contract, address them before you sign the document.

- Offer to bring in all necessary parties to resolve the issues.

Path on CD-ROM: Hiring Others→Hiring, Contracting→Agency confirms terms→With revisions-1

HIRING / CONTRACTING

Letters about the contract

[Name]
[Company]
[Address]
[City, State ZIP]

Dear [Name]:

Thanks again for selecting [our agency] to handle your [upcoming Web site relaunch] and for sending us your [agency services] contract.

We have reviewed the document with our legal counsel. While we are in agreement with the overall spirit of the contract, we do have a few comments and questions about a number of specific issues, including [issue] and [issue].

We have indicated our comments on the enclosed draft and would like to discuss these issues with you (and, if you'd like, your own legal counsel) before signing and beginning work for [your company].

Please let me know when we might be able to walk through the contract together and discuss the various open issues.

We look forward to working with [you and your team]. Thank you.

Sincerely,

[Name]
[Title]

- If the client has provided a contract with minor problems, be delicate in expressing your concerns.

- Let the new client know how excited you are about working with them, but make it clear—politely—that you will not begin work until the contract issues are discussed and (ideally) resolved.

- Maintain a positive, polite, friendly tone throughout the letter. (Or call to bring up these issues rather than using a letter as the initial means of communication.)

Path on CD-ROM: Hiring Others→Hiring, Contracting→Letters about contract→With revisions-1

Confidentiality

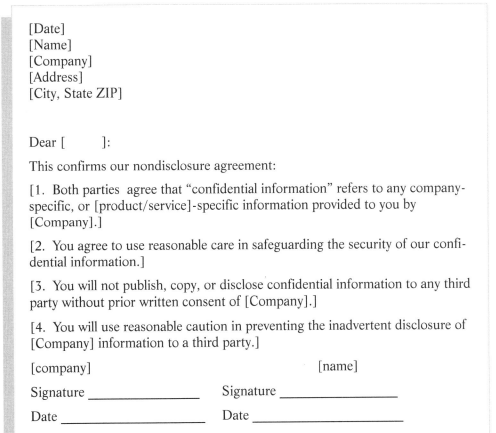

[Date]
[Name]
[Company]
[Address]
[City, State ZIP]

Dear [   ]:

This confirms our nondisclosure agreement:

[1. Both parties agree that "confidential information" refers to any company-specific, or [product/service]-specific information provided to you by [Company].]

[2. You agree to use reasonable care in safeguarding the security of our confidential information.]

[3. You will not publish, copy, or disclose confidential information to any third party without prior written consent of [Company].]

[4. You will use reasonable caution in preventing the inadvertent disclosure of [Company] information to a third party.]

[company]   [name]

Signature _____   Signature _____

Date _____   Date _____

- **This could be included as a clause in the nondisclosure portion of a contract with a freelance writer or agency.**

- **Also consider whether you want to add a noncompete clause or agreement, prohibiting the writer or agency from working simultaneously for one of your competitors.**

- **All legal agreements should be checked by your legal advisors.**

Path on CD-ROM: Hiring Others→Hiring, Contracting→Confidentiality→Generic-1

Agreements with freelancers

[Name]
[Company]
[Address]
[City, State ZIP]

Dear [   ]:

This letter will confirm our agreement with [WRITER] to write a series of [five] brochures for the [State Grocers' Association, a client of [company]]. The writer will deliver copy for these brochures by [DATE/YEAR].

Each brochure will consist of [one 1,200- to 1,500-word interview with a chef at an award-winning restaurant plus five to ten tips from the chef for cooks to use at home]. This material will be delivered on a computer disk and in double-spaced hard copy.

Payment of [$1,250] will be paid within [30 days] of delivery of satisfactory copy for the [five] brochures. If the writer fails to deliver the brochure copy by the due date or if the copy is unsatisfactory in the judgment of [company], payment will not be made. The writer will also receive [five each of the five printed brochures].

This assignment is a work for hire. The [State Grocers' Association] will own the brochures, including copyright and all other rights. The writer grants [company] the right to condense or edit the brochure copy as it deems appropriate.

The writer represents and warrants that the brochures are original work and do not infringe on or violate any copyright, trademark, right of privacy, or other rights of any individuals or organizations. The writer also warrants that the brochures shall contain no libelous or unlawful statements nor recipes or other instructions that may cause harm or injury.

The writer agrees to indemnify and hold [[company] and the State Grocers' Association] harmless in the event of any breach of the representations above and to cooperate in the defense of any legal action resulting from publication of the [five] brochures.

Agreed by:

[Name]
[Title]
[Company]

- **Letter of agreement specifies due date, payment, amount and type of copy, and how it is to be delivered.**

- **Agreement also specifies a work for hire and includes an indemnification clause.**

Path on CD-ROM: Hiring Others→Hiring, Contracting→Freelance agreements→Association-1

Review of agency

[Name]
[Company]
[Address]
[City, State ZIP]

Dear [Name]:

My [brand managers] have shared a number of agency-related concerns with me over the past few months. Considered individually, none of the issues they've brought to me is tremendously important. When viewed in their totality, however, the concerns I've heard do suggest that we need to get together to address them.

I would like to propose a somewhat formalized agency performance review so that the various members of my marketing team can voice their concerns in a dispassionate, organized manner. Please be aware that I am not looking to replace the agency or bring on a second one. My objective is simply to bring various problems to light so that we can discuss them—and solve them—together.

Over the next [two weeks] I will meet formally with my [brand managers] to hear their concerns. I will also ask each of them to fill out a standard agency review form [that I've used at previous jobs]. Once I have received all of their comments, I would like to meet with you and your team to go through the reviews in detail.

I'll give you a call [before the end of the month] so we can set aside a day to meet to address the various issues. Thanks for your cooperation. I'm sure it will help get us back on track.

Sincerely,

[Name]
[Title]

- **If there is a pattern of internal grumbling about the agency, consider formalizing the complaint/review process and sharing the results with the agency.**

- **Assuming the overall agency relationship is positive, use this letter to alert the agency that the review is imminent, but assure them that they are not at risk (at this point) of being replaced.**

- **Make clear how you wish to handle the logistics of the review.**

Path on CD-ROM: Hiring Others→Ongoing Maintenance→Review of agency→One-time-1

Change in client contact

TO: [Name@company.com]

FROM: [Name]

SUBJECT: Expansions to the Marketing Department

Dear [Name]:

In light of the tremendous growth that [Red Lodge Fashions] has experienced over the past two years, I am thrilled to announce that we will be expanding our Marketing department staff significantly. I wanted to let you and the rest of the agency know that we have already put two new people in place with whom you will be working very closely on the 2001 campaigns.

I have added two Directors of Marketing who will each report to me and will each be responsible for roughly half of [RLF's] product line, including all advertising and communications functions.

[John Heinz] joins us this week from [High Style Inc.] as our new [Director of Marketing for men's wear]. [Renee Campos] will be on board by [the end of this month]; [she] comes to us from [Camouflage Hunting Gear] and will be our new [Director of Marketing for women's wear]. (Please forward the attached organizational chart to your staff; all phone numbers and e-mail addresses are provided there.)

[John and Renee] will now be your primary contacts here at [RLF], though I will remain involved in [advertising discussions] for the next few months until my new hires are up to speed.

Please join me in welcoming [John and Renee] to our team.

- In this case, the writer is announcing the "passing of the torch" from him/herself to new employee(s). Make clear how responsibilities will be split between the new people and how you, the writer, will or won't remain involved.

- Provide phone and e-mail contact information.

Path on CD-ROM: Hiring Others→Ongoing Maintenance→Change in client contact→New contacts-1

Change in agency contact

TO: [Name@company.com]

FROM: [Name]

SUBJECT: New Phone Numbers at [George & Washington]

Dear [Name]:

Just a quick note to inform you and your staff about changes we're making to our phone system and phone numbers here at the agency.

We're switching to a phone system that will provide each member of our staff with direct dialing, making it that much easier for you and all of our clients to reach us at any time. This change will necessitate a new general switchboard number for [G&W] as well.

Our new general number, effective the [20th of next month], will be [(777) 555-5555]. Direct-dial numbers will be simply [(777) 555-xxxx, where "xxxx" represents a staff member's personal 4-digit extension].

A complete list of our personnel, along with each person's extension, direct-dial number, and e-mail address, is attached as a Word document.

We anticipate a few technical glitches while we're switching over to the new system, so please bear with us during the transition period. (If you do encounter problems reaching us by phone over the next few weeks, please e-mail us and let us know—our e-mail system will NOT be changing!)

We're sure that once everything's up and running, we'll be able to serve you better than ever.

- **Describe the change in progress as well as any rationale for the change; give practical advice as to how to use the new system.**

- **Attach complete information as a separate document if there is too much information to include in the body of the e-mail letter itself.**

- **Anticipate possible complaints by admitting that there may be a short transition period, and provide an alternative way for the reader to reach you during that period.**

Path on CD-ROM: Hiring Others→Ongoing Maintenance→Change in agency contact→New addresses-1

Change in agency rates

[Name]
[Company]
[Address]
[City, State ZIP]

Dear [   ]:

We would like to meet with you to propose a new compensation system for agency services.

In short, we are proposing moving away from the current media-commission-based system and toward adopting a fee-based system. We'll get into the details with you when we meet, but the bottom line is this: In an age when less and less of an ad agency's service to its clients is related to size of media billings—and more upon strategic planning, consulting, Web development, and other "beyond the line" expenses—a compensation system based upon media billings is not only increasingly irrelevant but can be downright harmful to an agency's financial stability.

We are putting together a detailed proposal that we would like to present to you before beginning contract discussions for the coming fiscal year. I will call you later this week to set a meeting date.

Sincerely,

[Name]
[Title]

- Use a letter to introduce compensation discussions, but not to actually set rates; save that for in-depth, in-person discussions.

- Give an overview of the direction you're heading in and some of the rationale; ask for a meeting date to go through details together.

Path on CD-ROM: Hiring Others→Ongoing Maintenance→Change in agency rates→Fees-1

Change in client plans

TO: [Name@company.com]

FROM: [Name]

SUBJECT: Shift in Media Priorities

Dear [Name]:

We've just completed an extensive research study on our consumers' media habits. In light of the study's key finding—that the average member of our target audience spends 6 hours a day online but only 1 hour a day watching television—I believe we should be allocating more of our advertising budget to Internet media (and our own Web site) and less of the budget to TV.

A change of this sort is obviously a significant one, as it has far-reaching implications for this coming season's media planning, creative development, and budgets.

I would like to meet with you and your media team later this week to get your point of view on this issue and, ideally, to start attacking it in depth. Please give me a call later today so we can set a meeting date and time. Thank you.

- **Information of the sort discussed in this letter can have many far-reaching effects. Ask for the agency's point of view before moving forward if possible.**

- **Request a meeting to discuss details in person, in depth.**

Path on CD-ROM: Hiring Others→Ongoing Maintenance→Change in client plans→New media-1

Change in client plans

TO: [Name@company.com]

FROM: [Name]

SUBJECT: Change to Advertising Start Date

Dear [Name]:

I just got a call from Operations with some very good news: The Spring product line will actually be available to ship a full month ahead of our current schedule!

In light of this news, we need to start our TV and print advertising in March rather than April, as is currently planned. I am meeting with my finance group this afternoon to determine what sort of incremental budget I will have available for the extra media needed for an earlier launch and will be able to give you that information tomorrow.

I'll call you once I have budget figures confirmed; in the meanwhile, please begin exploring March TV and print availabilities. Thanks, [Name].

- **Good news for you may not necessarily be as good for the reader. Convey your excitement but anticipate possible resistance.**

- **If certain information remains to be made available, advise the reader and let him/her know when you expect the missing pieces to fall into place.**

Path on CD-ROM: Hiring Others→Ongoing Maintenance→Change in client plans→Date-1

Dissatisfied with agency performance

[Name]
[Company]
[Address]
[City, State ZIP]

Dear [   ]:

I have a concern that I need to bring to your attention.

We are not getting the good, solid strategic thinking from [AD&F] that we need from our ad agency. While the creative is often clever and the team you have running our account is good with the day-to-day details, we feel [AD&F] falls short in terms of its ability to analyze the marketplace as a whole, antici-pate competitive challenges, and offer us smart, original strategic counsel. We need an agency that will bring consumer insights to us before we think of them ourselves, an agency that will work hand-in-hand with our own top strategic thinkers and take us to places that we might not get to on our own. Without that level of strategic input, the creative work you develop, arresting as it can often be, is not based on anything substantial and therefore, we fear, will not take us to the next level as a [software] company.

I imagine that [AD&F] and its parent company have some strategic planners on staff; perhaps the issue is that they haven't been putting enough time—or any time—against our business. I would hate to think that there's no one in your stable who can bring us the kind of top-level thinking our account deserves.

[Pete], why don't you give me a call so we can talk about this in more detail and figure out what needs to be done? Thanks.

Sincerely,

[Name]
[Title]

- This letter is friendly, reflecting a healthy relationship between writer and reader, yet also conveys the seriousness of the issue and suggests that the writer may be considering drastic steps.

- Suggesting sources for help on this issue serves to both stimulate the reader's action as well as signal the writer's frustration with the situation.

Path on CD-ROM: Hiring Others→Ongoing Maintenance→Dissatisfied→Strategic-1

Dissatisfied with agency performance

[Name]
[Company]
[Address]
[City, State ZIP]

Dear [   ]:

I have a serious concern that I need to bring to your attention.

While the creative work and media plans you have developed for our print and broadcast campaigns have generally been quite good, and we've been more than pleased with the overall handling of our account, our concern is that [your agency] is not currently equipped to offer us the kind of support we need in terms of new media. As a [software manufacturer], it is critical that we reach our target audience via nontraditional media, including [computer information sites and search engines]; further, our own Web site is a crucial medium for us.

As I see it, I have two choices at this juncture: I can meet with you and your department heads to discuss ways your agency can address my company's needs in this area, or I can engage another agency to develop [my company's] Web site, online creative work, and online media plans. Before considering the second option, why don't we get together later this month to review the resources you and/or your affiliated agencies can provide us? Let's set a date and see if we can't make this work.

Sincerely,

[Name]
[Title]

- While this letter addresses a serious issue, the consequences of failing to solve the problem are not as severe (keeping the overall assignment with the current agency while using another supplier for the specific needs outlined) in the short term. Nevertheless, the writer does expect that a solution from the current agency is within the realm of possibility, hence the friendlier (although still businesslike) tone.

- Letter clearly lays out the two choices before the writer so that reader can understand his/her plight (and potential consequences).

Path on CD-ROM: Hiring Others→Ongoing Maintenance→Dissatisfied→New media-1

Satisfied with agency performance

[Name]
[Company]
[Address]
[City, State ZIP]

Dear [   ]:

Thank you, thank you, thank you!

[Lucy], since the new commercial for [Bumpy Potato Chips] broke last month, we have not been able to keep the darn things on grocers' shelves!

Based on the most recent retail numbers, reflecting product movement since the campaign broke, sales are up [45%] vs. last year. It just shows what can happen when you've got an agency that can develop great creative work based on sound strategic thinking, and then run that work in all the right places. Well done!

Please let everyone at the agency know how thrilled all of us here at [Bumpy] are with your terrific work.

Sincerely,

[Name]
[Title]

- **Agencies hear complaints far more often than praise; feel free to be over enthusiastic if you'd like.**

- **Give specific results if you have them.**

- **Let the reader know who besides yourself is grateful for the agency's good work.**

Path on CD-ROM: Hiring Others→Ongoing Maintenance→Satisfied→Sales-1

Terminating an agency

[Name]
[Nonprofit Association]
[Address]
[City, State ZIP]

Dear [   ]:

When our charitable organization signed the contract with your marketing agency, we envisioned a smooth working relationship between your agency and our office. Unfortunately, the arrangement has not worked out. [Besides frequent miscommunications between agency professionals and our PR staff, agency expenses have run 25 percent or more above the estimates for each of the past four months.]

This letter provides the 30-day written notice of the termination of our agreement, as specified in the contract. Our organization will pay for agency services through the end of the month and will expect to receive the [completed, stage-two press packet by that date, as well as all photos, artwork, and ancillary materials developed in support of our ongoing $5-million capital campaign].

We regret that our agreement did not work out as we all had hoped it would.

Sincerely,

[Name]
[Title]

- **List expectations firmly but not in a challenging manner.**

- **State the unhappy facts without blaming any particular individual.**

Path on CD-ROM: Hiring Others→Termination→Termination of agency→Charity-1

Termination of agency

[Name]
[Organization]
[Address]
[City, State ZIP]

Dear [Name]:

It is with some regret that I must inform you of [company's] decision to end our relationship with [your agency], effective [date, year].

When we hired you as our agency [early last year], we were all very excited about working with you as we were familiar with your fine creative work and thought you showed an exceptional understanding of the challenges facing our business. While we have not been disappointed in [agency's] performance in either of those regards, the day-to-day process of dealing with the agency has been a difficult one.

As I have mentioned to you over the past few months, several members of my marketing department have expressed the frustration they regularly experience when dealing with your account management staff. My team feels that its concerns are not being addressed and its requests are not being taken seriously or followed up. Further, the account management team consistently misses deadlines, often fails to return my people's phone calls, and does not inform my group about budget overages or changes in project specifications. The difficulties the marketing department must face in order to get our advertising produced by [your agency] far outweigh the generally good creative work that eventually results, and despite repeated discussions with you and your team about these issues, the situation has not improved. Consequently, we have decided to seek advertising counsel elsewhere.

We will, of course, pay for agency services through [the termination date] as agreed in our contract. Please feel free to call me if you would like to discuss this matter in more detail.

Sincerely,

[Name]
[Title]

- **Get to the point of the letter immediately.**

- **List specific issues and concerns that led to the termination decision.**

- **Confirm that terms of the contract regarding termination will be adhered to.**

- **Offer the opportunity to discuss the issue in person or by telephone.**

Path on CD-ROM: Hiring Others→Termination→Termination of agency→Account mgmt-1

Agency leaving a client

[Name]
[Title]
[Organization]
[Address]
[City, State ZIP]

Dear [Name]:

I regret that I must inform you that after careful review of our current situation, [The Big Timber Agency] will no longer be able to provide advertising services to [your company], effective [30 days from today] as provided in our contract.

While it has been a pleasure working with you and your staff and we have enjoyed developing advertising for your print and television campaigns, we find that we can not provide the level of service your company demands and work within your budget parameters in a way that delivers a profit to the agency.

As you know, we have done whatever a given situation has demanded in terms of manpower, cost-saving efforts, and hard negotiating with our subcontractors, as we would with any client, and we have made more than the usual number of sacrifices in order to service your business. However, we find ourselves in the position of losing money on your account, a situation that is unacceptable to the agency as well as unhelpful to your own business—an agency that is financially healthy can provide far better service to a client than one that is not. While we understand your need to protect your company's financial stability and profit goals, surely you must appreciate that an ad agency has similar concerns.

I wish you and your team the best of luck. If there is anything I can do to help you in your search for a new agency, please do not hesitate to call me.

Sincerely,

[Name]
[Title]

- **Get to the point quickly but tactfully, explaining that you cannot continue to service the client under the circumstances, not that you no longer want to do so.**

- **Make clear the specific business reasons for the decision in a non-antagonistic way that the client can empathize with.**

- **End on a positive note, offering help with the client's next agency search if appropriate.**

Path on CD-ROM: Hiring Others→Termination→Agency leaving client→Budgets-1

Request for advertising rates

[Date]
[Name]
[Company]
[Address]
[City, State ZIP]

Dear [   ]:

I picked up a copy of your magazine, [*U.S. Antiques and Collectibles*], at your booth at the [Collectors Antique Fair in Indianapolis last week], and it seems like an ideal advertising vehicle for our [AntiqueMart software, which automates cash transactions, records dealer commissions, and offers an antique mall tax program for both sales and income taxes].

Please send a current rate card, including information on both small display ads (3 inches by 4 inches) and the type of classified advertisements that appear in your "Resource Section." I am interested in black and white advertisement only and also would like information on how to be included in your "Reader Response Card."

If your rates match our budget, I would like to run all of these types of advertising on a monthly basis, beginning with your issue of [November 1].

Thank you.

Sincerely,

[Name]
[Title]

- **Information about the writer's business makes this request a very credible one.**

- **Letter specifies advertising schedule and a start date.**

Path on CD-ROM: Hiring Others→Request for Rates→Print-2

Request for advertising rates

[Name]
[Company]
[Address]
[City, State ZIP]

Dear [   ]:

Our firm, [which produces time management and call tracking software], recently completed its marketing plan for the year ahead. We intend to purchase advertising on several business Web sites and are considering the addition of your magazine's Web site to our advertising mix.

Please send your Web site advertising rate card, including rates for a one-time monthly listing and multiple month listing options. In addition, we would like to know the number of hits your Web site has received for each of the past six months and whether there is a price discount if we also advertise in your print magazine. If there is a discount for advertising in both media, please also send an advertising rate card for the print publication.

Many thanks for your prompt response. We will begin our new advertising campaign two months hence.

Sincerely,

[Name]
[Title]

- **Writer saves time later by listing all the questions he needs answered now.**

- **Letter is specific and brief.**

Path on CD-ROM: Hiring Others→Request for Rates→Web-1

Internal Memos

Have you ever been a customer of a company you would consider world-class? What was it like interacting with their sales staff? Most likely, you found them knowledgeable and helpful. The cold truth is that nothing can do your company more harm than to have a customer call in response to an ad or letter and have the person answering the phone be unaware of what's going on.

That's why a significant portion of this book is devoted to the kinds of sales and marketing communication that should be occurring internally in all companies.

Many of the categories here cover the usual: updates about marketing activities (promotions, introductory offers, special events, advertising campaigns), changes in brochures, changes in product or service pricing, etc. But there are other types of information sharing that can help your sales staff do a better job:

- **Changes in policies and processes,** which affect how their work should be done and ensure there aren't any crossed wires within the work group.
- **Sales performance updates**. This is particularly critical, and not only for the reasons you might think of at first. Of course people like to know how they are doing personally, but information about how sales *as a whole* is going serves several purposes: (1) It lets everyone get a sense of how effective your company's sales practices are; (2) It can help stimulate creative thinking about how to do a better job.
- **Product and service updates,** and especially opportunities for the staff to educate themselves about them. Knowing your products and services actually work in practice will help your sales staff identify with your customers and their challenges.

The final two categories in the chapter deserve special consideration. The first deals with communication between the sales department and other internal departments, particularly finance/accounting and information services. These memos emphasize the message that sales is not an island unto itself; decisions you make affect other departments in your organization and vice versa.

The last category is devoted to the types of internal communication that should happen within an advertising agency, such as client updates, account management updates, and so on.

The underlying theme in all these letters is that companies must be able to enter the information age with ease. Business information is no longer a protected resource that should be restricted to only a few people. With very few exceptions, the more your sales staff knows about your business, it strategies, its customers, and its products or services, the more effective they will be in helping to increase sales, satisfy customers, and maintain your customer base.

COUPON PROMOTIONS

Explanation of coupon promotion

TO: [Loans@TrustBank.com]

FROM: [Name]

SUBJECT: Coupon promotion

The new coupon promotion for our [new automobile loan rates] will be starting [June 1]:

- The coupon offers customers a [25%] discount on the [published loan rate] for [new automobiles].

- The coupon expires on [September 1].

- The offer is subject to credit approval on behalf of the applicant.

- The coupon will be mailed to all current [TrustBank] customers on [May 25]. We will also be mailing coupons to selected area residents who are not yet [TrustBank] customers.

- This offer is not retroactive to loans secured prior to [June 1].

Note: This offer does not guarantee any specific rate to applicants since our published loan rates may change during the three-month period of this promotion. Encourage early sign-up in case the interest rates should rise.

- **Be sure to highlight any key aspects of the promotion (what qualifies, conditions of use, etc.).**

- **Coupon offers are rarely retroactive, but it pays to mention this to staff since customers who recently made a purchase may ask.**

Path on CD-Rom: Internal Memos→Coupon Promotion→ Explanation of promotion→Discount-6

Explanation of coupon promotion

MEMORANDUM

TO: [All staff]

FROM: [Name]

SUBJECT: Get 1 Free coupon promotion

The new coupon promotion for our new [Traveler series of luggage] will be hitting the market on [March 1]. Just to recap:

- The coupon offers customers a [free toiletries kit] for each set of [Traveler] luggage.

- There are four different sets of [Traveler] luggage being offered for sale; see the promotional flyer handed out last week for details.

- The offer is also good if the customer purchases at least $300 of luggage, even if they mix and match pieces from different sets.

- The coupon expires on [April 31].

- It is good at the time of purchase only—customers cannot get the free kit for sets purchased before March 1.

- It will be distributed through [the Sunday newspaper inserts and Weekly Shoppers].

Questions?

- **Describe all the ways that customers can qualify for the offer.**

- **Including a description of where the coupons will be distributed will help sales staff identify valid coupons.**

Path on CD-Rom: Internal Memos→Coupon Promotion→ Explanation of promotion→Get 1 free-2

COUPON PROMOTIONS

Change in coupon promotion

TO: [Sales@Centimeter.com]

FROM: [Name]

SUBJECT: Change in coupon promotion

The previous memo about the coupon promotion for our [precision non-mercury thermometers] had an error.

It was stated that only purchases of $250 or more would qualify. That figure should have been $150.

Also, the order entry code has been changed. The old code was [NoMerc-13721]. The new code you should use is [NoMerc-13725] [only the last digit is changed].

Questions?

- **State the change as simply as possible.**

- **Sometimes the change requires a change in processes as well (such as an order entry code). Be sure to mention any associated changes.**

Path on CD-ROM: Internal Memos→Coupon Promotion→Change in promotion→Qualifying-3

Results of promotion

MEMORANDUM

TO: All Staff

FROM: [Name]

SUBJECT: Coupon promotion

All the orders resulting from our coupon promotion on the [Complete Kleen] office cleaning service have now been processed. Unfortunately, it did not do as well as projected.

- We had 13 new and current customers qualify for the 5% discount, compared to a projection of 25.

- We had 18 new and current customers qualify for the 10% discount, compared to a projection of 35.

Overall, only 12 new customers were signed up, compared to projections of 25 (the rest of the orders were for continuing customers).

Still, having even 12 new customers will justify the hiring of additional cleaning personnel, so expect to see some new recruits around here in the next few weeks.

Thanks to everyone for their hard work on this effort. The Marketing group will be interviewing customers who did not choose to take advantage of this offer to see if we can figure out why.

The company's performance is still strong overall, however, and we don't anticipate any major negative impact of these disappointing results.

- **When results are negative, find some element that you can praise—even if it's just to praise everyone's hard work (usually the failure is not the result of lack of effort on the part of staff).**

- **Be as honest as you can about the impact of the disappointing results.**

Path on CD-Rom: Internal Memos→Coupon Promotion→Results of promotion→Disappointing-1

INTRODUCTORY OFFERS

Explanation of introductory discount

MEMORANDUM

TO: [All Sales Staff]

FROM: [Name]

SUBJECT: [CustomCopier Hits the Street!]

The world of photocopiers is about to be revolutionized! The release date for our new [CustomCopier] is scheduled for [June 15]. Starting on that day, our customers will be able to buy a copier custom-tailored to their needs.

We have a full PR blitz planned. A full-color brochure is at the printers and will be available within three weeks. You should start calling all your customers soon and using the promotional package to make pre-release sales. Any orders made before the release date will qualify for a one-time only 10% discount.

Also, we'll be hitting the airwaves with radio and TV ads beginning [in the middle of June], so you can expect to start receiving calls soon after the release date. In addition, you should contact your current customers.

During this special promotion period you should use a sales code of [CC2001] in the order entry screens. After the promotion period, use a code of [CC2002]. The first code includes the 10% discount, so you won't need to adjust the invoice.

If you have questions, contact [Carla] at extension [314].

- **Describing current promotions helps sale staff anticipate when they will start receiving calls about the product and identify what prompted the call.**

- **Describe where/how people can get acquainted with a complex product.**

Path on CD-ROM: Internal Memos→Intro Offers→Explanation of intro discount→Copiers-1

Explanation of introductory discount

MEMORANDUM

TO: [All Customer Service and Support Staff]

FROM: [Carla]

SUBJECT: [New Product Hits the Market]

At last! The new [product] you've all heard so much about is being released on [date].

The sales and marketing staff have already been informed of a special introductory offer available to all customers: a 10% discount through [date] off the purchase price to all retail customers. The retail price will be [$]. The special sale price is [$], a savings of [dollar amount] to the customer.

The discount applies only to the [new product], not to any other products ordered at the same time.

The discount does not affect the service you should provide to customers in any way, but we wanted you to know in case customers quote different prices for the [new product].

If you have questions, contact [Carla] at extension [414].

- **Sometimes knowing that a change doesn't affect you is just as important as knowing that it does.**

- **Provide enough detail so support staff aren't confused when they talk with customers.**

Path on CD-Rom: Internal Memos→Intro Offers→Explanation of intro discount→Generic-1

INTRODUCTORY OFFERS

Change in introductory discount

MEMORANDUM

TO: All Sales Staff

FROM: [Rico]

SUBJECT: [Change in Docu-Track discount offer]

We announced recently that customers who ordered the new [Docu-Track] service would receive a 10% discount off the one-year membership fee.

Starting immediately, this discount applies only to those who purchase a two-year membership.

Customers who have already placed orders at the reduced rate will receive their discounted one-year membership (that is, we will not be charging them more). However, you should call all these customers and explain that they can save money now buy upgrading to the two-year membership (otherwise, they will end up paying full price for the second year when their original membership expires).

- **Explain clearly what the change is.**

- **Explain how the sales staff should deal with customers who have already placed orders.**

Path on CD-Rom: Internal Memos→Intro Offers→Change in intro discount→Qualifying-2

Change in introductory discount

TO: [support@copier.com]

FROM: [LaShawn A.]

SUBJECT: [CustomCopier Hits the Street!]

As originally announced, orders made before the release date of our new [CustomCopiers] were eligible for a one-time only 10% discount.

The discount has now been increased to 15%.

Sales is taking care of notifying customers who have already purchased at the 10% discount that they are eligible for an additional 5% off. However, you may get calls from people who have heard about the increased discount. All such calls should be forwarded to [Carla [x104]].

If you have questions, contact [me] at extension [213].

- **Explain how staff should handle problems they cannot resolve themselves.**

- **Include a contact person's name and phone number.**

Path on CD-Rom: Internal Memos→Intro Offers→Change in intro discount→Discount-1

Explanation of introductory offer

TO: [Sales@company.com]

FROM: [Name]

SUBJECT: [Product Release Celebration & Announcements]

Hey, gang! The release date for [Handy Hammer] is set for [August 1]! We'll be having a brief celebration down in shipping to recognize everyone's contributions at [10 A.M.] that day. Hope you can all make it.

There's a special introductory offer you all need to know about: Customers can get 1 free [Handy Hammer] for every [$100] worth of products they order. (The [$100] can include any products, not just [Handy Hammer].)

To qualify, the orders must be received by [September 30].

This offer will be featured on our Web site ([www.HandyHammer.com]) and is described on our new fax cover sheets and order forms. Also, be sure to mention this offer to any customers you speak with during this time.

If any orders come in during this time using the old order form that doesn't indicate the special promotion, call or e-mail the customer to see if he or she would like a free [Handy Hammer].

If you have questions, respond via e-mail or call [Vic] at [x1357].

- When discounts or promotions involve more than one product, make sure you explain how a customer can qualify.

- Describe expectations of sales staff around making sure customers are aware of the promotion.

Path on CD-Rom: Internal Memos→Intro Offers→Explanation of intro offer→Hardware-1

Explanation of introductory offer

MEMORANDUM

TO: All staff

FROM: [Name]

SUBJECT: [Membership Drive Set to Start]

Our first ever fund drive is set from [date] to [date]! The Finance Committee has identified four levels of membership that will be available:

[Level 1] = [donation level1] = no premium

[Level 2] = [donation level2] = [premium2]

[Level 3] = [donation level3] = [premium3]

[Level 4] = [donation level4] = [premium4]

The basic membership includes a subscription to our bimonthly newsletter and [other benefits].

The kickoff will occur via [event] to be held on [date] from [time] to [time]. The [event] will be advertised on local TV and radio stations beginning [date], so we expect a big turnout.

We need volunteers to sign up to [activities]. Get your friends and families involved, too!

[Name] is coordinating all these efforts. Please see [him/her] to sign up!

The more memberships we can get, the better off we'll all be, so I expect everyone to pitch in. Thanks for your support so far. Your efforts on behalf of [organization] are greatly appreciated.

- **Sound excited about the event.**

- **Be specific about what you're asking people to do.**

Path on CD-ROM: Internal Memos→Intro Offers→Explanation of intro offer→Nonprofit-1

INTRODUCTORY OFFERS

Change in introductory offer

MEMORANDUM

TO: All Sales Staff

FROM: [Name]

SUBJECT: [Change in introductory offer of Handy Hammer]

As recently announced, customers could get 1 free [Handy Hammer] for every [$100] worth of products they order. The deadline is [September 30].

When asked, most customers have said they plan to give bonus [Handy Hammer] away as a gift, so we are now offering a special gift wrapping option for $7.50.

The order entry screens have been modified to include a check box for the gift-wrapping option. Be sure you ask each customer whether he or she wants this option.

If you have questions, respond via e-mail or call [Vic] at [x1357].

- Remind people what the original offer was.

- Describe how the change affects the order-entry process.

- This change shows the company was paying attention to customers and how they used their product and the accessory.

Path on CD-ROM: Internal Memos→Intro Offers→Changes in intro offer→Hardware-1

Change in introductory offer

TO: [Staff@UrbanWild.org]

FROM: [Leopold]

SUBJECT: [Membership Drive Set to Start]

Our [first ever] fund drive will still be held from [October 15] to [October 30]!

However, we've found that the poster we wanted to offer as a premium will not be ready in time, so we are substituting custom-designed T-shirts instead. The membership levels stay the same.

[Raven = [$10–$24] = Free Urban Wilderness greeting card]

[Heron = [$25–$49] = **Free Urban Wilderness T-shirt**]

[Goldfinch = [$50–$99] = Set of 25 Urban Wilderness cards]

[Osprey = [$100 or more] = Contributors get their name on our benefactors placard, plus the set of 25 cards and **T-shirt**]

These T-shirts are really great—a nice heavy cotton with a colorful design. In fact, every volunteer will get one for their own...so sign up now!

[John M.] is still coordinating these efforts. Please see him to sign up!

- **If your e-mail program allows it, highlight the changes with underlining or bold so people can zero in on what's new.**

Path on CD-ROM: Internal Memos→Intro Offers→Changes in intro offer→Hardware-1

Results of discounts or offers

TO: [Staff@company.com]

FROM: [Name]

SUBJECT: [TitanPro Introductory Offer]

The early results from our special introductory offer on the new [TitanPro golf club] is disappointing. Sales only reached [#] units, well below our projections.

Marketing will be conducting interviews with customers and retail outlets to see if there are any obvious explanations.

We are still very excited about this product and plan to continue offering it to the public. We may decide to revamp the ad campaign or conduct a different promotion in the future. Stay tuned for results.

- **When sales are disappointing, you may as well acknowledge the fact openly within the company—everyone will know anyway!**

- **If the company still stands behind the product, say so explicitly.**

- **Indicate what's being done to understand the causes of the poor sales performance.**

Path on CD-Rom: Internal Memos→Intro Offers→Results of discounts, offers→Bad news-1

Announcing a special event

MEMORANDUM
TO: [All Staff]
FROM: [Name]
SUBJECT: [1st Annual Fitness Fest]

The management team has just accepted the [Customer Recognition team's] suggestion that we hold a reception at each [Round-the-Clock Fitness Center] to thank our customers for their past support. We're calling this event the "1st Annual Fitness Fest.'

The target date is [Saturday, May 8]. Hours are [10 A.M. to 5 P.M.]

The [CR] team—which includes representatives from each [fitness center] as well as the home office—will be coordinating schedules, arranging refreshments and family-oriented activities, putting up decorations, and purchasing token gifts that will be handed out.

During the day we will need staff to help greet customers at the door, hand out the gifts, and run family activities and games. People who normally work on weekends will have their duties shifted to cover some of these responsibilities, but extra help will also be needed. For that reason, hourly and salaried staff who do not normally work on weekends are asked to sign up for at least one 4-hour shift. The hours will count as overtime for hourly staff. Sign-up sheets will be posted in the lunch room at the home office and in the office of each [fitness center] starting next week.

The family nature of this event is extremely important to us because a large percentage of our customers have children. Everyone is welcome to bring along their own spouse and children to partake in the day's activities.

Extra help may also be needed to help put up decorations on that [Friday, May 7]. If anyone can help out that night, please contact [Carmen Ramirez].

Further details will be communicated as our plans firm up. Until then, if you have any questions, please contact your local representative of the [Customer Recognition team].

- **If the event calls on people to put in overtime, describe if/how they will be compensated.**

- **Make sure staff know what is expected of them and how they should get involved.**

Path on CD-Rom: Internal Memos→Special Events→Announce→Club-1

Announcing a special event

TO: [All Staff@FTB.com]

FROM: [Name]

SUBJECT: Grand Opening of [Feed the Birds]

Good news!!! The interior construction is nearly finished on our new [Feed the Birds] store and the final countdown to the Grand Opening has begun.

Here are the start dates for some final key activities:

- [February 1]—Clean up interior
- [February 15]—Begin moving in equipment, supplies, and products
- [Ongoing]—Hiring and training of staff
- [March 3]—Final testing of HVAC systems, electrical systems, phone systems
- [April 15]— Run-throughs with staff; final stocking and clean up
- [May 1]— Open to the public
- [May 8]—Grand Opening

The Grand Opening promotion will last for a month. We'll be running specials on [all feeders, seed, and nature gifts], plus have drawings each day. We will also have a series of lectures from local and national [birding experts], and free demos from [the binocular and telescope sales reps]. Kids can sign up to win a free [Backyard Birdwatcher kit].

Further details will be forthcoming. For now, please make sure all of your To Do lists are targeted for completion before the Grand Opening date!

Thanks to all for your assistance. With your help, it will definitely be a Grand event!

- **Share the excitement that goes along with a grand opening; providing details can help people start talking up the event with friends, families, and customers.**

- **Listing several key dates /milestones will help staff plan out their own schedules.**

Path on CD-ROM: Internal Memos→Special Events→Announce→Store-1

Change in special event

TO: [Sales@company.com]

FROM: [Name]

SUBJECT: [Meet the Expert]

We've had to cancel the [Meet the Expert] day originally scheduled for [date]. The expert we wanted to bring in, [name], has [an illness in the family] and will not be able to attend that day.

Signs will be posted in the store alerting customers to the change in plans.

We would still like to hold this event and are trying to reschedule with [expert] or find other experts for alternative dates, but nothing firm is arranged at this time. You will be notified as soon as anything definite is known.

Thanks to all who were working hard on this effort—and don't throw away any plans you've worked on. They'll probably come in handy in the near future.

- **There's no need to go into tons of detail about why an event was canceled; keep the explanation short.**

- **If people had already put in time on the event, thank them for their effort.**

- **Mention whether the event will be rescheduled.**

Path on CD-Rom: Internal Memos→Special Events→Change in→Store-2

Change in special event

TO: [All Staff@FTB.com]

FROM: [Name]

SUBJECT: Change in Grand Opening of [Feed the Birds]

When was the last time you saw a bald eagle up close and personal?

You'll get the chance at our Grand Opening scheduled for [May 15]. We recently learned that a wildlife rehabilitation expert is available to come to the store and show off some spectacular birds for our customers. We're all very excited. It should be a great show for old and young alike!

To make room for the Birds of Prey exhibit, we will be moving some shelves and kiosks from the middle of the store towards the edges.

This new activity is in addition to everything else that's being planned.

Everyone's done a great job so far, and the plans are coming together well. Thanks to everyone for their efforts.

- **An interim memo like this can be used to keep staff energized and excited about the event.**

- **Also take the opportunity to thank those who have worked hard to make the event happen; that will increase their pride of ownership.**

Path on CD-ROM: Internal Memos→Special Events→Change in→Store-2

Results of special event

TO: [Sales@company.com]

FROM: [Name]

SUBJECT: [Meet the Expert]

I don't know about you all, but I heard LOTS of great comments from customers who attended our [Meet the Expert] day [on Saturday]. Of course, there were some complaints because the lines were so long and not everyone got to talk with [expert], but they enjoyed [his/her] opening talk. And most importantly, we increased foot traffic [xx%] compared to other [Saturdays].

So thanks to everyone who pitched in, and especially the staff at [location] who coordinated all the logistics. Everything went smoothly.

[The raffle was won by a customer from [city/neighborhood]. We got a great photo of [him/her] that we'll be posting in the store along with a display of [product types] endorsed by [expert].]

- **Avoid too much detail, but provide enough so that even staff who weren't there have a basic idea of what happened.**
- **Thank people who helped out.**
- **Describe the results of any giveaways associated with the event.**

SPECIAL EVENTS

Results of special event

TO: [Names]

FROM: [Name]

SUBJECT: [Results of kickoff event]

Thanks to everyone who helped put together the [product kickoff event]. Everything went very smoothly, and people seemed very enthusiastic.

Preliminary sales figures are not particularly strong, but it is still early in the game. We don't want to overreact, so we will continue watching the figures very closely. If sales do not improve by [the end of [month]], we will probably look at developing new marketing strategies.

In the meantime, thanks again to everyone who put in so much work on the [kickoff]. Great job, everyone!

- Try to find something to praise even if sales results aren't great yet.

- Thank people for their effort.

- Don't hide the negative results, but explain how the situation will be handled.

Path on CD-ROM: Internal Memos→Special Events→Results→Poor-1

Explaining a bonus program

TO: [Name@company.com]

FROM: [Name]

SUBJECT: New promotion

Now is the time that our customers do much of their vacation planning, so we're about to launch a new promotion. By special arrangement with [luggage company], we're going to be offering the following free gift to all our customers who book tickets valued at [$xxx] or more. Here's how it's being described in letters and promotional advertising:

SPECIAL BONUS: If you've traveled by air lately, you know the airlines are really enforcing the "must fit under the seat" rule! Well, now you won't have to worry that yours WILL fit with your FREE Carry-on tote from [brand name]. You'll be amazed at how much you can carry. And high-quality craftsmanship assures that this tote will last for years and years—and thousands of miles!

The tote bag has our logo on it and can be embroidered with the customer's initials for an additional price.

[Luggage company] is holding these tote bags for us. We will give customers a coupon that they will have to take to the [luggage company] themselves.

If you haven't seen these [brand name] tote bags, stop by my office to take a look! They're very well constructed and durable, so you can be proud to offer them to our customers.

Any questions?

- **Using the same language that's being used in advertisements, posters, etc. lets staff hear exactly what customers hear.**

- **Describe what the staff's responsibility is during the promotion.**

Path on CD-ROM: Internal Memos→Bonus Program→Explain→Travel-1

BONUS PROGRAMS

Explaining a bonus program

TO: [Name@company.com]

FROM: [Name]

SUBJECT: Watch for start of FREE MONTH offer

Starting on [date], we'll be running our annual "Free Month" of service offer—this time linked to our new [SonicWeb™ Service].

The [IS] department is fixing our ordering screens so this offer will automatically appear when you enter a new order. There will also be reminders on each screen to make sure we mention it to each and every new customer who calls.

We'll be holding a training session next week on [weekday] at [time] to review the features of this new service and role-play how to best present it to customers. If you can't attend, please contact your supervisor so we can make other arrangements.

- **Describe what staff will encounter during the promotion that's different from usual (e.g., banners on the computer screen).**

- **If the subject is too detailed to describe in an e-mail, arrange a meeting or training session so staff will be prepared when the promotion starts.**

Path on CD-ROM: Internal Memos→Bonus Program→Explain→Cable Web-1

Change in the bonus program

TO: [Sales@company.com]

FROM: [Name]

SUBJECT: Change in bonus offer

[Due to a high response rate], we have run out of stock of the [product name] that was being given away to customers who ordered through our Web site. Since we still have [## days/weeks] left in the initial offer, we have decided to continue the promotion but give away [product name2] as the free item instead.

The ad on the Web site has been changed accordingly.

If you take calls from customers who saw the initial order and wanted the original free item instead of the substitute, tell them we do not know if or when we will get additional [product name] in stock. If they don't want the substitute item, offer to take [$x] off their purchase price.

Questions?

- **Briefly describe the reason for the change.**

- **Describe what impact, if any, it will have on customers and on sales staff.**

- **Describe options for dealing with customers.**

Path on CD-ROM: Internal Memos→Bonus Program→Changes→Generic-1

Results of bonus program

TO: [Name@company.com]

FROM: [Name]

SUBJECT: Results of Buy One/Get One Free Promotion

Our "buy one, get one free" offer just ended, and preliminary sales figures show that we fell short of our projections. We had hoped the offer would increase foot traffic and sales [xx%] over a comparable non-promotion period, but figures show we actually were below the usual foot traffic.

[I'd like all the sales staff to meet tomorrow at 8:30 to do a quick debrief to see if we can identify anything obvious that would account for these disappointing results. I'll be particularly interested in how we can test whether it would be worthwhile to rerun the promotion at a later date or if we need to try an entirely new approach.]

In the meantime, we will carry through with our plans of marking down merchandise that didn't move through this promotion.

- **Be upfront about disappointing results.**

- **Describe as much as you can about what will be done to follow up, especially if staff will be involved.**

- **Discuss if anything is being done immediately or if the promotion will continue as planned.**

Path on CD-ROM: Internal Memos→Bonus Program→Results→Clothing-1

Announce new ad campaign

TO: All Employees

FROM: [Name]

SUBJECT: New Advertising Campaign

Recent marketing research studies we've conducted have indicated that consumers perceived [our product/service] as [problematic attribute] and [other attribute], despite the [product/service] reformulations we've made over the past [time period]. In short, perception is lagging behind reality.

To correct this perception problem, and revitalize flagging sales, we have developed a new advertising and marketing campaign positioning [product/service] as [new, desirable attribute]. The campaign, developed by [agency name], will break on [date], utilizing [medium], [medium], and [medium] directed at [target audience(s)]. Additionally, we have [created/revised] our Web site to reflect this new [new attribute] positioning.

We're all very excited about this new direction for the [brand/line/service]. If you'd like to see samples of the advertising or review the media plan, which lists all programs, publications, and Web sites that will be running the new [product/service] creative work, please contact [employee] in [appropriate department].

- **The decision to reposition an item, line, or service is often motivated by lagging sales and/or changing marketplace realities, but also, unfortunately, by boredom or managerial whim. Provide substantive rationale for the repositioning as well as its intended results.**

- **Contrast the old/current position with the new one about to be communicated.**

- **Provide campaign details: start and end dates (or duration), media, target audience(s), Internet/Web site activity; let readers know how they can see campaign materials and schedules.**

Path on CD-ROM: Internal Memos→Ad Campaigns→New campaign→Repositioning-1

Announce new ad campaign

TO: All Corporate and Branch Employees

FROM: [Name]

SUBJECT: Advertising Campaign Launch

This is to advise you that advertising announcing the availability of our new [no-fee brokerage] services will break [next Monday].

Advertising describing the benefits of the new service offerings, and their superiority to those offered by our competitors, will begin appearing in print next week; we'll be in major-market and financial newspapers as well as selected national newsmagazines and business/money books. TV and radio will be used in selected markets beginning a month from today. We have also updated our Web site to highlight these new services, and we will be running banner advertising on financial Web sites and selected search engines.

Please contact Corporate Marketing if you would like a copy of the complete advertising schedule listing all programs, publications, and Web sites in which the campaign will run.

- **Announce the date of the advertising start and the purpose of the campaign.**

- **Describe or list campaign components (media, dayparts, publication type/target, Internet activity, Web site changes/ additions).**

- **Provide internal or external contact information so readers can see/obtain copies of advertisements and media schedules.**

Path on CD-ROM: Internal Memos→Ad Campaigns→New campaign→Announcing-1

Announce new ad campaign

TO: All Employees

FROM: [Name]

SUBJECT: Product Relaunch

In light of [reason/motivation for relaunch] and [changes in marketplace], we will be relaunching the [brand name] [brand/product/service], which was [pulled/discontinued] from the market [time period ago] for [reason for discontinuation].

A new advertising campaign, announcing the [return/relaunch] of [brand] will begin on [date]. The campaign consists of [medium], [medium], and [medium], which communicate the familiar [benefits] of [product] while placing a new emphasis on [new benefit/reason for purchase]. Advertising/marketing communications will target [target audience].

If you would like to see any of the [medium, medium, or medium] advertising that will be running, or review a copy of the media schedule, please contact [employee] in [department].

- **Provide brief background information that led to the relaunch decision (marketplace conditions, consumer demand, consumer research, etc.); if appropriate, you might also remind readers of reasons for the product/ service's previous discontinuation.**

- **Give details about the new campaign: dates, media, target. Briefly describe similarities and differences between previous campaigns and the new effort.**

- **Provide contact information so readers can obtain creative work and media plans for their own review.**

Path on CD-ROM: Internal Memos→Ad Campaigns→New campaign→Relaunch-1

AD CAMPAIGNS

Announce new ad campaign

TO: All Employees

FROM: [Name]

SUBJECT: Advertising Launch

Now that the New and Improved [product] has replaced the original at [retail locations], we are ready to roll out our consumer marketing effort! Advertising announcing the introduction of New and Improved [product/brand] begins on [date].

Advertising will assure [target] that [product] is the same great [category] they've always trusted for [users], while highlighting [product's] new [feature/benefit], [feature/benefit], and [feature/benefit].

We will be using [medium], [medium], and [medium] in [locations] to support the refreshed product. The first wave of the campaign goes through [date]; the second wave begins [time period] into [date] (See [person] in [department] if you need copies of media plans or [campaign creative elements].)

Please join me in congratulating [internal department(s)] and [agency] for the fine work they've done on the campaign for the [refreshed/revised/improved] [brand/product].

- New advertising is frequently developed to announce changes to an established product/brand/ service.

- It is important to convey to both consumers and employees that the core values/ benefits of the old brand have not been lost or discarded; rather, enhancements have been made to improve quality and appeal.

- Provide campaign details—media used, start and end dates, specific target audience(s)—and internal contact information.

Path on CD-ROM: Internal Memos→Ad Campaigns→New campaign→Benefits-1

Change in ad campaign

TO: All Employees

FROM: [Name]

SUBJECT: Change to Advertising Campaign

I am sorry to advise you that we will be making some changes to our current advertising campaign in response to feedback we and our agency have received from a significant number of consumers.

Several segments of the television audience are apparently uncomfortable with some of the "action" sequences in our commercials. We have received a number of letters from individuals as well as consumer watchdog groups stating their displeasure with what they perceive to be "excessively violent" depictions of automobile accidents. Despite our position that such scenes are necessary to communicate the efficacy of our product in preventing such accidents, we have been threatened with boycotts and negative publicity campaigns in the press and are forced to take these threats seriously.

Our advertising agency is aware of the situation and is currently developing proposed TV commercial revisions for our review within the next 10 days. I will advise you of our progress in effecting the necessary changes

- **Advertisers respond differently to consumer complaints and threats—assess how important those complaints are to your business and consider the implications of ignoring the threats—but remember that there will ALWAYS be someone complaining about something; put the complaint in perspective.**

- **Advise your readers of specific "hot buttons" in the advertising that motivated the protest. If solutions are already at hand, say so.**

AD CAMPAIGNS

Change in ad campaign

TO: All Employees

FROM: [Name]

SUBJECT: Change to Advertising Campaign

I have just been advised by our legal counsel of a change that we must immediately make to our current ad campaign in order to avoid legal action by our largest competitor.

All side-by-side product demonstration scenes in our television commercials must be removed or substantially revised. Because [competitor] has discontinued the product shown in our advertising and replaced it with a model they claim to be "new and improved," their position is that our product demos depict a competitive comparison that is no longer appropriate or valid because we are contrasting our current model with their former model.

I have informed our agencies about this requirement and they will be getting back to us with their recommendations and cost estimates for commercial revisions. Rest assured that any changes we effect in our advertising will not compromise the integrity of our communication or in any way dilute the thrust of our product superiority message.

Please feel free to contact me if you have any questions.

- **Competitors can often impede a marketer's advertising plans—all's fair in love and war, but not in advertising!**

- **Communicate which specific elements of the advertising are in dispute and how you intend to resolve the challenge.**

Path on CD-ROM: Internal Memos→Ad Campaigns→Change in campaign→Competitor-1

Change in ad campaign

TO: All Employees

FROM: [Name]

SUBJECT: Revisions to Advertising

As you know, the campaign we've been running for the past six years has been quite successful in generating trial and repeat purchase.

However, given how long our commercials have been airing, we are concerned that they may be losing their impact in terms of memorability or ability to break through. Because we are hesitant to fix what clearly is not broken but are also sensitive to the need to put fresh advertising in front of our consumers, we have decided to make several modest changes to our TV commercials while maintaining those elements that have worked so well for us.

Consequently, beginning next month all TV advertising for [Happy Catsup] will feature new and more contemporary music, faster pacing, and more visually exciting graphics. Working from the existing film footage, the agency has re-edited the commercials to give them more drive and excitement while maintaining the [Happy Catsup] product promise.

We will be screening the new advertising at next week's sales meeting. I look forward to hearing your reactions.

- **When executional refreshment is merited but budgets are tight, revisions can be the way to go. Don't wait until sales are declining to make such changes, though! Anticipate possible decreases and get ahead of the curve.**

- **Describe both the changes to be made as well as elements that will remain as is.**

- **Consider screening or previewing revised advertising for the staff prior to air.**

Path on CD-ROM: Internal Memos→Ad Campaigns→Change in campaign→Creative-1

Change in ad campaign

[TO:]

[FROM:]

[SUBJECT:]

[DATE:]

A review of our enrollment statistics recently completed by our advertising agency suggests that a slight revision to our marketing target is in order.

While our student body has historically been overwhelmingly female and the vast majority of our student-enrollment advertising and marketing directed toward [working women], fully [40%] of the student body is male. This suggests that if we were to target men and women equally, or even dedicate a certain small percentage of our marketing budget toward reaching men specifically, we could increase our enrollment—and revenues—considerably.

I will be speaking with our advertising and public relations agencies about the implications of this target shift for our marketing efforts. I welcome your questions and comments.

- Memo opens by announcing that a change is being considered but does not (yet) give specifics of the proposed change.

- Second paragraph provides historical context, contrasted against current situation.

- Memo closes with indication of action steps (actual and potential).

Path on CD-ROM: Internal Memos→Ad Campaigns→Change in campaign→Targeting-1

Results of ad campaigns

TO: All Employees

FROM: [Name]

SUBJECT: Results of Advertising Campaign

Results of the third-quarter advertising campaign have just been tabulated. I regret to advise you that we were not completely successful in achieving our objectives.

The objectives we had set for the campaign prior to launch were:

- increase wholesale $ volume over last year's third-quarter level by 15%
- retain number two market share position
- increase Premium line share of total company unit sales from 25% to 35%

Our Sales Analysis group reports that Q3 dollar volume rose by 4%, and that the unit sales of the Premium line remained unchanged at 25%.

On the positive side, we still hold the number two share position in the category.

We will be studying the situation in more detail to determine the reasons for these results: studying the competition's sales/pricing strategies, meeting with our advertising agency to review creative work and media plans, speaking to retailers, etc. We will provide you with a complete analysis by the end of this month. In the meantime, please call me with any questions.

- **It's never easy to deliver bad news. Be as dispassionate as possible.**
- **Be sure to point out any positive results that did emerge.**
- **Describe what will be done next: analysis, revisions, strategic shifts, etc.**

Path on CD-ROM: Internal Memos→Ad Campaigns→Results of campaign→Negative-1

Announce new agency

TO: All Company Employees

FROM: [NAME]

SUBJECT: New Internet Agency

This will advise you that we are engaging the services of a new media agency to bring [Archaic & Obsolete Products] into the twenty-first century.

We have just hired [Flashy Young Turks], who I'm sure you've all read about in the trade press. [FYT] will begin working for us immediately on a variety of projects: designing [A&O's] first Web site, developing online advertising, and advising us on Internet media planning and buying. (In the longer term, we are hoping to have [FYT] work with our own technical staff on setting up an e-commerce division, although that's still a way off at this point.) [FYT] will work closely with our traditional advertising agency, [Agency name], to ensure synergy in all company communications.

Marketing and MIS will be meeting with the [FYT] account management team next Tuesday to begin discussions about the [2001] campaign. Please make [Sara Smith, Director of Marketing] and [Ann Anderson, Director of MIS] aware of any issues you'd like them to address with the new agency before the end of this week.

- **Describe specific assignments the new-media agency will be handling as there may be confusion among your staff as to the purpose of the new hire.**

- **Provide the opportunity for staff input in advance of initial meetings.**

Path on CD-Rom: Internal Memos→Ad Campaigns→New agency→Internet-2

Change in policy

To: [Group@company.com]

From: [name@company.com]

Re: [Policy change]

This is to advise you of a change in policy regarding [topic].

Due to [factor/problem/abuse], we will no longer [offer/allow] the [use/option] of [service]. This change is effective as of [date].

Please advise your [clients/customers] of this change but assure them that we will [offer alternative solution/service].

Please call me if you would like to discuss this matter in more detail or if you encounter any [customer/client] resistance to this [change/policy].

Sincerely,

[Name]

- **State the change, its effective date, and reason/rationale for the change.**

- **If readers need to take specific action (such as notifying customers of the change), say so.**

- **Provide alternative solutions that they can offer customers/ clients.**

CHANGES IN PROCESSES & POLICIES

Change in processes

To: [Group@company.com]

From: [name@company.com]

Re: [New policy on decision making]

After careful review, we've decided to give more decision-making authority to staff. We think this will speed up our ability to respond to customer requests and make us more efficient.

This policy change will be implemented in two stages: Initially, we will ask each salesperson to report on his or her key decisions during the weekly staff meeting. The purpose is NOT to rethink those decisions, but rather to help all of us reach a mutual understanding of decision guidelines. After a [three month] period, these weekly reviews will be discontinued, and staff will be encouraged to informally check in with the sales team and supervisors as needed.

The proposed decision-making changes are:

[describe old and new decision-making authority limits]

We will discuss this new policy and its implication at this week's staff meeting. It will become effective [date].

If you have any questions, bring them to the meeting or send me e-mail.

- Give the reason for the change.

- Describe in some detail specifically what will happen.

- Compare the old and new policies.

- Inform staff how they can voice their questions or concerns.

Path on CD-ROM: Internal Memos→Processes & Policies→Processes→Sales reps-1

Change in processes

To: [Group@company.com]

From: [name@company.com]

Re: Use of internal design services

Effective immediately, all requests made to the [studio/ graphics dept./design dept.] for [internal/interdepartmental] design services must be made using the attached request form. As you will see, the form requires the inclusion of a client-billable or interdepartmental billable job number as well as a supervisor's signature.

We hate having to formalize the process of working with the [studio], however, in light of the higher-than-usual number of internal requests, we find ourselves unable to complete client-billable jobs on deadline. Thanks for your cooperation with this new policy.

- Internal departments can be taken advantage of; policies designed to protect these departments from abuse may be necessary. Explain why the policy is being put into effect.

- Indicate the level of authorization needed for internal requests.

Path on CD-ROM: Internal Memos→Processes & Policies→Processes→Design-1

Changes in roles or responsibilities

[TO:]

[FROM:]

[SUBJECT:]

In light of (a) our recent budget cutbacks and (b) the departure of our Manager of Inventor Relations, the responsibility of meeting with outside product inventors will now be divided among the members of the Marketing Department.

Requests from inventors for meetings with the company will be routed to the Marketing Director, who will then assign a product manager to conduct the initial meeting. In most cases, the product manager selected will be the one whose category most closely fits the candidate submission. (If an invention does not cleanly fit any of our department's existing categories, more than one product manager may be asked to attend the initial meeting.) Should the candidate product be given a preliminary green light, the product manager will be responsible for working with the inventor on product modifications.

Please let me know if you have any questions.

- **Budget cuts and resignations often force reassignment or diffusion of current responsibilities among the remaining staff.**

- **Provide a logical rationale for the new logistics.**

Path on CD-ROM: Internal Memos→Processes & Policies→Roles, responsibility→Diffusion-1

Change in travel policy

[TO:]

[FROM:]

[DATE:]

[SUBJECT:]

In order to contain our continually escalating travel expenses, it has become necessary to make the following changes to our travel policy:

1. A maximum of [#] members of the [Client Service] team will be allowed to attend out-of-town client meetings/functions involving non-billable lodging costs.

2. A maximum of [#] members of the [Client Service] team will be allowed to attend out-of-town client meetings/functions requiring non-billable domestic air travel.

3. A maximum of [#] members of the [Client Service] team will be allowed to attend out-of-town client meetings/functions requiring non-billable international air travel.

We recognize that there will be occasions when certain key personnel must attend a given meeting and that such occasions will involve exceeding the allowable limits. Such occasions must be reviewed individually by [senior management] prior to booking hotels and flights.

Thank you for your cooperation.

- **Be explicit about limits relating to lodging and various types of air travel.**

- **Acknowledge, but do not encourage, the possibility of exceptions.**

Path on CD-ROM: Internal Memos→Processes & Policies→Travel policy→Staff-1

Change in commissions

[TO:]
[FROM:]
[SUBJECT:]
[DATE:]

In order to simplify our compensation system and provide you with bigger commissions, we will be going to a flat-rate system, effective [date].

Rather than offering [8% commissions] on [item A], [9%] on [item B], and [11%] on [item C], the commission rate for all items in the line will be a flat [10%].

We will review the sales and commissions-paid results after [six months]. Should it turn out that more members of the sales force are earning more under the new system—as we predict will be the case—it will be retained. If you're making less money—which we think unlikely to happen—we will consider revising the system.

Please contact me if you have any questions.

- **Give reasons for the change.**

- **Provide specific examples of how the new system will work.**

- **Anticipate negative reactions, and show that you're willing to review the new system after a reasonable amount of time.**

Path on CD-ROM: Internal Memos→Processes & Policies→Commission→Flat-1

Changes in territories

[Date]

[Name/Title]
[Business/Organization Name]
[Address]
[City, State ZIP]

Dear [   ]:

This letter announces a redistribution of sales territories for all associates working on the [JetPac account]. We have reviewed everyone's recent sales records and have adjusted plans in an attempt to better cover the market. In no way should this redistribution be construed as indicating dissatisfaction with your performance. We have confidence in your abilities; otherwise, you would not have received this letter.

Changes effective [November 1] are as follows:

[• Sheila Marcus will move from our northeast to our southeast sector in an attempt to revitalize sagging sales in the market. Don Gelding, former sales manager of the southeast section, is no longer with the firm.]

[• Bob Brand has been promoted to national sales manager and will supervise all regional sales managers. Bob's former position as midcentral sales manager will be handled by Mary Bradley.]

[• Northwest manager Dennis Punzo and southwest manager Astrid Kirche will switch positions, a measure designed to increase sales dynamics within the two regions.]

All positions will continue reporting directly or indirectly to [the chief operating officer, Beatrice Potter]. Questions may be directed either to your immediate supervisor or to me.

Sincerely,

[Name]
[Title]

Path on CD-ROM: Internal Memos→Processes & Policies→Territories→Redistribution-1

CHANGES IN PROCESSES & POLICIES

Changes in technology

[TO:]
[FROM:]
[SUBJECT:]
[DATE:]

This is a reminder of the policy regarding the use of personal e-mail on the company's server.

All e-mail coming from or going to [company.com] must be business related.

We realize that sales and marketing staff are often on the road for extended periods of time and need to send and receive personal e-mail to family members, etc. While we have no objection to your using the company-provided laptops for such correspondence, we request that you use a personal e-mail account/address to do so. (As you probably know, you can get free personal Web-based e-mail accounts through Yahoo, Hotmail, or any of a growing number of other search engines; or you can use whatever e-mail system your personal ISP offers.)

Thank you for your cooperation.

- **If you are restricting the use of your company's server, provide suggestions for alternatives.**

- **Thank the staff for their cooperation with the policy.**

Path on CD-ROM: Internal Memos→Processes & Policies→New technology→E-mail policy-1

Changes in technology

[TO:]

[FROM:]

[SUBJECT:]

[DATE:]

Our new intranet is up and running!

The intranet will make your life easier in just about every way.

You'll be able to check on product prices, quantity discounts, special deals, product availabilities, shipping schedules, commission rates, and just about every other detail concerning product, pricing, and income.

You'll be able to send and receive internal memos.

You'll be able to log in orders, changes to orders, and updates on customer payments.

You'll even be able to [other feature/benefit].

And what all this means, of course, is more sales—more commissions—and faster payments to you!

Go to [address/URL] now and check it out.

- **Turn what could be a daunting technological innovation into something that offers direct advantages to the sales staff.**

- **List features of the intranet, linking them to personal benefits.**

- **Include the address/URL.**

Path on CD-ROM: Internal Memos→Processes & Policies→New technology→Intranet-1

Change in advertising

TO: [Sales@company.com]

FROM: [Name]

SUBJECT: Change to Advertising Start Date

I just got a call from Operations with some very good news: the Spring product line will be available to ship a full month ahead of our current schedule.

In light of this news, I will be advising the Agency that we need to start our TV and print advertising in March rather than April, as is currently planned. I am meeting with Finance this afternoon to determine what sort of incremental budget I will have available for the extra media needed for an earlier launch. Once the budget number is in hand, I'll need to get your recommendations on product spending priorities; only then will we bring the agency into the loop.

Let's meet in the large conference room at 10:00 tomorrow morning to discuss spending priorities and also any challenges you anticipate may arise (packaging, PR plans, etc.) as a result of advancing the advertising calendar.

- **Provide the good news as well as specifics about dates.**

- **Set the meeting time and place and let the readers know what specific information they should be prepared to discuss at the meeting.**

Path on CD-ROM: Internal Memos→Processes & Policies→Advertising→Start-1

Change in advertising

TO: [Sales@company.com]

FROM: [Name]

SUBJECT: Change in Strategic Direction

In light of the recent consumer research study indicating that:

(1) our target market prefers the taste of [Happy Porky Hot Dogs] over the competition by a margin of more than two to one; and

(2) price is irrelevant to our most loyal customers,

(3) we need to discuss changes to the strategy that the agency is moving forward with for the fall campaign.

Before any advertising is developed and presented to us, the agency needs to know that the "taste" message now takes precedence over the "value/price" communication. I want to get the agency's point of view in this, too, of course. I'd also like to get their recommendation on including references to the research findings in the advertising.

Please give me your thoughts on these issues, then get in touch with the agency about this to have them stop the presses and to set up a meeting with them for some time next week. Thanks, [Bob].

- **Changes of strategy are not uncommon but are often met with resistance internally and from the agency. Providing support for the change and soliciting points of view from colleagues and the agency will help the process.**

- **Anticipate specific tactical/ executional changes necessitated by the strategic change and be ready for budget overages!**

- **Request a meeting date to discuss strategic issues in person.**

Path on CD-ROM: Internal Memos→Processes & Policies→Advertising→Direction-1

Media relations

TO: All Company Employees

FROM: [NAME]

SUBJECT: Media Relations Policy

This will advise you of the company's media relations policy.

Under no circumstances are you to speak with members of the press about company business. This includes but is not limited to issues such as company profits and losses, new product launches, expansion or consolidation plans, advertising or public relations campaigns, budgets, staff additions or deletions, vendor or supplier contracts or relations, etc.

Refer all inquiries from the media to [Mark Morris at extension 565] in our public relations department or [Laura Thomas, (555) 555-5555] at our outside public relations agency.

Please let me know if you have any questions about this policy.

- **Many employees are not prepared for press inquiries, so be explicit about the sorts of issues that are off-limits for discussion with the media.**

- **Provide names and phone numbers for both internal and external parties who are authorized to deal with the press.**

Path on CD-ROM: Internal Memos→Processes & Policies→Media relations→Manufacturer-1

Internal changes to share with clients

[TO:]

[FROM:]

[DATE:]

[SUBJECT:]

The company will soon be undergoing a reorganization to allow us [to focus more of our attention on our core business].

While many of the details remain to be worked out, the critical fact to be aware of at this time is that the vast majority of organizational changes being considered will not affect your day-to-day dealings with your clients. In fact, should everything go as smoothly as planned, the clients themselves need never know that any changes have taken place here.

Nevertheless, should clients ask about our new corporate structure, you should feel free to share with them [any information they request, as none of the planned changes are secret in any way]. And be sure to let them know that none of the changes we're instituting in our own internal workings will detract from our ability to continue serving them in any way—indeed, the only changes they may notice will be improvements!

Once all of the specifics of the reorganization are nailed down, we will hold a series of internal meetings to bring the entire staff up to speed. Thank you for your cooperation.

- **If rumors are floating around, consider issuing a memo to restore sanity and order.**

- **Let staff know how the reorganization will or won't affect client service—and what to tell clients if they ask about it.**

- **Thank the staff for their cooperation.**

Path on CD-ROM: Internal Memos→Processes & Policies→Internal changes→Reorganization-1

CHANGES IN PROCESSES & POLICIES

Internal changes to share with clients

[TO:]

[FROM:]

[DATE:]

[SUBJECT:]

This is to confirm that we will be moving into our new offices at [address] on [date].

While the actual move will take place over a weekend in order to maximize our productivity and our ability to serve our clients with as little disruption as possible, there will still undoubtedly be some of the usual frenzy that accompanies any significant change.

Please inform your clients of our scheduled moving date as soon as possible, and let them know that there may be unexpected temporary annoyances such as phone or e-mail problems that will be fixed as soon as possible and ask them to bear with us. (I'm not promising that such problems will occur; I'm just trying to anticipate what could happen!)

You may wish to give your clients your home and/or cell phone numbers just in case there are any difficulties in reaching us during our first few days in the new office. This will not only allow business to continue as normally as possible, it will also let your clients know how committed you (we) are to serving them.

Thank you for your cooperation.

- **Moving disrupts not only your own company's life but that of your clients.**

- **Put backup plans in place and advise staff on how to implement them.**

Path on CD-ROM: Internal Memos→Processes & Policies→Internal changes→Move-1

How to handle leads

[TO:]

[FROM:]

[SUBJECT:]

[DATE:]

This will advise you of the company's [new] policy regarding commission payments on sales that are generated from leads in one territory that result in business in another territory.

It is obviously in everyone's best interest to share or pass on leads even if the discoverer of the lead is not the closer of the deal. In fact, it's one of the best ways to grow the company.

We want to encourage you to share leads across territories—and we will reward you for doing so.

Effective immediately, any lead from one region that results in a deal in another region will result in both salespeople/regions getting a share of the commission. If salesperson A provides a lead to salesperson B that results in B closing a deal, both A and B will receive commission: A will get [35%] and B will get [65%].

We feel that this commission split will provide a substantial incentive for every member of the sales force to share or pass on leads while at the same time providing the salesperson who pursues and closes a sale with an appropriate reward.

Good luck to all!

- **Show how the policy benefits all involved parties.**
- **Provide rationale for the decision.**
- **Do not openly invite questions or comments; if the policy provokes rancor, you'll hear about it!**

Path on CD-ROM: Internal Memos→Processes & Policies→How to handle leads→Commissions-1

BROCHURES/CATALOGS

New marketing prices

TO: [sales@company.com]

FROM: [Name]

SUBJECT: New brochure to drop [date]

The revised brochure is set to drop on [date], which means you should start to receive calls around [date].

Most of the brochure is the same as the last one, but there are a few things I wanted to highlight:

- [Discounts are now offered on the total purchase price, not the purchase price of any individual training product. This means customers who order a little bit of a lot of things can qualify for a discount. As you know, before customers only got discounts if they ordered [$$] or more on an individual product. BE SURE TO EMPHASIZE THIS AS A NEW BENEFIT FOR CUSTOMERS.]

- [We no longer have prices for the Improvement Series in the catalog. Instead, it says "call for quote." In the next staff meeting, we'll go over how to handle these calls.]

- [For the first time, we have quotes and testimonials from customers in the brochure. In case there is any question, these are real quotes from real customers!]

- [Descriptions of our consulting services are now intermixed with products that cover the same topics, so our Management Training section covers the books, self-study workshops, and consulting rather than having the consulting set apart as a separate item. This is a new tactic for us, so it will be important to keep track of whether this helps or hurts our consulting sales.]

Look for the new brochure to appear in your mailboxes within the week. If you don't receive yours, contact [Manny] at [x23].

- **A memo like this would be just one element of a sales training effort intended to adequately prepare your sales staff to handle sales calls.**

- **Be specific on how any changes affect what people should do or how they should do it.**

Path on CD-ROM: Internal Memos→Brochures, catalogs→New prices→Training firm-1

Changes/corrections to catalog

TO: [Sales@company.com]

FROM: [Name]

SUBJECT: Change in seminar dates

Due to a problem with [room availability], we've had to change the dates for the [title of seminar/event] seminar originally scheduled for [date] in [city].

The new date is [date]. [And we've had to move it to [location] in [city] instead of the original location.]

We already had [##] participants signed up, and those customers have already been contacted. If they were unable to attend on the new dates, we offered them a full refund or the ability to apply the fees paid to a different seminar.

Please be sure to make notes to yourself to mention the date and location changes whenever customers come in.

We've prepared a new fax cover page that lists the correct dates and location for the seminar, and you can send that to customers if they want to see it in writing.

- Be clear about the change and the reason behind it.

- You may want to add text that describes how sales staff should describe the change with customers. You certainly don't want them saying anything like, "We couldn't get organized and had to cancel the May meeting!" Tell them what to say instead.

Path on CD-ROM: Internal Memos→Brochures, catalogs→Changes to catalog→Wrong date-1

CHANGE IN PRICING

Price decrease

TO: [Group@company.com]

FROM: [Name]

SUBJECT: Lower prices on high-ticket items

We will soon be announcing to our customer base a new pricing policy for our high-ticket items. As a competitive move—and to increase retail volume on higher-priced merchandise—we will be deeply discounting selected high-end items in every department: computers, stereo components and systems, digital cameras, etc.

Communication with our current customers—and advertising to prospects—will highlight the fact that this new pricing move isn't a sale but rather a continuing policy of offering top-of-the-line equipment at lower-than-normal prices. We believe that this approach to high-end equipment will create a unique position for our store within the online retail community.

Please contact me if you have any questions about this policy or the customer/prospect-oriented communication announcing it.

- **Provide information about the upcoming decrease and rationale for its institution.**

- **Allow staff to follow up with you with any questions.**

Path on CD-ROM: Internal Memos→Prices, Pricing Structure→Price decrease→Online retailer-1

Price decrease

TO: [Group@company.com]

FROM: [Name]

SUBJECT: Deeper discounts on top sellers

With the unchecked appearance and growth of competing e-retailers offering books and CDs, it has become critical that we offer our consumers a true point of difference versus the competition.

To that end, we will now be selling all *New York Times* bestsellers for 60% off the cover price and all Billboard Top 100 CDs for 50% off list price. While these items will no longer be as profitable for us on a per-unit basis, the additional volume we expect to generate for (non-bestseller) products as a result of this lower bestseller pricing is forecast to offset specific profit shortfalls.

This level of savings forms the cornerstone of our new "popular favorites" policy that will be communicated to both current and potential customers beginning next month. Other elements are still being worked out; however, it is crucial that we bring this news to consumers immediately in light of recent competitive announcements.

Please see me if you have any questions.

- **Drastic pricing policies on selected items may mean higher overall volume, offsetting per-unit profit decreases.**

- **Explain your rationale for the decrease and advise readers if additional policy changes are to follow.**

CHANGE IN PRICING

Price increase

To: [Group@company.com]

From: [Name]

Re: Higher commissions

As part of the contract negotiation process with [client] for the coming year, I am proposing an increase on our commission on [business area] from [x%] to [y%] and raising our fee on [other business area] from [$a] to [$b].

Please be aware that I am not proposing these increases out of sheer greed. Repeated budget cuts by [client] have decimated our bottom line and we are operating the account at barely break-even levels.

While I do expect some resistance from [client] to these proposed increases, I intend to fully explain to [him] the need for our business—specifically [his] account—to be a profitable one, just as it is for his company.

I will advise you of the outcome of our discussions.

- **Raising fees for client service is fraught with peril but often must be done if a client-service company is to remain viable.**

- **Advise the reader of your expectations, rationale, and results.**

Path on CD-ROM: Internal Memos→Prices, Pricing Structure→Price increase→Generic-1

Price increase

To: [Group@company.com]

From: [Name]

Re: Rate increase

This year's cost-of-living adjustment for all life-insurance policies is [x%]. Adjustments go into effect on [date] for all policyholders who choose to accept increased coverage.

Agents should advise all policyholders of the estimated increases to both their coverage and their monthly premium, providing them with complete instructions for accepting or rejecting the increase as well as potential consequences for rejection. (See the attached document for complete information and recommended methods for communicating this information.)

Please contact me with any questions you may have.

- **Routine yearly increases should not pose a problem for the staff, but newer members may need assistance in communicating increase information and implications to their customers.**

- **Make yourself available to guide staff through the process if necessary.**

Path on CD-ROM: Internal Memos→Prices, Pricing Structure→Price increase→Insurance-1

CHANGE IN PRICING

Change in pricing structure

[TO:]

[FROM:]

[DATE:]

[SUBJECT:]

[The company] will be adjusting its rates effective [date] in order to [keep pace with inflation and allow us to remain within our profit guidelines].

Key changes are as follows:

- our rate for [service] will be [$xxx/hour]
- our commission for [service] will now be [y%]
- the flat fee for [service] will be [$zzz]

We will be issuing new client-service contracts within the next [time period] that will allow clients to review the new pricing structure in detail. As we will point out—and as you may wish to state to your clients should they raise objections—all of our increases are [in line with inflation and are either equal to or lower than the increases that the clients themselves have instituted on the products they sell. In other words, these increases are neither unjustified nor excessive.]

We will provide copies of the new contracts for your review by [date]. Please feel free to contact me with any questions you may have. Thank you for your cooperation.

- **Give key details upfront.**
- **Provide ample notice to staff and advise them as to how clients will be informed.**

Path on CD-ROM: Internal Memos→Prices, Pricing→Pricing structure→Structure-1

New product

[TO:]

[FROM:]

[SUBJECT:]

[DATE:]

We will be modifying the launch schedule for the new [product/service] based on recent consumer input.

As you may know, the original launch date for [product/service] had been set for [date]. Consumer focus groups held [last month] in order to serve as a final "disaster check" did indeed reveal several important user concerns that we feel are worth addressing. Consequently, [R&D and Marketing] will be making some minor readjustments to the [product/service feature] in order to avoid potential consumer resistance.

While we're all understandably disappointed about not being able to make our original deadline, the changes we'll be making will result in a far more attractive [product/service]. The delay will be more than worth the trouble it may cause. We expect the revised [product/service] to be ready to [ship] by [date].

Thank you for your cooperation.

- **If staff is expecting a new product/service launch by a certain date, it is critical that they be informed about delays.**

- **Briefly explain the nature of the problem.**

- **Assure staff that the modifications being made are important enough to alter the launch schedule.**

New service

[TO:]

[FROM:]

[DATE:]

[SUBJECT:]

Effective [date], we will be adding an important new element to the roster of [financial services] we can offer our clients.

Due to [law/regulation/policy change], [category] firms such as ours will be able to offer [discount brokerage services] to our clients in addition to our current package of [financial services]. This addition will make us not only more valuable to current clients but should also help us to penetrate new market segments that we have been unable to reach to date.

We will be holding a series of in-depth seminars to educate all client-service staff on the new [services]. In the meantime, please let each of your clients know that [discount brokerage services] are soon to be an important part of [company], which will make working with us a more convenient and complete [financial] experience than ever before.

- **Communicate effective dates and new services to be offered.**

- **Give a brief explanation of the larger changes that motivated this internal change.**

- **If your staff is not yet fully ready to offer or communicate the new service, you may still want them to give their clients a "coming soon" announcement to pre-empt competitors from offering similar services.**

Path on CD-ROM: Internal Memos→Product or Service Updates→New product or service→Offering-1

Change in existing product

TO: [Sales@company.com]

FROM: [Name]

SUBJECT: Change to Product Name

Dear [Name]:

Legal has advised me of a problem with the intended name for one of the key items in the 2001 product line. Apparently [our biggest competitor] has already trademarked the name [Magic Sweep] for their line of [brooms], meaning that it's not available for our use. We will be changing the line name to [Mystery Sweep], which Legal assures me is available and protectable.

Since all of our new commercials have already been shot using [brooms] with the [Magic Sweep] name, I will be advising the agency that they will need to revise the advertising to now say/show [Mystery Sweep]; they will get back to me with cost and timing estimates. Meanwhile, I need you to advise the product design, package design, public relations, and internet teams about this necessary change as well.

Please get back to me by the end of the day tomorrow and advise me of your progress.

- **Clearly explain the nature of the change and the reason behind it.**

- **If you've already taken action, communicate that to the reader. Let him/her know which specific steps he/she needs to take so that there is no duplication of effort (and also to avoid any critical action from falling through the cracks).**

Path on CD-ROM: Internal Memos→Product or Service Updates→Changes→Name-1

Change in existing service

[TO:]
[FROM:]
[SUBJECT:]
[DATE:]

Due to unexpected delays on the part of our suppliers, we will not be able to offer [color copying and scanning] to our customers until at least [date].

Since we have been announcing the arrival of these anticipated services [in advertising and in-store displays], we are certain to have at least a few disgruntled customers. In order to keep the disappointment level at a minimum, we will temporarily [lower the cost of all black-and-white copying and scanning costs]. [Prices for black-and-white services will be restored to normal levels upon arrival of the new color machines.]

Please assure customers that we will be offering [color services] as soon as possible and point out the (temporarily) reduced [black-and-white] costs in the meantime.

Thank you for your cooperation.

- Explain the cause of the temporary setback.
- Offer a backup plan to keep customers happy.
- Enlist the cooperation of your staff.

Path on CD-ROM: Internal Memos→Product or Service Updates→Changes→Service-1

Discontinuation

[TO:]

[FROM:]

[SUBJECT:]

[DATE:]

Despite the best efforts of Marketing and Sales to improve the retail performance of the [Zesty] product line, consumers are not responding. Consequently, senior management has decided to discontinue production and sales of [Zesty] effective [date].

All [Zesty] product remaining in our inventory will be offered to [off-price jobbers] at significant discounts. Since [next year's] catalog has not yet gone to press, we still have time to remove all references to [Zesty]. Retailers with stock on hand will [have the option of returning product to us or offering it to their customers at highly competitive price points].

Although it is always difficult to discontinue a product/line, and it is natural to feel that we have failed on a personal level, I would like to acknowledge the tremendous job done by every member of this company in helping to fight what was ultimately, and unfortunately, a losing battle. Thank you for your hard work and better luck next time to us all.

- **Provide a rationale for the discontinuation decision.**
- **Touch on the resulting logistics.**
- **If appropriate, thank/ acknowledge staff for their efforts.**

Discontinuation

[TO:]
[FROM:]
[SUBJECT:]
[DATE:]

In light of insurmountable resistance from [the media and consumer groups], we are forced to announce the discontinuation of the [Chain-Saw Charlie action figure line].

While we experienced strong initial orders from our [toy store and department chain] customer base, since the line has been available at retail the backlash from [the press and from several well-organized parents' groups] has made our retail partners reluctant to keep the product on their shelves. Not surprisingly, this has cut reorders down to nearly zero.

When we first considered offering the line we expected some controversy, but nothing approaching the reaction we've gotten. While our usual rule of thumb is "there's no such thing as bad publicity," this case has proven that there is an exception to just about any rule. Consequently, in the best interests of the company as a whole, we have made the decision to pull the line and [will allow retailers to return unsold product to us].

Thanks to everyone in Product Design, Sales, Marketing, and Operation for your tremendous efforts in getting the line to market.

- **Describe the issues leading to the decision.**

- **Frame the decision in the context of the company's overall philosophy regarding issues of this sort.**

- **Thank all involved for their efforts.**

Path on CD-ROM: Internal Memos→Product or Service Updates→Discontinuation→Backlash-1

Training opportunities

[TO:]

[FROM:]

[SUBJECT:]

[DATE:]

Product development, manufacturing, and shipping of the [2003] line are complete! The line will be launched at retail stores beginning [in June], supported by [TV, radio, magazine, and online advertising nationwide].

Everyone involved with the development of the ['03] line agrees that it is not only the most [extensive] ever offered by [company] but also the most [innovative and customer-friendly]. Indeed, the breadth of the line, which includes [products] to fit virtually every budget, should help propel [company] to the forefront of the [category] category.

Given the importance of the line to our company, it is imperative that [all members of the sales force] be intimately acquainted with all products, price points, benefits and features. Marketing and R&D will be leading a series of sessions [next month] that will familiarize you with the individual products and the key functional and selling points of each.

The sessions will be held on [date, date, and date]. Your attendance is mandatory. Please contact [person] in [Marketing] to reserve your slot in the training sessions. Thank you.

- **Introduction of a new line requires extensive training.**
- **Allow for multiple training sessions and stress the importance (requirement) of sales force attendance.**

Path on CD-ROM: Internal Memos→Product or Service Updates→Training→Designer-1

PRODUCT AND SERVICE UPDATES

Training opportunities

[TO:]

[FROM:]

[SUBJECT:]

[DATE:]

Effective [date], we will begin offering [Web hosting and development] to our [residential customer base]. Being able to offer this important service will help us compete against the various local ISPs who currently offer [only Internet connections and e-mail].

Since it is crucial that all customer service and technical staff be fluent in these areas when speaking with customers, we will be holding [a full-day meeting] covering the basics of these areas. The meeting will take place on [date], from [time] to [time].

Please call my assistant, [name], at extension [234] to confirm your attendance. Thank you.

- **Include specifics about service offerings and effective date.**

- **Make clear the importance of customer-contact staff having familiarity with the new service offerings even if they will not be actually selling or installing the services.**

- **If there is only one training session planned, ask staff to call to confirm attendance.**

Path on CD-ROM: Internal Memos→Product or Service Updates→Training→Internet-1

Helping co-worker

[Reader's first name]:

I've noticed that you seem a bit [mood] lately, and I've been concerned.

I know you've been [negative emotion] because of [presumed work-related cause] this [time period]. While [specific work parameter] could be [better/stronger/improved], I'm confident that you can turn things around—after all, you're one of our best [job title/description], and your [work] has been [word of praise] over [time period]. I'm sure this is just a temporary setback.

Why don't you [see/visit/call] me if you'd like to talk about what's going on with [work-related issue] or anything else that's on your mind. You know I'm here to help.

[Your first name]

- **Acknowledge that there's an apparent problem with the reader's mood and/or performance.**

- **If you suspect a direct link to a job-related issue, say so. (IMPORTANT: If you suspect that the problem is personal or not directly work-related, you may wish to speak to the person directly as a first step rather than writing a memo.)**

- **Reassure the reader that his/her work is generally good and express your confidence that good performance will quickly resume.**

- **Make clear your availability to listen, talk, help.**

Path on CD-ROM: Internal Memos→Miscellaneous Internal Correspondence→Help co-worker out of slump→Slump-1

MISCELLANEOUS CORRESPONDENCE

Congratulations

MEMORANDUM

TO: [Names]

FROM: [Name]

SUBJECT: [We Did It!!!]

I didn't think it was going to be possible to [describe accomplishment]—but we did. And I just got a call from the customer saying how happy they were with [product or service type/name]! So congratulations to everyone who pitched in!

The [Management Team] asked me to tell you how pleased they are with your effort and how important they believe it is that we continue to do whatever it takes to make our customers happy. Strong customer loyalty is the key to success in a business like ours, and it's the company that is able to solve a customer's problem quickly that will thrive in this market.

I'm hoping to arrange a [pizza] lunch next week for the whole staff—stay tuned for further details. [Client contact name] even said [she/he] would love to come by and express [his/her] thanks in person!

Way to go everyone!

- **Describe the reason for saying congratulations.**

- **Mentioning staff names in a positive light to your bosses or fellow executives is always a welcome sign.**

- **To help reinforce this behavior around the company, find ways to publicly recognize the effort.**

Path on CD-ROM: Internal Memos→Miscellaneous Internal Correspondence→Congratulations→Solve problem-1

Congratulations

TO: [Name@company.com]

FROM: [Name]

SUBJECT: Congrats on continued success!

We've just looked at the numbers for the past [8 months] and your sales figures have been consistently above those of all the other staff. Congratulations, and keep up the good work!

I know you've been very generous with sharing your tricks with your coworkers, and I wondered if you'd be interested in making it a more formal arrangement. I'd like to discuss the possibility of having you provide a series of in-service sessions so everyone can benefit from your expertise. I was thinking this could either be a temporary assignment or a permanent promotion to a position like Senior Sales Associate.

Give me a buzz or drop by my office so we can set a time to discuss these opportunities. And congratulations again on your fine performance!

- **Describe the occasion for the congratulations.**

- **Use the opportunity to see if you can get the top performer(s) in your company to share their expertise with others so everyone can increase sales.**

Sharing client information

TO: [Group@company.com]

FROM: [Name]

SUBJECT: [Client company] makes the news!

Just wanted to let everyone know that [client company] was in the most recent issue of [name of newspaper, magazine]. The article discusses [type of activity at client].

I don't think there's much here that will affect us, but I thought anyone who does business with [client name] should read the article so they can congratulate their contacts.

Let me know if you need a copy of the article.

- **Describe briefly when and where you saw the article about the client.**
- **Describe if/how the news might affect your business with the client.**
- **Either file a copy of the article in a central location or offer to give copies to people who want to read it.**

Path on CD-ROM: Internal Memos→Miscellaneous Internal Correspondence→Sharing client information→Newspaper-1

Sharing client information

TO: [Group@company.com]

FROM: [Name]

SUBJECT: [Criticism overheard]

When I was at [event] [yesterday], I overheard a former customer of ours criticizing our [product/service] when speaking with another attendee. [S/he] was saying how disappointed they were in the [quality] and thought the [product/service] was too expensive for what you got.

Has anyone else heard similar criticisms about us? I'd like to get a handle on how big of an issue this is. I don't want to overreact to a single customer, but I don't want to ignore something that may indicate a bigger problem, either.

In the meantime, I've scheduled an interview with this customer to hear exactly what [her/his] experience was with us. Perhaps that can give us some insights on how to improve our [product and/or service].

- **Briefly recap what you heard under what circumstances.**

- **Be a role model by demonstrating positive action in the face of bad news.**

- **Invite others to share what they've heard so you can work together to make sure you keep on top of negative feelings in the marketplace.**

Path on CD-ROM: Internal Memos→Miscellaneous Internal Correspondence→Sharing client information→Criticize-1

MISCELLANEOUS CORRESPONDENCE

Motivating staff

TO: The Staff

FROM: [NAME]

SUBJECT: Summer Hours

The days are getting longer (and hotter!) and we're all looking forward to getting away on the weekends, spending more time outdoors with our families and friends, and recapturing that "no school for three whole months!" feeling that stays with us no matter how distant our childhood actually was. Summer is often the hardest time to stay focused on work. Unfortunately, it's also the busiest time of year in our [industry/ sector/ company].

Not to worry. We know how critical it is that everything get done for the upcoming fall season, and we also know how itchy everyone is to spend as little time in the office as possible. So we're instituting a special summer-hours schedule—effective the third week in May through the second week in September—that we think everyone will like. Details are as follows:

- Starting time (Mon—Fri) will be a half hour earlier than normal

- Quitting time (Mon—Thurs only) will be a half hour later than normal

- Quitting time (Friday only) will be at noon. This will be strictly enforced. The office will be officially closed and you will be REQUIRED to leave the office at noon on Fridays.

Additionally, we will observe the three major summer holidays (Memorial Day, Independence Day, and Labor Day) as FOUR-day weekends: the Friday AND Monday of each of these three weekends will count as (paid) company holidays.

We're all looking forward to a warm, sunny, enjoyable—and productive—summer!

- **Many companies have summer Friday policies. Lengthening the Monday–Thursday workday hours in exchange for a longer weekend is a trade-off many companies (and employees) are happy to make as a way of maintaining productivity and focus during the summer.**

- **Acknowledge that your employees— and you yourself— are human, that you get itchy in the summer and wish you could be a kid again (in certain ways). You can't give/ get the entire summer off, but you can steal a piece of it.**

Path on CD-ROM: Internal Memos→Miscellaneous Internal Correspondence→Motivating staff→Summer Fridays-1

Memos about ad agency

TO: [Sales@company.com, Marketing@company.com]

FROM: [Name]

SUBJECT: Agency Account Team Personnel Changes

This will advise you of staff changes on the account team handling our business at [Thomas & Jefferson].

After we voiced our concerns about the team that's been handling our business, management at [Thomas & Jefferson] has decided to put a completely new account group in place for us, effective immediately.

The team consists of [five] individuals, each of whom has been with [T&J] for years. I applaud this decision as it will make certain elements of the transition period that much smoother. [Jerry Smith] will run the account as Management Supervisor, reporting directly to [Paula Jones], the agency's head of account services. Under [Jerry] will be two Account Supervisors; each AS will be supported by an Account Executive. (The attached Word document shows the organizational structure and provides direct-dial phone numbers and e-mail addresses for each team member.)

[Paula] assures me that each of these new account managers are outstanding professionals as well as great people to know and work with.

Should any of you encounter any difficulty with the new team (beyond the usual bumps that can be expected at first when dealing with new contacts), please bring it to my attention immediately. Thank you.

- **Since the personnel changes here were motivated by the writer and/or the writer's colleagues, there's no reason to omit this information and show that the agency was responsive to the complaints that had been voiced. However, don't dwell on this; move quickly to the relevant new information.**

- **Be concise about the new people's names, titles, reporting relationships, and contact infor-mation. Forward any supporting materials you've received from the agency so that your staff has all the information they need (and won't have to hound you for it!).**

Path on CD-Rom: Internal Memos→Miscellaneous Internal Correspondence→Memos about ad agency→Team-1

Firefighting

TO: [Sales@company.com]

FROM: [Name]

SUBJECT: Back orders

The back orders for [product name/model] are piling up, and we still don't have a promised delivery date from [the plant]. They're hopeful of getting the items to us by [date].

This is an awkward situation, but we don't want to risk angering our customers by misleading or ignoring them. Even if we lose a few sales on this particular item, my goal is to keep these people as our customers. So here's what I want to have happen:

- All sales staff should call their customers and explain that the item is still on backorder.

- It's OK to say we hope to have it in stock by [date], but DO NOT PROMISE a specific delivery date.

- Ask the customer if he or she would like to keep or cancel the order.

- If the customer chooses to cancel, describe [alternative products/models] that he or she may want to consider.

- If they do not want to substitute another item, ask if it's OK if you keep track of their order and contact them when [product/model name] arrives in case they have not yet found an alternative.

- If the customer keeps the order, promise him or her overnight delivery when we receive our stock.

- No matter what the outcome, thank the customer for doing business with us.

Remember, we want to keep the customer even if we lose the sale.

If there are any questions, please let me know. And keep me posted on the results of your phone calls.

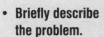

- **Briefly describe the problem.**

- **Provide detailed instructions on how to handle it.**

- **Emphasize your overall goal.**

Path on CD-ROM: Internal Memos→Miscellaneous Internal Correspondence→Firefighting urgent issues→Backorder-1

Firefighting

[Date]

[X] pages this fax

TO: Territory Manager

FROM: General Sales Manager

RE: [ ]

Dear [   ]:

Right before you left we finished the last interview, and we've just completed checking references on our top three candidates. As soon as you get back in the office, let's meet to make a decision about who will be the [new sales representative working the [section] section of your territory].

As we have discussed, we want this [new sales person] to [know the industry well and also have a track record of developing slow areas]. In addition, we wanted to find a personality match with the rest of your team.

Would you be sure to bring the style indicator results on the candidates to our meeting? The pages following this cover are the summary evaluations on each of the candidates we're still considering. Please review them [on your flight back tomorrow]. Can we expect you in the office by [time]?

If you have any questions, please call me right away.

Sincerely,

[Name]
[Title]

- **Explain the decision that needs to be made.**

- **Consider phoning to make sure the fax went through.**

Path on CD-ROM: Internal Memos→Miscellaneous Internal Correspondence→Firefighting urgent issues→Staffing-1

Tradeshow planning

TO: [Sales@company.com]

FROM: [Name]

SUBJECT: [Process for handling foreign orders at trade shows]

As you all know, technically we're not allowed to sell anything at the [trade show name] show. A question has come up about how we will handle foreigners attending the show who want to pay on the spot and take the product home with them.

I've spoken with the trade show organizers, and we're safe as along as we don't process orders on the trade show floor. Here's what to do:

- [Give customers an order form. Tell them to fill in what they want and provide a credit card number. They can hand the filled-in form back to us anytime during the show.]

- [Periodically, we will fax these forms back to the home office and have sales staff here process these orders. They will let us know if the payment is OK'd.]

- [If yes, we will give customers the product(s) they wanted.]

We are only taking a very limited supply of product with us to the show, so this method is to be used only for foreign nationals. All other customers will be instructed to call the home office or log onto our Web site to order.

Any questions?

- **Describe the problem.**
- **Describe in detail how staff should handle the situation.**
- **Leave the door open for people to ask questions.**

Path on CD-ROM: Internal Memos→Miscellaneous Internal Correspondence→Trade show planning and execution→Foreign orders-1

Good news

TO: [   ]

FROM: [   ]

SUBJECT: [   ]

They said it couldn't be done—but they were wrong!

I'm happy to report that sales of our [dripless candles] are up by more than [xx%] over last year. And as you know, we haven't changed the product line or lowered its price.

This tremendous increase in unit sales is due primarily to an innovation recommended by Sales and executed by Marketing. As recommended by [Becky Hall and Sara Brooks] at last year's regional sales meeting, we have begun [selling our candles on the Internet] in addition to [using our traditional retail channels]. By adding this new media weapon to our arsenal, we have been able to add [$$$] to the bottom line without decreasing the amount of revenue we realize from our retail accounts.

This is a terrific reminder that innovation can come from any area—Product Design, Operations and, of course, Sales and Marketing. Thanks, [Becky and Sara], for this important contribution.

- **The memo opens with a catchy opening sentence.**

- **Remind staff that there are many potential contributors to sales success.**

- **Acknowledge the key individuals involved.**

Bad news

TO: [   ]

FROM: [   ]

SUBJECT: [   ]

I have bad news to report regarding our new [voice-messaging feature].

Since we started offering [the feature as an optional add-on to local telephone service], sales have been nothing short of abysmal. We projected that [10% of current customers and 20% of new customers] would [add voice-messaging to their local phone-service packages] by the end of [the fiscal year]. The actual sign-up rates, just received from Sales, show that only [2% of current customers and 5% of new customers] have elected to add or include this feature.

We are currently reviewing the competitive field to determine [the costs of our closest rivals' comparable service]. We are also [researching purchase trends for answering machines].

I expect to have a recommendation as to how to proceed with our [voice-messaging feature] marketing—should we decide to continue to offer the feature at all—by the end of the month. In the meantime, please do not hesitate to contact me with any questions.

- **Open by getting right to the point.**

- **Provide not only actual data but comparisons to forecast.**

- **Describe what's being done to understand and potentially correct the situation; if the product/service/ line might be discontinued, consider mentioning that if appropriate.**

Path on CD-ROM: Internal Memos→Updates on Sales Performance→Bad news→Very poor-1

Bad news

TO: [   ]

FROM: [   ]

SUBJECT: [   ]

[The agency] has completed its sales and advertising analysis of the [4th quarter campaign].

Their conclusion, with which I agree, is that the sales decrease we experienced vs. last year's [4th quarter] is due primarily to [our decision to remove television from our media plan while continuing to use radio and newspapers]. Given that [all other key factors—creative message, advertising budget, product pricing, competitive offerings, retail distribution, consumer performance, and preference ratings—remained more or less constant during this 4th quarter vs. last], it does seem reasonable to conclude that the one factor we did vary is related to the sales decline.

[The agency and the marketing department] are developing a recommended media plan for [next quarter]. I understand that [television will be restored to the plan, most likely in concert with radio and print]. We expect that this will help restore sales to their previous levels.

I will keep you updated on our plans and the subsequent results at retail.

- **Attribute a conclusion to its source; indicate your agreement or disagreement.**

- **If you suspect one factor is critical, comment on how other factors did or did not come into play.**

- **Offer to keep the reader informed.**

Path on CD-ROM: Internal Memos→Updates on Sales Performance→Bad news→Media-1

Mixed news

TO: [   ]

FROM: [   ]

SUBJECT: [   ]

The [three] regional sales managers have just submitted their monthly movement reports to me. I am happy to announce that every item in the [Zippy] product line is moving well at retail—at least [10%] over projection, as a matter of fact.

While the retail situation is obviously quite positive, one issue I need to bring to your attention is that of inventory at our end.

As you will recall, when we first previewed the [Zippy] line for the trade, their response was extremely positive. This led us to increase our unit-sales projections and, correspondingly, our production capacity. We now see that the line is indeed moving quite well at retail, but not at the exceptional levels that would allow us to clear out all of our inventory.

Consequently, we need to work out a way to move even more [Zippy] product out of our warehouses and into the channel. I would like to meet with the department heads from Sales, Operations, and Marketing [at 3:00 this afternoon in my office] to determine ways to achieve this objective. Thank you for your cooperation.

- **Lead with the good news, then get into the drawback of the situation.**

- **Provide your understanding of the cause of the situation without overtly placing blame.**

- **Offer a solution or ask key colleagues to work with you on developing one.**

Path on CD-ROM: Internal Memos→Updates on Sales Performance→Mixed news→Overstocked-1

Finance/accounting

TO: [Name@company.com]

FROM: [Name]

SUBJECT: [Effect of changing discount policy]

My team and I have been discussing a proposal that we want to go over with someone in Accounting. A number of customers have complained that we only offer discounts on a per-item basis, not based on the total purchase prices. We'd like someone to help us answer the following questions:

1. If we compared orders of a given dollar amount, what percentage of those customers are buying little bits of lots of things vs. large quantities of a few things. (That is, how many of those customers qualified for a quantity discount?)

2. What would be the effect of changing our policy to offering discounts based on total dollar amount of the order instead of quantity discounts offered per item?

Can you help us out, or is there someone else over there who could?

Thanks,

—[Name]

- **Describe the purpose of the overall effort.**

- **Describe specifically what you're asking of the other person.**

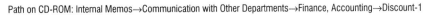

Path on CD-ROM: Internal Memos→Communication with Other Departments→Finance, Accounting→Discount-1

COMMUNICATION WITH OTHER DEPARTMENTS

Finance/Accounting

TO: [Name@company.com]

FROM: [Name]

SUBJECT: [Eliminate quantity discount level]

In discussions with my staff, we think the [xx%] discount level on [product(s)] isn't doing much good—it doesn't seem to kick people up from a lower quantity. What we'd like to recommend is just eliminating that discount level all together—that is, extending the [lower XX%] discount up until [quantity].

What do you think about this idea?

—[Name]

- **Indicate the decision is tentative pending input from the other person.**

- **Provide a rationale for the recommendation so the other person can better judge whether an alternative will work better.**

Path on CD-ROM: Internal Memos→Communication with Other Departments→Finance, Accounting→Discount-2

Information services

TO: [Name@company.com]

FROM: [Name]

SUBJECT: Changing definition of "active" customer in [software] database

[The Sales department] has been tracking data lately on how long our customers usually go between orders. That is, if they haven't ordered [for 5 months], are they still "active" customers or is it unlikely that they would order again?

We've discovered that the cutoff point seems to be around [8 months]. That's about the longest that "regular" customers go between orders. Currently, we have the [software] database set up to label as "inactive" only those customers who haven't ordered in a year.

What we'd like to do is change that definition and, in fact, add another category called "lapsing." We want to be able to search the database and pick up any customers who have gone, say, [7 to 9 months] without ordering so we can make a special effort to contact them and hopefully get them to order. Any of these customers who don't order within a month or two—plus those who have gone longer than 8 months—should automatically be rolled over into "inactive" status.

Is it possible to do this? Can you or someone else in IS help us get the program set up right?

Thanks.

- **Describe what you want to be able to do.**

- **Provide sufficient detail to let the recipient judge the scope of the request.**

INTERNAL AD AGENCY CORRESPONDENCE

Termination with client

TO: All Agency Employees

FROM: [NAME]

SUBJECT: Termination of (X) Account

In light of several recent rumors in the trade press that we have been pursuing the [competitive company name] business, I must inform you that [our current client] has terminated their relationship with us effective immediately.

It is unfortunate that they were forced to make this decision. As you know, [client] had been very pleased with the creative work we had developed for them over the past [x] years, and they'd always expressed positive comments about the account group's handling of the day-to-day relationship. However, our reported (potential) involvement with [competitive company] represented a direct conflict with their interests and they felt they had no choice but to end their relationship with us.

While I am not placing blame on any member of the staff, losing a client because of trade press rumors is something I do not wish to have repeated. All of you should be familiar with our media relations policy, which, in short, states that you are to direct all press inquiries to our PR department rather than speaking with reporters yourselves. Further, you are not to initiate dialogue with the media. I am hoping that no one at the agency provided any sort of leak to the press in this situation.

Please see me if you have any questions about agency press policies or about this particular situation.

- **Acknowledge the reason for the termination.**

- **Express your disappointment in the client's decision as well as your understanding of their reasoning.**

- **Remind staff of any existing policies whose adherence might have prevented the termination.**

Path on CD-ROM: Internal Memos→Internal Ad Agency Correspondence→Termination of account→Policy-2

INTERNAL AD AGENCY CORRESPONDENCE

Media relations

TO: All Agency Employees

FROM: [Name]

SUBJECT: Media Relations Policy

This will advise you of the Agency's media relations policy.

1. Agency Business:

Under no circumstances are you to speak with members of the press about Agency business. This includes issues such as billings, profits, account wins and losses, prospective accounts, and upcoming pitches. All inquiries you may receive from reporters should be directed to [John Smith, extension 122] in our Public Relations Department or to [Mary Jones], the head of the public relations agency we engage for such matters. ([Mary's] number is [(555) 555-5555].)

2. Client Business:

Under no circumstances are you to speak with members of the press about client business. This includes issues such as new campaigns that have not yet broken, new products that clients are about to introduce, media plans the Agency has developed for clients, clients' profits and losses, client company revenues, client company expansion or consolidation plans, etc. Should you receive inquiries from the press about matters such as these, do not answer any questions or share any information. Refer inquiries to the client's own public relations manager; if you do not know who handles press relations for your client, call me immediately.

Please let me know if you have any questions about this policy.

- **Make clear all restrictions on providing information to the press; the issue of inquiries concerning client business is particularly sensitive.**

- **Provide names and phone numbers for internal and external contacts who are authorized to handle press inquiries.**

INTERNAL AD AGENCY CORRESPONDENCE

Staff updates/changes

TO: [AllStaff@company.com]

FROM: [Name]

SUBJECT: New Account Team on [NECG]

We've made some staffing changes on the [New England Cattle Guard] account, effective immediately.

While top management on the team is new to this account, they're no strangers to the agency, having all been with [T&J] for years. [Jerry Mander], who's been doing a terrific job on the [Belgrade Cappuccino] business, will remain on that business and also head up the [NECG] team as [Management Supervisor], reporting directly to me.

[Jerry] will be supported by [two Account Supervisors]: [Suzie Kew], who also adds [NECG] to her [Belgrade] responsibilities; and [Joe Bloh], who's been on the [Three Forks China] account. ([Jerry, Suzie, and Joe] will move down the hall into the offices that had been occupied by the former [NECG] account team, but their phone extensions will not change.) [Suzie and Joe] will each supervise an [Account Executive]; once these spots have been filled, we'll let you know.

We're very excited about the changes we've made to the account staff, as is the client. We're certain this new team will run the [NECG] business with the professionalism and good judgment this important account deserves. Please join me in congratulating [Jerry, Suzie, and Joe] on their new roles.

Sincerely,

[Name]
[Title]

- **While this staffing change has been made as a result of a client request (due to dissatisfaction with the previous team), there's no need to drag (former) staff members' names through the mud; just deliver the news factually and dispassionately.**

- **Be clear about each person's new responsibilities and contact information.**

Path on CD-ROM: Internal Memos→Internal Ad Agency Correspondence→Staff updates→Staffing-1

INTERNAL AD AGENCY CORRESPONDENCE

Account management memos about media

[TO:]

[FROM:]

[SUBJECT:]

[DATE:]

[Client] will be launching a new product [next year] that will be marketed to [target audience]. Since this represents the first time [client] will be developing a product for this audience, they need our help in educating them on the various media vehicles this new target group [reads/watches/listens to].

I propose that we put together a [presentation/document] that will provide [client] with an overview of the [target group] media world. This will help familiarize [client] with this category of [magazines/programs] before we present actual media plans to them; this familiarization should help us get our plans approved that much more easily.

Let's meet [at 4:00 today] to discuss ways we might tackle this project. Thanks.

- **Provide an overview of the situation and put it in context.**

- **Recommend a way to address the client need and show how it will benefit the agency in the long run.**

- **Suggest an internal project kickoff meeting.**

Path on CD-ROM: Internal Memos→Internal Ad Agency Correspondence→Account management to media→Information-1

INTERNAL AD AGENCY CORRESPONDENCE

Account management memos about media

[TO:]

[FROM:]

[SUBJECT:]

[DATE:]

I just got off the phone with [client]—it appears that they're almost ready to approve the [2002] media plan we presented last week.

In order for [client] to feel completely comfortable with the [magazine portion of the] plan, we will need to supply them with [media kits and readership statistics for each of the publications we recommended]. Please contact the various [magazine sales reps] and forward the requested information [directly to the client]. Once [client] has had a chance to review those materials, I'm sure we'll have an approval!

Thanks for your help.

- **Focus the opening and closing on the good news (the pending approval, not the missing information).**

- **Clearly state what's needed and what effect you expect it to have.**

- **Thank your colleagues for their help.**

Path on CD-ROM: Internal Memos→Internal Ad Agency Correspondence→Account management to media→Information-2

INTERNAL AD AGENCY CORRESPONDENCE

Account management memos to creative staff

[TO:]

[FROM:]

[SUBJECT:]

[DATE:]

We need to discuss changing the target of our [Crunchy Sweet breakfast cereal] advertising.

Retail sales of [Crunchy Sweet] are down significantly since our [adult-directed TV commercials] began running. After lengthy discussion with [Marketing and Consumer Research], I have convinced [client] to let us develop [new/revised] advertising for the [Crunchy Sweet] brand, targeted directly toward [children], the primary consumer.

We agreed to approach this assignment from two angles:

(1) [revise the existing commercials so as to make them appealing to children]

(2) [develop all-new, kid-directed advertising]

I would like to meet with you [tomorrow morning at 11:00] to discuss this in more detail. Please let me know if that time works for you. Thanks.

- Introduce the topic of the memo in the opening sentence.

- Provide brief background, then get to the client direction/agreement.

- If the project/issue is significant enough, ask for a meeting to discuss it in detail.

Path on CD-ROM: Internal Memos→Internal Ad Agency Correspondence→Account management to creative→Target-1

Account management memos to creative staff

[TO:]

[FROM:]

[SUBJECT:]

[DATE:]

I just got some bad news: [Client] has rejected the [newspaper ad] entirely and would like us to go back to the drawing board.

I want to meet with you to go through [client's] comments in person as they're rather extensive. Painful as it will be, the process of walking through the issues together in detail will give us a far better understanding of what will and won't work for the client.

Since the insertion date is [date], we don't have much time. Let's meet at [time] in [meeting room].

- **Get right to the point.**

- **Do not put specific criticisms in writing to the creative team; save those for the in-person meeting.**

- **Point out the advantages (if any) to having this unpleasant information.**

Path on CD-ROM: Internal Memos→Internal Ad Agency Correspondence→Account management to creative→Rejection-1

INTERNAL AD AGENCY CORRESPONDENCE

Account management memos to entire staff

[TO:]

[FROM:]

[SUBJECT:]

[DATE:]

I just received an important call from [name] at [client company].

Due to [problem], [client company] has decided to discontinue the production and sale of [product/line], effective [immediately].

This obviously affects us significantly:

- [All creative work and production development on [product/line] should halt immediately.]

- [Media plans including advertising for [product/line] need to be immediately revised to reflect the deletion of the [product/line] and resulting lowered total budgets.]

- [Agency income forecasts will need to be recalculated to reflect the loss of income that [product/line] advertising had been projected to bring in.]

I will be speaking with [Name] in more detail over the [next few days] to determine if anything can be salvaged. I will update you all as soon as I have more information.

- **Explain the situation and its cause.**

- **Lay out how each department of the agency is affected.**

- **Let team members know if there will be further developments in this area and what they are to do (or not do) in the meantime.**

INTERNAL AD AGENCY CORRESPONDENCE

Media department memos to account management

[TO:]

[FROM:]

[SUBJECT:]

[DATE:]

We've received a proposal from [magazine] for a [combination insertion, merchandising, and Web site] package that may be of interest to the [client] client.

I've asked the [magazine] rep to make some minor revisions and come back to present the proposal to us on [date]. I'd like to invite you [and other members of the account team] to their presentation, which will take place on [date] at [time] in [my office].

Please let me know which members of your team will be able to attend. Thanks.

- **Open with a simple description of the proposal and explain why you're sharing it with the account team.**

- **Communicate the status of the project/proposal as well as next steps.**

- **Ask for the account group's attendance.**

Path on CD-ROM: Internal Memos→Internal Ad Agency Correspondence→Media to account management→Recommendation-1

INTERNAL AD AGENCY CORRESPONDENCE

Memos to account management

[TO:]

[FROM:]

[SUBJECT:]

[DATE:]

The [21-month] contracts with [performer's name] and [other performer's name], who appear in the ["title"] commercial for [product], expire on [date].

Should the client wish to continue airing ["title"], we will need to renegotiate with [performer and performer]. Based on conversations I've had with their agents, I expect that an increase of [$x,000 or xx%] above the current rates will be requested.

Please contact the client and advise him/her of this impending expiration date and anticipated rate increase as soon as possible so that we can begin the renegotiation process (or drop the commercial). Thank you.

- **Open with a simple declaration of key facts: performers, title, product, expiration date.**

- **Lay out options and prices (actual and anticipated).**

- **State the action the account rep needs to take.**

Path on CD-ROM: Internal Memos→Internal Ad Agency Correspondence→Miscellaneous correspondence→Talent-1

Soliciting Customer Input

Chapter 6

Gone are the days when product developers sat around in closed rooms and decided what *they* thought customers wanted. Nearly gone are the days when companies thought they were doing enough if all they did was address customer complaints.

Today, companies know that they have to regularly—and proactively—gather the "voice of the customer" in order to stay ahead of the marketplace. In fact, these days it's not uncommon to have several different groups within a company contacting customers: the sales staff doing interviews to improve the sales experience, the research staff investigating new product alternatives, the marketing staff surveying large groups to identify future trends.

To avoid confusing your customers and frustrating them through repeated contact by different groups, it's important that all customer contact be coordinated, preferably by either the sales or marketing staff.

The letters in this chapter cover two key reasons why you would want to proactively contact customers: (1) to complete a survey or questionnaire, and (2) to involve them in various stages of the product/service development process. In all these letters, it is important to:

1. **Make the customer feel special.** Make it clear that they were chosen to be among a select group.
2. **Demonstrate an interest in and respect for what *that particular customer* has to offer.** The more the person feels they are just one of a crowd, interchangeable with others in the group, the less likely they are to think that their participation will add value. Naming the particular

knowledge or experience you think they have can help you convince the customer that you really want him or her to participate.

3. **Make it clear the customer is doing you a favor** by agreeing to participate. After all, *your* company depends on its customers to stay in business, so the customer really is helping you out.

4. However, you can balance #3 by **describing how the customer can also benefit from participation**—e.g., improvement of a product they use, gaining knowledge they can use on their own job, helping their company stay ahead of the marketplace, and so on.

The more time and energy you want from the customer, the more you should rely on multiple forms of communication: phone calls and e-mails, for example, in addition to letters. Be sure to plan out when and how letters get sent, and how they fit in with your overall communication plans.

Be prepared to repeat information. Remember that the customer is not involved in your marketing or development efforts every day, so in each letter provide a brief description of the big picture. ("Thanks for agreeing to participate in our effort to develop a new version of Product X....")

Cover letters

We Really Need Your Help!

[Name]
[Title]
[Organization]
[Address]
[City, State ZIP]

Dear [Name]:

A lot of companies say that they pay attention to customers, but [Custom Steel] is one of the few that really proves it! We've been able to keep providing you with leading-edge products because our customers have given terrific feedback on what they like and don't like.

That's why we need your help now. Enclosed you'll find our latest [2001] questionnaire, and we're hoping you could take a few minutes to fill it out. You can then return it to us in the enclosed postage-paid envelope, or fax it to [800-555-5555].

Your input will be collected with that of other target customers and used to help us make important decisions about [what specialty steel products we should be offering to the marketplace].

Thanks for participating! We greatly appreciate your input!

Sincerely,

[Name]
[Title]

- **Make it sound really important that the customer helps you.**

- **Use an attention-grabbing headline.**

- **Show how participation is in the customer's best interests.**

Path on CD-ROM: Soliciting Customer Input→Surveys and Questionnaires→Cover letters→Feedback-2

Cover letters

TO: [Name@company.com]

FROM: [Name]

SUBJECT: Annual questionnaire

Dear [Name]:

In the past year, [Company] has consistently maintained very high customer satisfaction ratings. And we're hoping you can help us keep up that trend!

Could you please take a few minutes to complete our online survey about what you like and don't like about doing business with us? It should only take you 10 to 15 minutes at most—and you'll have the satisfaction of knowing that you helped us improve our [product/service] based on YOUR needs!

Just click here to go to our survey. All your responses are COMPLETELY CONFIDENTIAL.

Thanks so much for taking the time to help us out.

Sincerely,

[Name]
[Title]

- **If you include a salutation in the letter, include the person's actual name; don't just say "Dear Valued Customer" or something generic like that because it counters the message you want to send that your company is concerned about that particular customer.**

Cover letters

TO: [Name@company.com]

FROM: [Name]

SUBJECT: Get a [FREE CD] from [HighNotes.com]!

Is [HighNotes.com] your favorite online music Web site? We want to know—one way or the other—and we're willing to pay for your opinion!

[HighNotes.com] is doing a survey of customer reactions to our new Web site, and we'd like you to participate. Everyone who completes a survey will receive an e-coupon good for a [FREE CD of your choice—up to an $18.00 value]!

Participating is easy! Just click here! And it shouldn't take more than a few minutes of your time.

And remember—get a [FREE CD]!

Sincerely,

[Name]
[Title]

- **The opener grabs attention by mentioning a reward.**

- **In an e-mail, people may not scroll down far enough to see a P.S., so mention the incentive again in the close of the letter.**

Path on CD-ROM: Soliciting Customer Input→Surveys and Questionnaires→Cover letters→Inventive-2

Cover letters

[Date]

[Name]
[Company]
[Address]
[City, State ZIP]

Dear [   ]:

It was a pleasure working with you last year on the [Kennet product launch]. We really enjoyed serving you and, even though we no longer [provide advertising services] for your company, we value your opinion.

Would you help us improve our services by completing the enclosed questionnaire? It is important that the survey be completed by the person most responsible for decisions affecting the purchase of [advertising services]. It will only take a few moments, and we would be most obliged if you would return it in the provided self-addressed stamped envelope by [date].

Thank you very much.

Sincerely,

[Name]
[Title]

- **Open with gentle compliments.**

- **Use a response-increasing strategy, such as asking for help.**

Path on CD-ROM: Soliciting Customer Input→Surveys and Questionnaires→Cover letters→Input-2

SURVEYS & QUESTIONNAIRES

Survey in a letter

[Name]
[Company]
[Address]
[City, State ZIP]

Dear [   ]:

Thank you for answering the following questions. Please return your questionnaire in the enclosed self-addressed stamped envelope by [date] or fax it to [555-555-5555].

A. Please list the top three reasons you do business with [Industro Tools].
1.
2.
3.

B. Over the past, year how often have you ordered from [company]? (Please circle one)
a) 0
b) 1–5
c) 6–9
d) 10 or more

C. Overall, how do you like doing business with us? (Please circle one)
a) very satisfied
b) somewhat satisfied
c) somewhat dissatisfied
d) very dissatisfied

D. How would you rate the quality of our products? (Please circle one)
a) best in class
b) very high
c) adequate
d) marginal
e) unacceptable

- **If the person had an unhappy experience, you can use the survey to open the door to resolve the situation.**

Path on CD-ROM: Soliciting Customer Input→Surveys and Questionnaires→Survey in letter→Company-2

Survey in a letter (cont.)

E. How would you rate our product support services (including complaint resolution)? (Please circle one)
a) extremely good
b) good
c) adequate
d) poor
e) very poor
f) never used any services

F. Compared to your other vendors, how does [Industro Tools] rate? (Please
circle one)
a) best in class
b) very high
c) adequate
d) marginal
e) unacceptable

• **Thank the person for participating and provide information on what to do with the completed survey.**

Thank you for taking the time to answer these questions!

NOTE: If you are unhappy with any of our products or support services, we
would welcome the chance to remedy the situation. We want all of our customers to be 100% satisfied! Please list your name and phone number below so
one of our service managers can contact you.

Path on CD-ROM: Soliciting Customer Input→Surveys and Questionnaires→Survey in letter→Company-2

Survey in a letter

TO: [Name@company.com]
FROM: [Name]
SUBJECT: Can we get your input, please?

Dear [Name]:

On behalf of [Company], I'd like to thank you for letting us be your [type or product/service] provider in the last year. And now I have a favor to ask of you. Each year we do a broad survey to get an overall picture of how well we're meeting our customers needs. And if you have about 15 minutes to spare, I'm hoping you can take the time to answer the following questions:

A. What do you like MOST about doing business with us?

B. What you like LEAST about doing business with us?

C. What is the most important strategic need facing your company in the year ahead?

D. What ONE thing could [Company] do to help make your life easier?

You can just reply to this e-mail, or print out this page and mail or fax it to the numbers shown below.

Thanks so much for your help!

Sincerely,

[Name]
[Title]

- Language like "doing business with us" will get you broader responses than questions focused on only products or services. You may find out, for instance, that the customer loves your product but hates your billing process.

- Similarly, asking questions about the challenges facing your customers' businesses can help you identify opportunities.

Path on CD-ROM: Soliciting Customer Input→Surveys and Questionnaires→Survey in letter→Open-ended-1

Thanks for participating

[Date]
[Name]
[Company]
[Address]
[City, State ZIP]

Dear [   ]:

Thank you so much for completing our recent [industry] industry compensation survey. Surprisingly, salaries for many positions have not increased as much as expected. The full survey results have been compiled into [Group's] annual Compensation Report.

This data-packed product has been a reliable source of compensation data for the [industry] industry for more than a decade. This year's manual is available to non-participants for $[amount]. As a survey participant, you may purchase it for the special discounted price of $[amount].

As a special token of our appreciation, please find enclosed a gift certificate for an additional $[amount] off when you order your copy of the survey results before [date].

Thanks again for helping us improve our products and services. We look forward to your feedback on the report.

Sincerely,

[Name]
[Title]

- **Use a salient survey result to sell the whole report.**

- **Say thank-you in several ways, including providing participants with special discounts.**

Invitation to participate in focus group

[Name]
[Title]
[Organization]
[Address]
[City, State ZIP]

Dear [Name]:

What went through your mind the last time you used [Fiskal's accounting services]? Were we on time? Did we treat you well? Were you disappointed in anyway? Well, we'd like to know, whatever your reaction is!

[Fiskal's Financial Services] is inviting a select group of customers to join us at a focus group from [11:00 a.m. to 1:00 p.m.] on [May 23]. The session will be run by [Trend Marketing, Inc. of Dallas]. During the session, they'll ask you to share what it's like to do business with [Fiskal]—what you like and don't like, and any suggestions you have for improvement. We've found that these types of discussions are invaluable as we look to the future.

Each attendee will be awarded a [$100] honorarium.

Won't you join us? Just call [800-555-5555] by [May 16] and ask for [Burt] at extension [222]. [He'll] provide you with specifics about where to meet.

Your opinion is very valuable to us. And I hope you'll have the time to join us on [May 23]!

Sincerely,

[Name]
[Title]

- Everyone is going to answer the opening question in their minds—which you hope will increase the odds that they'd want to share their opinion with a group.

- Keep the invitation simple and straightforward.

- Often focus groups are conducted by a third party; you'll need to decide if the invitation to participate comes from the third party on your behalf or directly from your organization.

Path on CD-ROM: Soliciting Customer Input→Involve Customers in Product Development→Invite to focus group→Accounting-1

Do you have an opinion about [topic]?
How would you like to get **PAID** for telling us about it?

[Name]
[Title]
[Organization]
[Address]
[City, State ZIP]

Dear [Name]:

[Company] wants to know what you think about [topic]—and we're willing to pay for it! On [date] from [start time] to [end time], we'll be holding a focus group at [location]. And we'll pay you [$$] for joining us!

The purpose of the evening is [purpose]. You'll be joining a select group of other [company] customers and be asked to share your thoughts about [topics]. We promise to start and end on time—and you'll go home [$$] richer!

Please RSVP by [date] so we know whether to count on you! Just call [800-555-5555] and tell the attendant you are responding to the focus group invitation.

Hope to see you on [date]!

Sincerely,

[Name]
[Title]

[P.S. Because this focus group starts in the early evening, we'll even provide a FREE dinner!]

- **Most focus group invitations are made by phone, but there may be times when you want to contact people via letter, e-mail, or fax first.**

- **Draw people into the letter with the promise of making money.**

- **Emphasize that you'll respect their time commitment by starting and ending on time.**

Path on CD-ROM: Soliciting Customer Input→Involve Customers in Product Development→Invite to focus group→Generic-1

Invitation to participate in testing

**How many times have you said,
"I could do a better job than these guys!"?**

[Name]
[Address]
[City, State ZIP]

Dear [   ]:

We're hoping you're one of those people who always seems to have a better idea than the ones you see in the marketplace. [Company] is launching an effort to develop the next generation of [home product], and we could use your help!

[Company] employs a lot of bright people, but we're well aware that we don't know everything that goes on in our consumers' minds. That's why we're putting together a [Customer Test Group] as we launch an effort to develop the next generation of [consumer product]. And we're hoping you will consider participating.

The [Customer Test Group] will meet [4] times over the next [6] months. During those meetings, we'll show you ideas, concepts, or test products, then ask you to share your reactions.

In other words, all you have to do is talk about what you like and don't like about what we're doing, and give us ideas on how to do better! What could be easier!

If you are interested in participating in our [Test Group], please call [800-555-5555] by [date] and ask for [Melissa]. She'll sign you up and answer any questions you have.

It's not often that someone ASKS for your ideas, right? But we're very serious here about hearing what you have to say. So please consider participating in our group.

Thank you for your consideration. We look forward to seeing you at the first [Customer Test Panel] on [date.]

Sincerely,

[Name]
[Title]

- **The headline captures a common sentiment, which should entice the reader into the body of the letter.**

- **A general consumer won't be aware of the product development process, so provide a brief sketch of how their input will be used.**

- **The close is a positive statement (we WILL see you).**

Path on CD-ROM: Soliciting Customer Input→Involve Customers in Product Development→Invite to product testing→Manufacturer-4

Invitation to participate in testing

Dear Customer:

You see that [product name1] that appears on page [x]? It was a customer's idea. Or the [product name2] on page [x2]? A customer suggested it to us. And the new [feature] on [product name3]? Our customers asked for it!

Got the idea? We LOVE to get customer suggestions, whether for an entirely new product or just making improvements to existing products. And if you have a unique idea that we decide to use, we'll pay you for it!

Think you've got an idea we can't live without? Let us know! It's easy to do. Just call [800-555-5555] or visit our Web site and click on [Suggestions].

Don't let your great ideas languish in your head! Write them down and send them to us! We know what to do with creativity!

Sincerely,

[Name]
[Title]

- **Open by describing products or features that came from customer suggestions. That lends the credibility that you do act on suggestions.**

- **Make it simple for them to submit ideas.**

- **If you offer monetary rewards, describe how the customer can qualify. You'll probably want to check with your legal advisor to make sure you don't end up owing money to everyone who submits an idea!**

Path on CD-ROM: Soliciting Customer Input→Involve Customers in Product Development→Invite to product testing→Get ideas-1

INVOLVING CUSTOMERS IN DEVELOPMENT

Confirmation of participation

[Name]
[Company]
[Address]
[City, State ZIP]

Dear [   ]:

Thanks so much for agreeing to come to our focus group on [topic] on [date] at [times]! We've lined up a great facilitator and are very confident it will be a fun session for everyone involved.

As I mentioned over the phone, the session will be held at [location]. [I've enclosed a map to help you get there.] The session starts at [start time] and ends at [end time]. We want to respect the time you're so graciously donating to us, so we promise we'll start and end promptly!

The discussion is going to focus on three main topics:

[topic 1]

[topic 2]

[topic 3]

You'll be breaking out into small discussion groups, and we expect there to be a lot of energy generated during the [evening].

If you have any questions at all, please give me a call! Otherwise, just be prepared to bring your creative energy on the [##th]! I look forward to seeing you there!

Sincerely,

[Name]
[Title]

- **The energetic tone and enthusiastic language is intended to get the participants excited about attending.**

- **Be sure to cover the basic what/where/when questions.**

- **How specific you get in discussing the session topics is a matter of judgment. You need to provide enough detail so the person knows generally what to expect. Whether you give more details depends on if you want to witness people's first reaction to an idea or concept or if you think the discussion will be more fruitful if they've had a chance to think about some ideas beforehand.**

Path on CD-ROM: Soliciting Customer Input→Involve Customers in Product Development→Confirmation→Confirm-2

Confirmation of participation

[Name]
[Company]
[Address]
[City, State ZIP]

Dear [   ]:

Welcome to the [Customer Input Panel] for [vendor's] new [product/service] development project. We're glad that you could join in on this important effort!

I wanted to take this opportunity to share a few details with you that we hadn't yet discussed. I believe I did mention that your primary role will be reacting to ideas and [prototypes] that our [R&D] team develops. To give you access to the ideas, we've set it up so you can gain access to a restricted portion of our Web site. Whenever there is something for you to react to, I will alert you via e-mail and give you the time frame (usually 5 working days) within which we would like your input. Each e-mail will list the project code and password you'll need to log into the Web site.

Your first task will start next week. For this initial pass, we will have a number of key [product/service] user questions that we'd like you to answer. You'll be able to enter your answers right on the Web site. We estimate it will take you about [10] minutes.

I'll let you know as further details are developed. In the meantime, thanks again for your time and input—and watch your e-mail next week for instructions on how to begin Task #1!

Sincerely,

[Name]
[Title]

- **Thank the person for participating.**

- **Provide sufficient detail so they know what to expect as the project unfolds.**

- **Tell them how/when to get the passwords they need to use the Web site.**

- **Provide the contact information.**

Path on CD-ROM: Soliciting Customer Input→Involve Customers in Product Development→Confirmation→Web access-1

INVOLVING CUSTOMERS IN DEVELOPMENT

Thanks for participating

[Name]
[Company]
[Address]
[City, State ZIP]

Dear [   ]:

On behalf of everyone here at [vendor], I'd like to thank you for all the effort you put into our recent [project title] project. I know that everyone on the team is disappointed because we didn't come up with a viable [product/service] idea, but I want to assure you that we in no way view this as a failure. Rather, we think of this as a very successful effort that has spared us the expense of developing a [product/service] that no one in the market wanted!

As a token of our appreciation, please accept the enclosed [token gift] with our heartfelt thanks.

It was great having you on our team, and I hope that we can continue doing business together in the future.

Sincerely,

[Name]
[Title]

- **Even if the project didn't achieve the intended results, there is usually an important positive aspect you can describe in the letter. This is very important. You don't want to leave the participant feeling like a failure or thinking that your company doesn't know how to run a project.**

- **If the project was particularly important, you may want to start off with the more formal "On behalf of" type of thank-you.**

Path on CD-ROM: Soliciting Customer Input→Involve Customers in Product Development→Thanks→Unsuccessful

Results of their participation

[Name]
[Company]
[Address]
[City, State ZIP]

Dear [   ]:

Just thought you'd like to know that we're about to launch [product/service name] in just a few weeks. We have a full description of it in the enclosed catalog that I thought you might enjoy—note that your name is listed as one of the customer reviewers! So if people start asking for your autograph, you'll know why!

Thanks for your participation in this effort. Though I'm sure the new [product/service] will be a success in the market, we learned so much in doing the project that it was well worth the investment no matter what the outcome.

If we can ever help you in any way, please let me know.

Sincerely,

[Name]
[Title]

P.S. Remember that as a developer of [product/service name], you can get a [$xxx.xx] discount off your first purchase. Just tell the sales rep to look up your name on the developers list!

- **People like to see a tangible result from their effort, either the product itself or its description in a catalog, video, etc.**

- **Put the sales pitch in the body of the letter (not the opening) or in a postscript so you don't leave the customer thinking the only reason you involved him or her was to sell product.**

Path on CD-ROM: Soliciting Customer Input→Involve Customers in Product Development→Results→Catalog-1

Distributors

In many businesses, distributors are a key link between a company and its customers. Maintaining good relationships with distributors, and keeping them well informed about your product lines, is just common sense.

When communicating with your distributors, keep in mind that customers' perceptions of your business are partly shaped by how well they are treated by those distributors. The more your distributors know about your products, and the better they are treated by *you*, the better they will be able to serve those customers.

The key in dealing with distributors is to treat them like customers. Customers who find it easy to do business with you are more likely to return; the same is true for distributors. The letters in this section are simple and direct—providing key information quickly and providing easy ways for distributors to get answers to their questions.

Release of new product

Dear Distributor:

Great news! [Company] is launching a great new product, [product name]. In preliminary test marketing, it has already proven a big winner with our customers. Here is just a sampling of what we've heard:

[• Quote 1]

[• Quote 2]

[• Quote 3]

We're certain you'll want to add this product to your lineup! [To help you understand its features and appeal to customers, I've enclosed a brief promotional video you'll want to watch, plus some brochures that you can share with your retailers. You can obtain more brochures, absolutely free, by contacting us at the phone number listed below.]

The enclosed information also shows the suggested retail price and distributor quantity discounts available at this time. Note that there is a special introductory offer we're making to our direct retail customers, and accompanying introductory discounts for distributors who place orders before [date].

I will call you in the next week to answer any questions you may have about [product name] and process your initial order.

Thank you for carrying [company] products. [Once you preview the enclosed video,] I'm sure you'll agree that [product name] is a great new addition to our lineup.

Sincerely,

[Name]
[Title]

P.S. We are continuing to carry all our current products at the existing published rates.

- **You need to sell a distributor on a new product before they will sell it to the public, and the way to sell to a distributor is to show that their customers will likely want this product. Providing actual customer quotes or providing multimedia tools (video, Web site previews) can help achieve this goal.**

- **With any new product, you will probably want to follow up with a phone call.**

Path on CD-ROM: Distributors→Communication with distributors→New product-1

COMMUNICATION WITH DISTRIBUTORS

Building partnerships

MEMORANDUM

TO: [All Distributors]

FROM: [Name]

SUBJECT: [New partnership initiative]

A recent analysis of our sales channels has shown that our [distributors] account for the majority of our sales. We would like to recognize the importance of these relationships by establishing new partnership arrangements with all our distributors.

As part of this partnership arrangement, [company] [has established a Distributor Hotline where you can place orders, check on the status of orders, voice your concerns and ideas, and receive instant answers to any questions you (or your customers) have about our products]. In addition, [company] is prepared to provide you with [sales literature and other promotional items at no extra charge, and our sales staff will gladly help you develop appropriate sales strategies for dealing with your customers].

We hope you will take advantage of these new services. Feel free to call our hotline at [800-555-5555] anytime!

- **A new approach is to recognize and encourage close relationships with distributors.**

- **Explain the new services available to distributors that will help them sell your product(s) to their customers.**

- **Provide contact information.**

Path on CD-ROM: Distributors→Communication with distributors→Partnerships-1

FIND MORE ON THIS TOPIC BY VISITING

BusinessTown.com

The Web's big site for growing businesses!

- ☑ **Separate channels on all aspects of starting and running a business**
- ☑ **Lots of info on how to do business online**
- ☑ **1,000+ pages of savvy business advice**
- ☑ **Complete web guide to thousands of useful business sites**
- ☑ **Free e-mail newsletter**
- ☑ **Question and answer forums, and more!**

http://www.businesstown.com

Accounting
Basic, Credit & Collections, Projections, Purchasing/Cost Control

Advertising
Magazine, Newspaper, Radio, Television, Yellow Pages

Business Opportunities
Ideas for New Businesses, Business for Sale, Franchises

Business Plans
Creating Plans & Business Strategies

Finance
Getting Money, Money Problem Solutions

Letters & Forms
Looking Professional, Sample Letters & Forms

Getting Started
Incorporating, Choosing a Legal Structure

Hiring & Firing
Finding the Right People, Legal Issues

Home Business
Home Business Ideas, Getting Started

Internet
Getting Online, Put Your Catalog on the Web

Legal Issues
Contracts, Copyrights, Patents, Trademarks

Managing a Small Business
Growth, Boosting Profits, Mistakes to Avoid, Competing with the Giants

Managing People
Communications, Compensation, Motivation, Reviews, Problem Employees

Marketing
Direct Mail, Marketing Plans, Strategies, Publicity, Trade Shows

Office Setup
Leasing, Equipment, Supplies

Presentations
Know Your Audience, Good Impression

Sales
Face to Face, Independent Reps, Telemarketing

Selling a Business
Finding Buyers, Setting a Price, Legal Issues

Taxes
Employee, Income, Sales, Property, Use

Time Management
Can You Really Manage Time?

Travel & Maps
Making Business Travel Fun

Valuing a Business
Simple Valuation Guidelines

STREETWISE® BOOKS

Newest Arrivals!

Low-Cost Marketing
$19.95 (CAN $31.95)
ISBN 1-58062-858-3

Business Valuation
$19.95 (CAN $31.95)
ISBN 1-58062-952-

Also Available in the *Streetwise®* Series:

24 Hour MBA
$19.95 (CAN $29.95)
ISBN 1-58062-256-9

**Achieving Wealth
Through Franchising**
$19.95 (CAN $29.95)
ISBN 1-58062-503-7

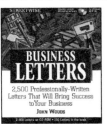

**Business Letters
with CD-ROM**
$29.95 (CAN $47.95)
ISBN 1-58062-133-3

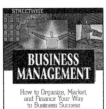

Business Management
$19.95 (CAN $29.95)
ISBN 1-58062-540-1

Complete Business Pla
$19.95 (CAN $29.95)
ISBN 1-55850-845-7

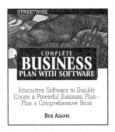

**Complete Business Plan
with Software**
$29.95 (CAN $47.95)
ISBN 1-58062-798-6

Complete Publicity Plans
$19.95 (CAN $29.95)
ISBN 1-58062-771-4

**Customer-Focused
Selling**
$19.95 (CAN $29.95)
ISBN 1-55850-725-6

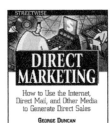

Direct Marketing
$19.95 (CAN $29.95)
ISBN 1-58062-439-1

**Do-It-Yourself
Advertising**
$19.95 (CAN $29.95)
ISBN 1-55850-727-2

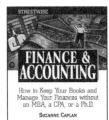

Finance & Accounting
$19.95 (CAN $29.95)
ISBN 1-58062-196-1

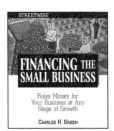

**Financing the Small
Business**
$19.95 (CAN $29.95)
ISBN 1-58062-765-X

Get Your Business Online
$19.95 (CAN $28.95)
ISBN 1-58062-368-9

Hiring Top Performers
$17.95 (CAN $27.95)
ISBN 1-55850-684-5

**Human Resources
Management**
$19.95 (CAN $29.95)
ISBN 1-58062-699-8

Independent Consulting
$19.95 (CAN $29.95)
ISBN 1-55850-728-0

Landlording & Property Management
$19.95 (CAN $29.95)
ISBN 1-58062-766-8

Low-Cost Web Site Promotion
$19.95 (CAN $29.95)
ISBN 1-58062-501-0

Managing a Nonprofit
$19.95 (CAN $29.95)
ISBN 1-58062-698-X

Managing People
$19.95 (CAN $29.95)
ISBN 1-55850-726-4

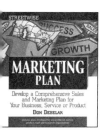

Marketing Plan
$19.95 (CAN $29.95)
ISBN 1-58062-268-2

Maximize Web Site Traffic
$19.95 (CAN $29.95)
ISBN 1-58062-369-7

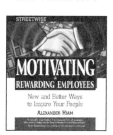

Motivating & Rewarding Employees
$19.95 (CAN $29.95)
ISBN 1-58062-130-9

Project Management
$19.95 (CAN $29.95)
ISBN 1-58062-770-6

Relationship Marketing on the Internet
$17.95 (CAN $27.95)
ISBN 1-58062-255-0

Restaurant Management
$19.95 (CAN $29.95)
ISBN 1-58062-781-1

Retirement Planning
$19.95 (CAN $29.95)
ISBN 1-58062-772-2

Sales Letters with CD-ROM
$29.95 (CAN $44.95)
ISBN 1-58062-440-5

Selling Your Business
$19.95 (CAN $29.95)
ISBN 1-58062-602-5

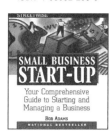

Small Business Start-Up
$19.95 (CAN $29.95)
ISBN 1-55850-581-4

Small Business Success Kit with CD-ROM
$24.95 (CAN $35.95)
ISBN 1-58062-367-0

Time Management
$19.95 (CAN $29.95)
ISBN 1-58062-131-7

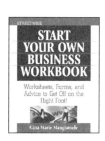

Start Your Own Business Workbook
$9.95 (CAN $15.95)
ISBN 1-58062-506-1

Available wherever books are sold.
For more information, or to order, call 800-872-5627 or visit www.*adamsmedia.com*
Adams Media, an F+W Publications Company, 57 Littlefield Street, Avon, MA 02322

Instructions for CD-ROM

Streetwise® Sales Letters with CD-ROM
(ISBN: 1-58062-440-5)

For Windows 95, Windows 98, or Windows NT

Note: The software must be used in conjunction with your own Word Processing Software.

Streetwise® Sales Letters was designed to serve as a comprehensive business resource, providing you with the letters you need to run your business in the real world.

These letters will help you to manage your finances, close sales, track employee performance, and much, much more.

This is not an interactive program. You do not need to install any part of the program onto your hard drive. You can retrieve any of the 2,500 samples directly off the CD-ROM through your own word processor.

If you want to find one of the letters highlighted in the book on the enclosed CD-ROM, simply insert the CD and follow the path outlined at the bottom of the letter you have chosen.

To find variations of the letter you're interested in, you can browse through the other letters located in the same folder on the CD.

Just open the letters and edit them in any text editor or word processor.

We recommend you rename the letters and save them to your hard drive before editing.

To customize any letter included with *Streetwise® Sales Letters*, follow these instructions:

1) Launch your word processing program.
2) Use the Open command and proceed to browse and select the file of the letter you wish to manipulate.
3) Rename and save the letter to your hard drive in order to manipulate it.
4) Begin the customization of your letter.

SYSTEM REQUIREMENTS

Minimum Requirements
486 PC compatible
Windows 95/98 or NT
6X CD-ROM
16MB of RAM
20MB of free hard drive space should you choose to load all 2,500 letters

How to Reach Us
By Mail: Adams Media
57 Littlefield Street
Avon, MA 02322
By e-mail: techsupport@adamsmedia.com

When you e-mail your questions, please provide the following information:
1) The type of computer you are using (486, Pentium, model, etc.)
2) The operating system software you are using (Windows 95, Windows 98, Windows NT)

Please note we will be unable to answer any questions concerning your word processing software; you must consult the manufacturer of the software directly.